Grafted In

the Jewish Olive Tree

ENDORSEMENTS

"The book "Grafted In" will challenge you no matter how much knowledge you may have of the Jewish People. This book is focused on how the Church and the Jewish people are interconnected and that the church should not forget it roots. Maureen's passion for the Jewish people and her research of the Jewish people is seen throughout this book, you will not be disappointed. This book is truly a book to be treasured."

Pastor Wayne Boersma, Dominion Gateway Center Church, Lethbridge, AB

"In our day and time is so important that we learn to pray and take a stand with Israel. This will be all the more strategic as the Last Days unfold. I encourage you to join with Maureen Moss to that very thing. May the Spirit of Revelation be upon you as you read 'Grafted In to the Jewish Olive Tree'."

James W. Goll
Encounters Network - Prayer Storm - Compassion Acts
Author of The Seer, The Coming Israel Awakening, The Prophetic Intercessor,
Empowered Prayer, Dream Language and many more.
www.jamesgoll.com

GRAFTED IN

the Jewish Olive Tree

RESTORING THE CHURCH'S ROOTS
IN GOD'S MISSION FOR ISRAEL

by E. Maureen Moss

Leeway Literary Works
Published by Leeway Artisans, Inc.
9468 Pep Rally Lane, Waldorf, MD 20603

Book & Cover Design by Mykle Lee

ISBN: 978-0-9823349-6-6

Copyright © 04/2010 by Maureen Moss.

No parts of this book may be reproduced or used in any form or by any means, electronic or mechanical, including photocopying, recording, or by any information storage or retrieval system, without permission from the Publisher. All inquires should be addressed to:
9468 Pep Rally Lane, Waldorf, MD 20603.
ALL RIGHTS RESERVED

LCCN: Pending

First Edition
Printed in the United States of America.

TABLE OF CONTENTS

ACKNOWLEDGEMENTS   i

FOREWORD   iii

  Introduction   9
    A Note Regarding Bible Translations   14

PART 1   ESTABLISHMENT OF THE JEWISH OLIVE TREE THROUGH GOD'S SOVEREIGN COVENANTS

1 Introduction to God's Covenants   21

2 The Adamic, Noahic, & Abrahamic Covenants   25
    The Adamic Covenant   25
    The Noahic Covenant   27
    The Abrahamic Covenant   29

3 The Mosaic Covenant   41

4 The Davidic Covenant   49
    The New Covenant   52
    The New Jerusalem   58

PART 2   HISTORICAL SEPARATION OF THE CHURCH FROM JEWISH ROOTS

5 The Early Church   63
    Miracles, Signs and Wonders   63
    The Early Church   64
    The Gospel Taken to the Gentiles   68
    The Jerusalem Decree   70

6 The Roman Influence   73
    Persecution of Christians   73
    The Church under Constantine   75
    Pagan Influences   77
    "It is finished"   78

7 Paganism In The Church   79
   What the Bible Says   79
   Roots of Paganism   81
   Christmas   83
   Easter   88
   What about Halloween?   91

8 Protestantism   95
   The Moravians   95
   The "Reformation"   97
   The Growth of Lutheranism and Offshoots   101
   The Presbyterian Church in Scotland   104
   The Anglican Church In England   105
   The Huguenots   106

PART 3   DEFINITION OF GOD'S CUSTOMS AND JEWISH CUSTOMS

9 Back To God's Word   111

10 The Feasts Of The Lord   115
   Why Should Christians Be Aware of the Feasts?   115

11 The Spring Feasts   121
   Passover and Unleavened Bread (Lev. 23:4-8)   121
   Meaning of Passover   124
   The Church's Celebration of "Easter"   125
   Feast of Unleavened Bread (Lev. 23:4-8)   130
   The Feast of Firstfruits (Lev. 23:9-14)   131
   Passover as Celebrated Then and Now   132
   The Feast of Weeks - also called Pentecost
   or Shavuot (Lev. 23:15-22)   133

12 The Fall Feasts   139
   The Feast of Trumpets – Yom Teruah (Lev. 23:23-25)   139
   The Day of Atonement (Yom Kippur) (Lev. 23:26-32)   141
   The Feast of Tabernacles (Sukkot) (Lev. 23:33-44)   145

The Jewish Wedding and Jesus our Bridegroom	151
13 Other Feasts and Special Days	159
The Feast of Dedication (Hanukkah or Chanukah)	159
Other Special Days	163

PART 4 GOD ESTABLISHES RELATIONSHIP WITH GENTILES

14 The Story Of Ruth	167
The Story of Ruth	167
Ruth and the Church	168
15 The Story Of Esther	173
The Significance of this Story	176
The Ongoing Conspiracy Against Israel and the Jewish People	178
16 Anti-Semitism Throughout History	181
Antiquity	182
Second century	182
Fourth century	184
Fifth century	186
Sixth century	187
Seventh century	188
Eighth century	190
Ninth century	190
Eleventh century	191
Twelfth century	192
Thirteenth century	195
Fourteenth century	200
Fifteenth century	202
Sixteenth century	205
Seventeenth century	210
Eighteenth century	212
Nineteenth century	214
Twentieth century	219

	Twenty-first century	228
	References from Wikipedia	233
17	**Hindrances To Understanding**	237
	Replacement Theology	240
	Dual Covenant Theology	242
	The Bottom Line	244
18	**The Olive Tree**	247
	The Unpreached Sermon	249
	The Olive Tree	253
	The "Mystery"	254
19	**Messianic Judaism**	259
	Beginnings	259
	Historically	260
	The 60s Revolution	261
	The 70s and the 'Jesus Movement'	261
	Messianic Judaism Today	262
20	**The Land And The Promises**	267
	Wars and Rumors of Wars	268
	We Need to Pray	269
Conclusion God's Heart For His People		271

ACKNOWLEDGEMENTS

I want to thank my Pastor, Wayne Boersma, for his encouragement with this project from inception to end. Thanks to Pastor Harry Holmquist, Messianic Rabbi Cal Goldberg and Pastor Wayne Boersma for their willingness to take the time to read my first draft and make suggestions.

A big thank you to my children, Jeff Oliver, Koby Gutoskie and Dulaine Lough for their love and encouragement through even the toughest of times. A special thank you to Lonnie Lane, who was not only willing to write the book's Foreward, but who also edited the manuscript for me, making very valuable suggestions.

Thank you to Robert Heidler and Sid Roth for their special permissions to quote from their works. I also want to thank my friends for their wonderful encouragement throughout this project. You know who you are.

A very special thank you to my daughter Dulaine for painting the cover artwork. Without each one of you this book may never have reached fruition.

FOREWORD

IT IS A RARE BOOK that gives such a panoramic view of what the church has been through for centuries that it allows its readers an opportunity to see beyond the limits of our own spiritual vision. Only through a proper picture of where the church went "off" can we find our way back to being fully "in His will." Maureen Moss has provided us with such a picture in this book.

As has often been said, we must be aware of our history in order not to repeat it. Maureen has done a masterful job of weaving the critical aspects of history together with regard to the church's doctrines over the centuries and as they relate to the Jewish people in order that we do not maintain the errors or repeat them. As this comprehensive recounting of church history makes clear, the church over the centuries has often had its own agenda and preoccupation with its position of power which resulted in doctrines which God had not initiated.

If we look at the church of the Book of Acts as our model, it becomes clear that we have lost our way and deviated from the effectiveness of the original church. Even a casual glance at church history makes it clear that the power of the Holy Spirit which was so mightily upon the early church had soon dissipated. The question is why. Church history soon reveals that when the church outlawed all things Hebrew in the Bible, including rejecting the Jews at the same time, the Holy Spirit who had inspired Hebrew men to write the Hebrew Bible withdrew and was no longer evident in the church. They did not realize that with rejecting the Jews they were rejecting the God of the Jews at the same time. Torah, the first five books of the Bible, was meant to be a light to all mankind through the Jews. Having essentially turned off this Light, this act of independence from God, plummeted the church – and the world with her – into the Dark Ages.

As a result, within a few hundred years following the resurrection of Jesus, the church slid into a pond of despond when it entwined pagan practices with Christianity. This decision changed the concept of "church" from which we have not completely recovered. Instead of a sin-forgiven born-again Spirit-led church, now anyone who lived under Rome's dominion was considered a Christian, albeit a Christianity mixed with other religions. By the Middle Ages, the so called "church" had become a religion of mysticism, witchcraft and superstition bringing fear and oppression upon the populace. Had the church leaders considered the Hebrew Scriptures as valid for following God, particularly the commandments in the Torah, they would have found that God forbade many of the practices they had included, warning His people of what they would suffer if they looked away from Him to "other gods."

The church went from being a powerful influence for righteousness, truth and justice and having great impact on the entire Roman Empire, to almost complete spiritual powerlessness and riddled with corruption. There is no explanation other than having turned from the Word and violating what was commanded by God, including "cursing" the Jews. However, centuries of Christianity have proved Jesus' words to be true that "*…the gates of Hades will not overpower it*" (Matthew 16:18). It is because of God and not man that the church has survived even the Christians!

Today, as in other times, we are a church that is largely impacted by the world rather than being the standard-setters of righteousness and justice. In order to find our way back to His presence and power, especially if we are the generation to welcome His return, if we are to be God's instruments of healing in a damaged world, we must first, each of us, decide if that's what we want. Do we want the Spirit to rule our lives? If so, then we must surrender our lives to Jesus wholly and completely, just as the early church members did. We must believe what His Word really says and choose to live accordingly. And we must become aware of where the church has deviated from the whole counsel of God, both with regard to church doctrines in general, as well as those doctrines which affected the Jewish people.

Why is this matter of the Jewish people so important to the church today? Because God made a covenant with Abraham that extended to his descendants, a covenant that still maintains today. God's promise to Abraham was this, *"I will bless those who bless you, and whoever curses you I will curse; and all peoples on earth will be blessed through you"* (Genesis 12:3). Pretty strong words, aren't they? Do they still apply today? Take another look through history and you will see that nations, ethnicities and even empires have perished, but the Jews remain. There cannot be the fullness of the blessings of God for *"all the peoples on earth"* unless and until there is peace with Israel and the Jewish people. Will that happen before His return? Perhaps not politically, but for those who long for the presence of God to return to His people in fullness, there must be a recognition of the place of Israel and the Jewish people in the heart and plans of God. Those who are at peace in their hearts with God will likewise be at peace in their hearts with the Jewish people and with Israel. This is not a political statement, but a spiritual principle. We who are His will love what God loves (and hate what God hates).

We live in a time when more prophecies are being fulfilled regarding Israel than ever before. The News reads like pages from Israel's prophets in the Bible. At the same time, there is a polarization taking place among the Believers regarding Israel. Some can only see her in the political colors in which the media has often painted her, while others see her in relation to God's Word. For the nations that turn away from the Jewish people and from

Israel they will suffer the consequences. It was once said of England that the sun never set on the British Empire. Today they are but a small island. Could this be due to their oppression of the Jews as they were becoming a nation in 1947 and 1948, and the disallowing of Jews into the land so that they had to sneak in or die?

The Word tells us that *"the spiritual is not first, but the natural; then the spiritual"* (1 Corinthians 15:46). In other words, that which takes place in the natural will then have a corresponding event take place in the spiritual realm. As relates to our discussion and the subject of this book, the natural relates to Israel and the corresponding spiritual aspect is what subsequently takes place in the church. Perhaps, dear reader, you are familiar with the correlation between Israel being declared a State by the United Nations in 1948, and the healing evangelist movement that developed in the church. Israel was back in her land and healing came back into the church in the same time frame. With Israel once again in the Land God promised to them, a restoration was beginning to take place.

In 1967, the Six-Day War occurred when five Arab nations attacked little Israel. Miraculously, with God's help, Israel won the war and all of Jerusalem was once more in Jewish hands for the first time in 1,878 years since the destruction of the Temple by Rome in 70 A.D. Following this, the Holy Spirit came back into the church in power with the Charismatic Movement moving upon the people, not just upon the leaders, just as it had been in the beginning in Jerusalem, two millennia earlier. First the natural, then the spiritual.

What we see taking place today is another kind of restoration. There's a growing awareness by many in the church of the importance of the "whole counsel of God," and that the Old Testament is as much from God to the church as the New Testament is. In fact, the New Testament stands on the shoulders of the Old Testament and cannot be adequately or fully understood without it. As you read through this book, you will see how the errors of the church deviated from God's Word and His ways and therefore placed the people outside of the blessings of Abraham, which is to say outside of the blessings of God, especially when taking a stand against the Jewish people.

Many believers expect that we are living in the last days before Jesus' return. Things are coming into place and must before Jesus will return. Peter made it clear on the day of Pentecost what would precede God sending Jesus back to earth, " ...*that He may send Jesus, the Christ appointed for you, whom heaven must receive until <u>the period of restoration</u> of all things about which God spoke by the mouth of His holy prophets from ancient time*" (Acts 3:20, 21 my emphasis). Restoration means something was lost. It can also mean we are lost and must find our way back to the path that will lead to where we need to be when Yeshua returns. It is time for the restoration of the Kingdom of God as God intended, *"for the kingdom of God is righteousness and peace and joy in the Holy Spirit"* (Romans 14:17).

We have yet to really see what it is He's restoring because the church hasn't seen it for two millennia. He'll lead us, day by day and decision by decision. However, the restoration today of what we call the "Jewish roots" of the Gospel to a place of importance in the lives of many Believers indicates a sensitivity by the Body of Messiah, the Remnant of true believers, to the heart and mind of God that is found in His various commandments. These are not observed by any legalistic "have-to," but out of a love for God and His ways in the Spirit of Grace. They are not Jewish celebrations but "Godish" celebrations. They come from Him and are really "rehearsals" of the Messiah to come. Three of them, Passover, Sukkot (Tabernacles) and Shavuot (Pentecost) will be celebrated when Jesus returns so it is not surprising that they would begin to be celebrated once again.

Of the Old Testament, He said of Himself, *"These are My words which I spoke to you while I was still with you, that all things which are written about Me in the Law of Moses and the Prophets and the Psalms must be fulfilled"* (Luke 24:44). As was said, they are being fulfilled today. The completion of the restoration may well be taking place in our generation. But we must also make sure the restoration doesn't take precedence over our ultimate destination – Jesus Himself is and always must be our destination!

Lonnie Lane, Staff Writer
Sid Roth's Messianic Vision Ministries
August 1, 2010

Introduction

For as long as I can remember I've had a heart for Israel. I was born during the second world war, and when I understood the consequences of that atrocity, I was devastated. Ashamed because of my parents' German heritage, as I grew older, my response to questions regarding my nationality was always "Canadian." My mother was born in Canada, but my father was born in what was then called Bessarabia, Russia and came to Canada as a child with his family in 1924.

When I found out that Israel became a country again in 1948 I was overjoyed. Throughout the 50s and 60s I was always interested in any news about Israel. Their early statesmen and a woman named Golda became my heroes. If only there was another Golda on the present-day stage!

When I was about 4 or 5 years old, I recall standing outside our house one day with palpable knowledge that I was God's little girl. Sitting beside my mother in church on Sundays, I wanted to 'get a piece of God' as I watched people going to the front for Communion, but my mother would not allow it.

At age five I was allowed to go and sit in the front pew with the other little girls. In my excitement as I went forward at the appropriate time to 'get a piece of God,' I had no idea of the 'sin' I had committed, as I had no proper instruction.

In the Catholic Church, the regimentation confused this little girl's heart and mind. To a child full of questions and longing, "because the Church says so" was an insufficient answer in my bewildered mind. I was told that I was a 'bad girl' for receiving Communion because I was unprepared for my 'First Holy Communion.' I was promptly sent off to Kindergarten with the 6-year olds to do just that.

Kindergarten left an indelible mark on me. In class one day, the nun told us about some martyrs who were killed for their faith by having their tongues nailed to a table! That horrified me, and I was afraid that I could never love God enough to let anyone do that to me! The residue from that made me feel I could never be 'good enough' for God, and stayed with me a good part of my life.

As I grew older, I eventually left the Catholic Church. However, enough indoctrination 'stuck' that I figured if God wasn't in the "one true" church, He must be in the world. I searched for Him through different philosophies and psychologies, becoming lost in the process. Convinced that I wasn't good enough for God, I eventually found myself in a much-needed AA meeting.

Through the help of God and AA I sobered up in January of 1980. That was when I began to pray again, for the first time in about 15 years. When I did Step Three – Made a decision to turn my will and my life over to the care of God as I understood Him – God removed from me the desire to drink.

That was the beginning of a new life for me, as I sought sobriety through seeking God. He says in His Word, **"... seek the Lord your God, and you will find Him if you seek Him with all your heart and with all your soul"** (Deut. 4:29). It didn't happen overnight. But I am thankful that my sponsor told me at the beginning to ask for His help in the morning, and to thank Him at night to stay away from the 'first drink.'

Meanwhile, my ex-husband phoned one day, told me he had become a Christian, and asked if he could take the children to church. I said yes. Before long they were born-again. My son began telling me I needed Jesus, but I wasn't there yet. I was

Introduction

comfortable praying to my heavenly Father, as my thoughts of Jesus returned me to my childhood, where the large crucifix at the front of the church had filled me with guilt. I knew my sins had put Him there, but was never guided how to rectify that.

I began to ask the Father every morning to disclose His truth to me. I told Him I didn't want any truth but His. After praying this every morning for about a year, one morning in my quiet time Jesus spoke to me audibly. He said, **"I am the way, the truth and the life. No one can come to the Father but by Me."** Not as loud and less clearly, I heard Him say something about "... the Father draw him." I was excited and humbled that Jesus would speak to me, such a sinner!

Thankfully, I had bought a Bible in my first year of sobriety, although I had only read as far as the story of Abraham before being bogged down. I went to my bookshelf, and picking up the Bible, I said, "I think those words are in here someplace. If You want me to read them, You'll have to find them for me, because I haven't a clue where to look."

Then I just let the book fall open. My eyes landed on the words that Jesus had just spoken. I flipped once (several pages were turned) and my eyes landed on the verse, **"No one can come to Me unless the Father draws him."** I was trembling, and thanked my heavenly Father for His faithfulness in answering my prayer. I began reading all the words in red, because I wanted to know all that Jesus said.

I shared this experience with a Christian friend, and was told to ask the Holy Spirit to reveal His truth to me as I read the Bible.

That began a whole new life for me! As a Catholic, we didn't use a Bible, but a Missal, which contained only verses here and there from the Bible, lacking continuity or context. I read through the Gospels, then the epistles. Every Billy Graham program that came on TV, during the altar call, I would renew my decision to follow the Lord. My understanding of salvation became clearer.

I studied the Bible for four years, each time asking the Holy Spirit to reveal His truth to me. I wanted to make sure I knew what the Bible said before I would go to a church, as I did not want to be misled again.

Finally, I was ready to go and be baptized. I went to a Baptist Church for a while, and arranged to be baptized. The big day finally arrived, and the pastor's wife phoned me that morning and asked if I wanted to reschedule it, because there was no hot water.

I said, "No, I do not want to reschedule."

The water was cold, let me tell you, but I was baptized and joy flooded me!

My youngest daughter came from her Bible College for my big day. She said to me afterwards, "Mom, if you can become a Christian, anybody can!" Those are precious words to me, for I had lived a very sinful life!

It was particularly after my baptism that I began to notice changes taking place within me – not decisions I was consciously making for me. Inner changes. The first thing I noticed was my music preference. It changed from rock and roll to praise and worship. A small thing, perhaps, but significant to me.

Although more than 20 years have passed, I can remember that special day as if it were yesterday. Many significant changes have occurred because I came to know my Lord.

However, my love and concern for Israel and God's chosen people, the Jews, remains stronger today than it ever was. I've been told by a Messianic Jew that I have a 'Jewish heart,' and I think I have.

All of my life I have had a love for the Jewish people and things Jewish. Their humor, reading books by Jewish authors, whether historic or a novel… it has just always been a part of me. I believe God made me that way.

Reading the Bible and the covenants God made with His Jewish people had a great impact on me. When I read what Paul wrote regarding the Olive Tree in Romans 11, it made perfect sense to me – that some of the Jewish people at the time of Christ did not believe Him, so they were the cut-off branches; and that we Gentiles who believe in Him were grafted in. The Jews who did believe remained branches on their Olive Tree, and Jews who have later come to believe that Jesus is their Messiah have been grafted in again. The Olive Tree itself is Jewish, with the roots of it being the patriarchs and prophets, on which we gain our knowledge of God.

It is my prayer that God will use these words to bring understanding to the Gentile church of its Jewish roots, that we have a responsibility to 'pray for the peace of Jerusalem' (Psalm 122:6), and to become the 'one new man' that Paul spoke about in Ephesians 2:14-15 – Jew and Gentile together – and bring 'life from the dead', the great worldwide revival so many are waiting for.

Time is short. We are already beginning to suffer the 'birth pangs' of the end times as described in the gospels of Matthew, Mark and Luke.

> And do this, knowing the time, that now it is high time to awake out of sleep; for now our salvation is nearer than when we first believed. The night is far spent, the day is at hand. Therefore let us cast off the works of darkness, and let us put on the armor of light. (Romans 13:11-12)

A Note Regarding Bible Translations

I include this short section to make readers aware that as Christians we can often take too much for granted, and assume without checking deeply into facts. We can be too trusting or gullible at times.

Be aware that much history has taken place between the time that Jesus walked the earth, and this present-day. The Church did not spring forth as it is today without much tumult and compromise.

We often assume that our Bible translations accurately portray the intention of the original authors who, with the possible exception of Luke, were Jewish. Daniel Gruber, in his book *'The Separation of Church and Faith, Volume 1: Copernicus and the Jews'* suggests that misunderstanding grew out of the difficulty of the original writers who were writing in Greek and thinking in Hebrew. Sometimes there was not an accurate word in Greek to completely convey the intended meaning. As well, translators of the Bible from Greek to English or any other language would have encountered difficulties which would extend from that. Gruber states:

> "... the translator may have a different mind-set than the author, or a different mind-set than the audience. He, or she, may not understand what is being said, or what is being heard. He may assign incorrect meanings to the original words, because he does not understand the context in which they were used. Also, the language into which he is translating may not have any equivalent way of reproducing the original."[1]

Gruber continues:

Introduction

"Most translations of Matthew to Revelation contain such misrepresentations. They also contain systematic errors that come from a failure to recognize the original language and text. For the most part, this is not the result of either bad motives or lack of knowledge. It is the result of the translators' misperception of the very nature of the text. The translators translate as though they were dealing with a Greek text written in a Christian context. Neither assumption is correct."[2]

In the Hebraic Roots Version Scriptures[3], which were translated from the original old Hebrew and Aramaic by James Scott Trimm, the author states in his introduction that this edition of the New Testament was not rooted in a Greek Hellenistic text, but rather from the languages in which it was originally written.

It is commonly believed in Christian circles that the New Testament was written originally in Greek, and perhaps it was. If that is the case, Daniel Gruber makes some interesting points, a taste of which is seen above.

However, Trimm suggests the New Testament was originally written in Hebrew and Aramaic. He states in his introduction, "This is important because there are some passages in the NT which do not make sense at all in Greek, but only begin to make sense when we look at them in Hebrew and Aramaic."[4]

He uses Acts 11:27-30 as his first example. Verse 28 tells us that there is going to be a great famine throughout all the world. The next verse tells us that the brethren in Antioch decided to send relief to the brethren in Judea.

Trimm asks the question: why would those in Antioch send relief to those dwelling *in Judea* if the famine was to strike all *the world*? He suggests that the solution lies in the fact that the word for "world" in the Aramaic manuscripts is Strong's #772, which is the Aramaic form of the Hebrew word for Strong's #776. He goes on to say that this word can mean 'world' (as in Prov. 19:4), 'earth'

15

(as in Dan. 2:35) or 'land' (as in Dan. 9:15) and is often used as a euphemism for 'The Land of Israel' (as in Dan. 9:6). Trimm concludes, then, that the word in this Scripture is not meant to mean "world" but rather "land of Israel".

According to Strongs itself, #772 in the Hebrew/Chaldee dictionary from 'ara'(Chaldee) pronounced ar-ah´ means *the earth; earth; interior.* Strongs #776 – 'e-rets – pronounced eh´-rets; from an unused root probably means to *'be firm; the earth (at large or partitively); a land: - x common, country, earth, field, ground, land, X nations, way, wilderness, world.*[5] When I first saw the word 'erets' I immediately thought of "Eretz Israel' – the Land of Israel, as it is often referred to today.

Another example used by Trimm is from Matt. 26:6, referring to Jesus being at the home of Simon the leper. Because of the fact that lepers were not permitted to live among the rest of the population, but rather "outside the camp" according to Lev. 13:46, there must be some error here. Trimm suggests that since both Hebrew and Aramaic were written without vowels, that no distinction was made between the Aramaic words GAR'BA (leper) and GARABA (jar maker or jar merchant). He goes on to say, "Since in this story a woman pours oil from a jar it is apparent that Simon was a jar merchant or jar maker and not a leper."[6]

We are all familiar with the story of Phillip preaching to the Ethiopian eunuch. Trimm makes the point that the Torah forbids a eunch from becoming a proselyte Jew, as well as from worshiping at the Temple. Consequently, this verse does not make much sense, since it also says that he came to Jerusalem to worship. However, the word 'eunuch' in Aramaic manuscripts can mean 'eunuch' but can also mean 'believer' or 'faithful one'. There had been a Jewish presence in Ethiopia since the time of King Solomon and the Queen of Sheba, and this man had come to Jerusalem to worship.

Trimm cites more examples than those I have shared here. However, it is important for us to realize that all translations of the

Bible are not necessarily 100% correct. Ask Holy Spirit to grant you understanding as you read the Scriptures.

A word which causes misunderstanding is 'testament', a word which has even divided the Scriptures into two parts, the Old Testament and the New Testament. This is extremely unfortunate for both the Jews and for believers, as it suggests that the Old Testament was for the Jews and that the New Testament is for Christians. This false understanding has greatly contributed to our separation from our Jewish roots, and it has also contributed to the Jews' thinking that the New Testament is entirely a Gentile book, a different religion altogether. Essentially, the word 'covenant' would be more accurate to convey the truth, as it was in fact the New Covenant which Jesus introduced, and would therefore be more beneficial for the understanding of both groups.

PART 1

ESTABLISHMENT OF THE JEWISH OLIVE TREE THROUGH GOD'S SOVEREIGN COVENANTS

Chapter 1
Introduction to God's Covenants

OUR GOD IS A COVENANT-MAKING and covenant-keeping God. Beginning in the Garden of Eden, when Adam and Eve disobeyed His command not to eat the fruit of the tree of knowledge of good and evil, they, and subsequently mankind, is cursed by God and banished from the garden. After the death of Moses God promised Joshua that He would not leave nor forsake him, and He kept His promise. Joshua led the people into the Promised Land, and in many miraculous ways God helped them to overcome their enemies. In the book of Judges, we see numerous covenants God made with his people and the leaders of Israel, the rewards of keeping God's covenants and the judgment from breaking them. For example, God called on Gideon, declaring him a mighty man of valor. Gideon felt nothing like valor, and protested that he was weak. He bargained with the LORD, not once but twice. Yet again, God kept His promise, and even with a small army Gideon subdued the Midianites. Samson was bestowed incredible strength unlike any other man, and yet when he broke his Nazarite covenant with God, he was overcome by the Philistines.

An example of answered prayer is that of Hannah, who desperately wanted a child, and prayed to the Lord to open her womb, promising to give the child to the Lord. With a covenant established, God granted her desire, and Samuel is born.

God's faithfulness in keeping His promises is not limited to the Old Testament as there are many more examples throughout Scripture. In fact, some promises given in the Old Testament fulfill in the New. Perhaps the greatest of all was His promise through the prophet Isaiah about the promised Son.

> For unto us a Child is born,
> Unto us a Son is given;
> And the government will be upon His shoulder.
> And His name will be called Wonderful, Counselor, Mighty God,
> Everlasting Father, Prince of Peace (Is 9:6).

In keeping the promise of His Son, God established the greatest of all covenants, that of salvation for all people. In Paul's letter to the Romans he says *"if you confess with your mouth the Lord Jesus and believe in your heart that God has raised Him from the dead, you will be saved."* Rom.10:9

God keeps His promises. Numbers 3:19 says: **God is not a man, that He should lie, nor a son of man, that He should repent. Has He said, and will He not do? Or has He spoken, and will He not make it good?** God made covenants with various people to show Himself trustworthy, so they, and we, would trust Him and love Him. He also made covenants to establish His reign and sovereignty over all creation. You see when God makes a covenant to keep, He expects His creation to keep His commands. As you have read, disobedience to God's commands results in judgment. As wonderful as it is to be on the receiving end of His promises, it is equally awful to be judged for breaking covenant with God.

In the following chapters I want to examine six covenants God established with man in greater detail. These covenants are often referred to as God's "main" covenants with man. These are the

Adamic Covenant, the *Noahic Covenant*, the *Abrahamic Covenant*, the *Mosaic Covenant*, the *Davidic Covenant*, and the *New Covenant*. What are these key Biblical covenants, and with whom did God make them? Do they have any impact on our lives today?

Chapter 2
The Adamic, Noahic, & Abrahamic Covenants

THROUGHOUT THE SCRIPTURES we know as the "Old Testament" God made several covenants with His people – with Noah, with Abraham, to whom He also gave a Covenant of the Land, with Moses, with David, and finally the promise of a New Covenant. The word *"covenant"* is listed 292 times in Strongs Concordance, which gives us an indication of how important this concept is to God. In this chapter we are going to look at the covenants God made with Adam, with Noah, and with Abraham.

THE ADAMIC COVENANT

IN THE CREATION ACCOUNT, God called forth light, and He called the light Day and the darkness Night. Genesis 1:5 tells us, **So the evening and the morning were the first day.** God spoke to Jeremiah many years later and said to him, **"If you can break My covenant with the day and My covenant with the night, so that there will not be day and night in their season, then My covenant may also be broken with David My servant..."** (Jer. 33:21-22). Obviously, God considers this to be a covenant with His creation.

Although this early creation account and the story of Adam and Eve do not contain the word "covenant," the Garden of Eden contains other elements of a covenant. God gave dominion to Adam over all the earth which He had created in the first six days. God rested from all His work on the seventh day, and He sanctified it. As well, God gave Adam one command, which was not to eat of the tree of the knowledge of good and evil. It was then that God created Eve and established the covenant of marriage, as Scripture gives us the words in Genesis 2:24 **"Therefore a man shall leave his father and mother and be joined to his wife, and they shall become one flesh."** Since God had created Adam and Eve, they obviously did not have either father or mother.

However, Adam and Eve disobeyed God by eating the fruit of the tree of the knowledge of good and evil, resulting in consequences which have affected mankind ever since, including pain in childbirth for woman and hard toil for man. As a result of their disobedience whereby their eyes opened to sin, they recognized their nakedness, and God provided a blood covering for them by sacrificing animals in order to use their skins for clothing.

This early blood sacrifice was a foreshadow to the shedding of the blood of Jesus to cover the sins of mankind. This took place long before the word "covenant" was used by God.

Issues from this Adamic covenant are still in effect today. God desired obedience from Adam and Eve, but they disobeyed the one command He had given them: not to eat the fruit of the tree of the knowledge of good and evil. Eve was beguiled by Satan when he told her, "You shall not surely die. For God knows that in the day you eat of it your eyes will be opened, and you will be like God, knowing good and evil" (Gen. 3:4-5). Satan still lies to us today, and we often believe the lies.

Because of their disobedience, God cursed the ground telling Adam that it would require great toil for it to produce. As for Eve, God told her that childbirth would be painful, that her desire would be for her husband (man) and that her husband would rule over her.

Man still has dominion over God's creation, although, to be sure, we have made rather a mess of it. As well, the covenant of marriage still stands today, but again, mankind has perverted it and often disregards it.

The Noahic Covenant

AFTER ADAM AND EVE were ejected from the Garden of Eden they had children, Cain and Abel. Cain tilled the ground, and Abel looked after the sheep. Each brought an offering before the Lord, Abel the firstborn of his flock, and Cain an offering of the fruit of the ground. The Bible tells us that God accepted Abel's offering, but did not accept Cain's offering. However, it does not make clear why Cain's offering is not accepted; perhaps it was of poor quality, or perhaps it was not a 'firstfruit', which we later discover in Scripture is important to the Lord. Whatever the reason, God did not accept Cain's offering.

His jealousy got the better of him, and he killed his brother Abel. When the LORD asked him where his brother was, Cain's reply was sarcastic, saying, "I don't know. Am I my brother's keeper?" But he lied to the LORD, knowing full well where Abel's body was. So God cursed Cain for what he had done, and sent him away. Cain went and lived in the land of Nod, and took a wife and had children.

Over time, the population of the earth multiplied. The Bible tells us in Genesis 6 there were giants on the earth, when the sons of God came in to the daughters of men, and they bore children. However, it does not make clear exactly who these giants were, and there is much conjecture. Regardless of exactly who they were, the Bible does tell us that wickedness increased on the earth, to the extent that God was sorry He had even created man! (see Gen. 6:6). This is when God decided to destroy both man and beast (v.7)

"But Noah found grace in the eyes of the LORD." (Gen. 6:8)

The word "covenant" is first used with Noah in Gen. 6:18 when God said to him, **"But I will make a covenant with you; and you shall go into the ark – you, your sons, your wife, and your sons wives with you."** God protected Noah and his family, as well as all species of animals, from the great flood which swept over the earth. One may wonder why God decided to destroy all but a male and female of each animal, bird and creeping thing that He had made, saving only enough to procreate. An obvious reason for this is that not all would fit in the ark. Why then, one might ask, did He decide to cause such a deluge and flood to eradicate all the wicked from the earth? Could He have done this in a manner targeting only human beings, and not animals? Perhaps He could have, but personally, I can't think how. Or perhaps the wickedness of the people had somehow tainted the animals and they had become an abomination to Him. The bottom line here is that God is sovereign, and this is the way He decided to wipe out the wickedness from the earth.

After the waters receded Noah built an altar and offered burnt offerings to the LORD. The precedent for this blood sacrifice had previously been established when Adam and Eve had disobeyed God in the Garden and realized they were naked. God then killed animals for their clothing, as we have seen.

This offering of Noah pleased God, and He promised never again to flood the earth and destroy all flesh.

> "Thus I establish My covenant with you: Never again shall all flesh be cut off by the waters of the flood to destroy the earth." And God said: "This is the sign of the covenant which I make between Me and you, and every living creature that is with you, for perpetual generations: I set My rainbow in the cloud, and it

shall be for the sign of the covenant between Me and the earth."
Gen. 9:11 - 13

Today we can enjoy the beauty of the rainbow in the sky, and use it as a reminder of God's promise.

THE ABRAHAMIC COVENANT

GOD'S COVENANT WITH ABRAHAM is foundational to all other covenants which came after. Beginning with Abraham God has been calling out a people; and even prior to that, God elected only one of Noah's sons, Shem, to produce a pure line to Abraham (Gen. 11:10-26). The Mosaic Covenant and the Davidic Covenant as well as the New Covenant all stem from the covenant God made with Abraham.

Although Noah's other sons, Ham and Japheth, had offspring, it was through Shem's line that God cut covenant. The Bible tells us the sons of Japheth were Gomer, Magog, Madal, Javan, Tubal, Meshech, and Tiras (Gen. 10:2). We see some of these names again in the writings of the prophets Ezekiel and Hosea (Ezek. 38; Hos.1:2-3), and they are part of Gog's army in the last days, who war against God's people.

In Genesis 12:1-3 God told Abram to go to a land that He would show him, and He gave him seven promises: 1) that He would make him a great nation; 2) that He would bless him; 3) that He would make his name great; 4) that Abram would be a blessing; 5) that He would bless those who bless him; 6) He would curse those who curse him; and 7) that in him all the families of the earth would be blessed. This foreshadows the growth of the Jewish people through the patriarchs, the nation of Israel, and even the Messiah through Whom all people on earth could be blessed.

After Abram, Sarai his wife, and his nephew Lot arrived in Canaan, the LORD appeared to Abram at Shechem and said, **"To your descendants I will give this land"** (v.7). However, due to a famine in the land at the time, they continued to Egypt. The Scriptures do not say how long they remained in Egypt, but after a time they returned to Bethel in Canaan, the place where Abram had originally built an altar. Genesis 13:2 tells us that Abram was rich in livestock, silver and gold, so obviously God had blessed him materially. Abram and Lot separated, because the land could not support them both with all their livestock and shepherds.

> "And the Lord said to Abram, after Lot had separated from him: 'Lift your eyes now and look from the place where you are – northward, southward, eastward, and westward; for all the land which you see I give to you and your descendants forever. And I will make your descendants as the dust of the earth; so that if a man could number the dust of the earth, then your descendants also could be numbered.'" (Gen. 13:14-16)

In the fifteenth chapter of Genesis the word of the LORD came to Abram in a vision, saying, **"Do not be afraid, Abram. I am your shield, your exceedingly great reward"** (v. 1). When Abram responded by reminding Him he had no offspring, the LORD said, **"... one who will come from your own body shall be your heir"** (v. 4). Then the LORD took him outside and pointed to the stars and said in verse 5, **"Look now toward heaven, and count the stars if you are able to number them... So shall your descendants be."** Abram believed what the LORD told him, **and He accounted it to him for righteousness** (v.6). This belief, or faith, of Abram resulted in a legal reckoning as righteousness by the LORD, and that phrase is repeated later by both Paul and James as the basis for righteousness.

This set the stage for the "covenant-cutting" ceremony which followed. It is referred to as "covenant-cutting" rather than covenant-making, because blood was shed. The LORD told Abram to bring Him a three-year-old heifer, a three-year-old female goat, a three-year-old ram, a turtledove and a young pigeon. Abram brought them all to Him and cut the large animals in two, down the middle, placing each piece opposite the other, but he did not cut the birds. These "covenant-cutting" ceremonies were standard practice in the ancient near east, and in the Hittite suzerainty covenant, the inferior party would walk between the bleeding pieces of the animals, and take an oath of loyalty to the superior party, essentially saying, "May the gods do to me as I have done to these animals if I do not fulfill the terms of this covenant.[1]

As the LORD cut this covenant with Abram, He took the part of the inferior party, and as Abram fell into a deep sleep, the LORD told him of things that would happen in the future: that his descendants would spend four hundred years in a land that was not theirs, and be afflicted, speaking of the time they would be in Egypt. He also told Abram that he would live to a good old age.

When it was dark **there appeared a smoking oven and a burning torch that passed between those pieces** (Gen. 15:17), indicating the Shekinah Himself passed between them. It was God Himself Who was doing the promising, with no demands on Abram's part. He simply believed.

Sarai, meanwhile, had become impatient with regard to having a child, and suggested to Abraham that he go in to Sarai's Egyptian maid Hagar, thinking that perhaps she could obtain a child through her. Hagar conceived, but instead of being happy about it, Sarai became jealous and Hagar became proud. As a result, when Sarai treated her harshly, Hagar ran away.

As she was sitting by a spring on the way to Shur, the Angel of the LORD found her and spoke to her, telling her to return to her mistress and submit to her. He then gave Hagar a great promise:

"Behold, you are with child, And you will bear a son. You shall call his name Ishmael, Because the Lord has heard your affliction. He shall be a wild man; His hand shall be against every man. And every man's hand against him. And he shall dwell in the presence of all his brethren." (Gen. 16:11-12)

Ishmael, meaning 'God hears', is the first person in the Scriptures that is named by the Angel of the LORD. Modern-day Arabs claim descent from Ishmael.

So Hagar went back and bore Abram a son, when he was 86 years old.

When Abram was ninety-nine years old The LORD appeared to him again and changed his name from Abram to Abraham, **"for I have made you a father of many nations. I will make you exceedingly fruitful; and I will make nations of you, and kings shall come from you. And I will establish My covenant between Me and you and your descendants after you in their generations, for an everlasting covenant, to be God to you and your descendants after you"** (Gen. 17:5-7). In verses 10-11 the LORD said to Abraham, **"This is My covenant which you shall keep, between Me and you and your descendants after you: Every male child among you shall be circumcised; and you shall be circumcised in the flesh of your foreskins, and it shall be a sign of the covenant between Me and you."** Thus circumcision is the sign of the Abrahamic Covenant.

It was at this time also that God changed Sarai's name to Sarah, and told Abraham that he would have a son by her, who was to be named Isaac, with whom God would also establish His covenant.

Much later God tested Abraham's faith by asking him to sacrifice his only son, born in old age, as a burnt offering on a mountain in the land of Moriah. The Scriptures do not clearly indicate how old Isaac was at the time, but he was old enough to carry the wood for the fire. However, the Book of Jasher, which is mentioned in both Joshua 10:13 and 2 Samuel 1:18, tells us that Isaac was thirty-seven years old at this time (Jasher 22:41)[2]. The Book of Jasher also suggests that Isaac knew ahead of time that he was to be sacrificed, and he willingly offered his life as a burnt offering to the Lord (Jasher 23:50-56)[3].

This was a foreshadowing of God Himself sacrificing His only Son. However, the Lord stayed Abraham's hand and provided a ram for the offering.

> "By Myself I have sworn, says the Lord, because you have done this thing, and have not withheld your son, your only son – blessing I will bless you, and multiplying I will multiply your descendants as the stars of the heaven and as the sand which is on the seashore; and your descendants shall possess the gate of their enemies. In your seed all the nations of the earth shall be blessed, because you have obeyed My voice" (Gen. 22:16-18).

In a later chapter we will have a look at some of the ways that the Jewish people have blessed mankind.

This Abrahamic Covenant was confirmed with Isaac, as well as with his son Jacob.

Thus far we have seen that Abraham has fathered two sons, Ishmael by Hagar, and Isaac by Sarah. Later we will examine his other progeny.

The Covenant of the Land

As part of the Abrahamic Covenant, God first promised land to Abram in Genesis 12:1. He told Abram to get out from his father's house and his country and go **"to a land that I will show you."** He reiterated His promise of the land of Canaan several more times.

"And the Lord said to Abram, after Lot had separated from him: 'Lift your eyes now and look from the place where you are – northward, southward, eastward, and westward; for all the land which you see I give to you and your descendants forever. And I will make your descendants as the dust of the earth; so that if a man could number the dust of the earth, then your descendants also could be numbered. Arise, walk in the land through its length and its width, for I give it to you.'" Genesis 13:14-17

Genesis 15:18-21 tells us, **"On the same day the LORD made a covenant with Abram, saying, 'To your descendants I have given this land, from the river of Egypt to the great river, the River Euphates – the Kenites, the Kenezzites, the Kadmonites, the Hittites, the Perizzites, the Rephaim, the Amorites, the Canaanites, the Girgashites, and the Jebusites.'"** This took place after the blood covenant when the Shechinah glory passed between the pieces of the sacrificed animals.

Again in Genesis 17:5-8 the Lord said to Abram, **"No longer shall your name be called Abram, but your name shall be Abraham; for I have made you a father of many nations. I will make you exceedingly fruitful; and I will make nations of you, and kings shall come from you. And I will establish My covenant between Me and you and your descendants after you in their generations, for an everlasting covenant to be God to you and your descendants after you. Also I give to you and your descendants after you the land in which you are a stranger, all the land of Canaan, as an everlasting possession; and I will be their God."** Notice that the land mentioned here is an everlasting possession. That is right up to today and beyond today. Everlasting means forever.

It is also a much larger piece of real estate than what is presently considered to be Israel. If Israel continues to bow to pressures from

The Adamic, Noahic, & Abrahamic Covenants

world leaders to give-up land for peace, what remains could become indefensible against their enemies.

They have given away portions of the land they won in the 1967 war in hope of the peace promised, but all they have received is more war, threats of war, suicide bombings, and rockets launched at them. They have been threatened more than once that they will be "wiped off the map." This is an issue which requires the prayers of God's people. World leaders are trying to force Israel to divide Jerusalem, God's Holy City. Thankfully, the Prime Minister is standing his ground in declaring that Jerusalem will never be divided. May God grant him the grace to stay strong in this stance. When Jesus returns He won't be coming to Washington, or to London, or to Ottawa, or to Shanghai. He will be returning to Jerusalem, the City of David, God's Holy City.

It is important for Christians to understand God's covenant promise of the land in this day of world powers trying to force Israel to give away "land for peace." David tells us in the psalms to **'pray for the peace of Jerusalem'** in Psalm 122:6, adding a reward for those who do so, saying, **'May they prosper who love you'**.

Besides our responsibility as Christians to pray for the peace of Jerusalem, we need also to be aware of another part of God's covenant with Abraham, which tells us that God will bless those who bless Abraham and his descendants through the son of promise, Isaac, and He will curse those who curse them. Who are Isaac's descendants?

Genesis 25 tells us that Isaac's wife Rebekah had twins, Esau and Jacob, with Esau being born first. However, he sold his birthright to his twin for a bowl of stew. Genesis 25:30 tells us in the same verse: **Therefore his name was called Edom.**

The New Compact Bible Dictionary states the Edomites were the descendants of Esau. We know from Scripture that Edomites were enemies of the Jewish people. Both Saul and David fought against them.

Consequently it was Jacob who was the son of promise, and not Esau.

Therefore the descendants of Isaac to be the recipients of the covenant promise are the Jewish people through the line of Jacob. How do we bless the Jewish people? I believe the primary way to do this is to pray for them - for their physical safety in their land, and for them to come to recognize their Messiah, Yeshua (Jesus). We also need to be aware of critical issues facing Israel and her people at different times. For example, Israel is a desert country, much of it being barren. However, there are also forests and reclaimed land where they grow lush flowers, fruit and vegetables. They often need prayer for rain. Keep up to date regarding happenings in Israel, and pray for these issues. There are many resources available, both online and through magazines and newspapers. Also pray for wisdom for the leaders of Israel, especially the Prime Minister.

Another way in which we can bless them is to pray for Jewish people around the world to make *aliyah*; that is, to go to live in Israel. God is calling His people home. We can support ministries that make this possible.

Isaiah tells us in chapter 44, verses 5-6:

> "Fear not, for I am with you; I will bring your descendants from the east, And gather them from the west; I will say to the north, Give them up!' And to the south, 'Do not keep them back!' Bring my sons from afar, And my daughters from the ends of the earth.

In Isaiah 49:22-23 the prophet says:

> Thus says the Lord God: "Behold, I will lift My hand in an oath to the nations, And set up My standard for the peoples; They shall

bring your sons in their arms, And your daughters shall be carried on their shoulders; Kings shall be your foster fathers, And their queens your nursing mothers; They shall bow down to you with their faces to the earth, And lick up the dust of your feet. Then you will know that I am the Lord, For they shall not be ashamed who wait for Me."

In the second part of the next verse the Lord says:

For I will contend with him who contends with you, And I will save your children.

There are many issues regarding Israel that daily need our prayers, especially in these last days. I encourage Christians everywhere to keep up to date on the issues facing the Jewish people, both in Israel and around the world. For those with access to a computer there are many websites and ministries dedicated to what is going on in Israel.

We, as Christians, have been 'grafted in' to the family of God's chosen people, the Jews, through our belief in the Jewish Messiah, which I will explain in detail in a later chapter. May we be faithful members of His family!

God has promised to bless those who bless His people, the Jews. I can attest to that in my own life!

Partial Fulfillment of God's Covenant with Abraham

Has God fulfilled His promises to Abraham? In many ways He has. Although the Jewish people have suffered throughout the centuries, as we shall see in a later chapter, He has also blessed them.

He has brought them back to their own land, even though they have had to fight tooth and nail in order to hang on to it.

Consider the percentage of Jewish people who have won Nobel prizes through the years. It is enormous in comparison to other countries and peoples. According to Rabbi Jonathan Bernis in his book 'A Rabbi Looks at the Last Days', "although Jews make up only .2% of the world's population, Jews have won 23 percent of the Nobel Prizes since the award established in 1901."[4] They have excelled in the fields of medicine and technology.

Abraham's descendants have multiplied throughout the earth, although not all are Jewish, as not all are from Isaac's line. But Abraham also sired Ishmael through Hagar, as well as others through his second wife Keturah. The names of Ishmael's descendants are listed in Gen. 25:13-16: ... **The firstborn of Ishmael, Nebajoth; then Kedar, Adbeel, Mibsam, Mishma, Dumah, Massa, Hadar, Tema, Jetur, Naphish, and Kedemah. These were the sons of Ishmael and these were their names, by their towns and their settlements, twelve princes according to their nations.**

The names of his children from Keturah mentioned in Gen. 25:2-4: **And she bore him Zimran, Jokshan, Medan, Midian, Ishback, and Shuah. Jokshan begot Sheba and Dedan. And the sons of Dedan were Asshurim, Letushim, and Leummim. And the sons of Midian were Ephah, Epher, Hanoch, Abidah, and Eldaah. All these were children of Keturah.**

However, verse 5 tells us that **'Abraham gave all that he had to Isaac.'** Verse 6 goes on to inform us that **'Abraham gave gifts to the sons of the concubines which Abraham had; and while he was still living he sent them eastward, away from Isaac his son, to the country of the east.'** A footnote in the Spirit Filled Life Bible says "Some of these names are found today in ancient south-Arabian inscriptions. Midian appears often in the early books of the OT."[5] Some of these names are familiar to us through the pages of Scripture where they are mentioned, such as Sheba (1 Chron. 1:32), Dedan who, besides being a descendant of Abraham, was also

38

a people descended from Noah (Gen. 10:6-7), and Midian, whose descendants, the Midianites, had great wealth in the time of Moses, and whose leaders Gideon and his men chased down and killed (Judges 8). The New Compact Bible Dictionary suggests that Sheba's descendants, by intermarriage or otherwise, finally became identified with the descendants of the son of Raamah, son of Cush (Gen. 10:7; 1 Chron. 1:9), as well as with a son of Joktan, grandson of Eber (Gen.10:28; 1 Chron. 1:22).[6]

Since Abraham sent these children to the countries of the east, by looking at an ancient map they must have been sent to the lands of Bashan, Gilead, Ammon and/or Moab, or perhaps even farther east.

Chapter 3
The Mosaic Covenant

RECALL THAT WHEN GOD was cutting covenant with Abram he fell into a deep sleep, and at that time God foretold that his descendants would be strangers in a land and would serve their masters with affliction for four hundred years. God also foretold that He would judge this nation, and that His people would come out of it with great possessions (Gen. 15:13-15).

Moses was the man God chose to lead His people out of this bondage. In those days the Hebrew midwives were ordered by the king of Egypt to kill all sons that were born to the Hebrew women. However, the midwives feared God, and did not kill the male babies. When Pharaoh learned of this he was angry, and commanded that all the male babies should be thrown into the river.

Moses' mother kept her baby hidden for three months, but when she could no longer hide him she put him in a sealed bulrush basket and placed it by the reeds at the riverbank. The baby's sister stood out of sight to see what would happen to her baby brother. Pharaoh's daughter found the child and had compassion on him. His sister then came out of hiding and offered to find a Hebrew woman to nurse the child for her, and of course called on her mother. The child grew and was weaned probably sometime between the ages of three to five, giving his mother ample time to instruct him about the God of his Hebrew people. Then she gave him to Pharaoh's daughter who raised him as a son. She named him Moses because she had drawn him out of the water, from a Hebrew root meaning "to draw out."

Even though Moses lived in the palace, he had learned enough about his people at his mother's knee that he could not forget about them and their suffering as he grew to manhood. One day he went out to his people and saw an Egyptian beating a Hebrew. In his anger Moses killed the Egyptian and hid him in the sand. However, he had been seen and his deed known. When Pharaoh heard of it he sought to kill Moses, so Moses fled to the land of Midian.

The Midianites were descendants of Abraham through his second wife Keturah, as we have previously seen. Moses lived among them, took a wife, Zipporah, and had a son whom he named Gershom. In time Pharaoh died and the situation and suffering of the Hebew people in Egypt became much worse. They cried out to God in their bondage, and God heard their cry and moved with compassion.

It was at this time that Moses met the LORD at the burning bush, a very pivotal time in Moses' life. God introduced Himself, saying, **"I *am* the God of your father – the God of Abraham, the God of Isaac, and the God of Jacob"** (Ex. 3:6). God told Moses He had come to deliver His people from the hand of the Egyptians, and to bring them into a land flowing with milk and honey. He wanted Moses to go to Pharaoh and bring His people out from bondage. Moses felt unworthy to do this. He had questions for God, and wondered how he would answer the people when he said the God of their fathers had sent him. **And God said to Moses, "I AM WHO I AM." And He said, "Thus you shall say to the children of Israel, "I AM has sent me to you"** (Ex. 3:14), revealing Himself as absolute. In the Hebrew this name relates to the verb "to be," and is the source of the terms "Yahweh," Adonai, or LORD. In Exodus

34:6-7 this Name is explained in terms of His attributes, "**The LORD, the LORD God, merciful and gracious, long-suffering, and abounding in goodness and truth, keeping mercy for thousands, forgiving iniquity and transgression and sin ...**"

But Moses continued to balk. He asked, "What if they don't believe me?" He argued that he was a poor speaker, not eloquent, slow of tongue, and even pleaded that the Lord would send someone else. God was gracious, and even in His anger that roused against Moses, He did not change His mind about whom to send, and said that his brother Aaron could be his mouthpiece.

Thus Moses and Aaron went to Egypt and said to Pharaoh for the first of many times, "Let My people go." There followed ten plagues that God sent upon Pharaoh and the Egyptian people before he finally relented. It took the death of all the firstborn in Egypt before Pharaoh finally said, "Go!"

The Lord instituted the Passover, telling Moses and Aaron to have every man take a lamb without blemish for his household on the 10th of the month (of Nisan/Abib) and keep it until the 14th, when at twilight it should be killed. They were to take some of the blood and put it on the doorposts and lintels of their houses, and eat the lamb that evening with unleavened bread and bitter herbs.

> "And thus you shall eat it: with a belt on your waist, your sandals on your feet, and your staff in your hand. So you shall eat it in haste. It is the Lord's Passover. For I will pass through the land of Egypt on that night, and will strike all the firstborn in the land of Egypt, both man and beast; and against all the gods of Egypt I will execute judgment: I am the Lord." Exodus 12: 11-12

Verse 13 goes on, "**Now the blood shall be a sign for you on the houses where you are. And when I see the blood, I will pass over you; and the plague shall not be on you to destroy you when I strike the land of Egypt.**"

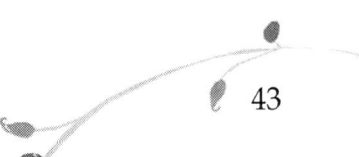

So again we have a blood covenant from the Lord. The Hebrews were protected from the Angel of death by the blood on the doorposts and lintels of their houses, just as in the New Covenant we are covered by the Blood of Jesus in our hearts.

When Pharaoh's firstborn was struck dead, he called for Moses and Aaron, and said **"Rise, go out from among my people, both you and the children of Israel. And go, serve the LORD as you have said"** (Ex. 12:31). The people left with silver, gold and clothing from the Egyptians and journeyed to Succoth, where the Lord again spoke to Moses, telling him to consecrate all the firstborn of both man and beast to the Lord, as a reminder that they were spared when all the firstborn in the land of Egypt were killed.

As they journeyed, the LORD went before them as a pillar of cloud by day and a pillar of fire by night.

The Lord provided another great miracle for them when they reached the Red Sea (or Sea of Reeds), and held the waters back after telling Moses to lift his rod and stretch it forth so that they crossed over on dry ground. The Lord had hardened Pharaoh's heart, and he and all his chariots pursued them. When they entered the dry riverbed where the Israelites had crossed, the Lord again told Moses to stretch forth his hand, and the waters came rushing back over the Egyptians, their chariots and horses.

After traveling for three months they arrived at The Wilderness of Sinai, where God called to Moses and told him to tell the people of Israel, **"You have seen what I did to the Egyptians, and how I bore you on eagles' wings and brought you to Myself. Now, therefore, if you will indeed obey My voice and keep My covenant, then you shall be a special treasure to Me above all people; for all the earth is Mine. And you shall be to Me a kingdom of priests and a holy nation"** (Ex. 19:5-6a).

Three days later Mount Sinai was covered in smoke as the Lord descended upon it in fire and gave the Ten Commandments to

Moses and explained the whole Law to him. This is recognized as the Constitution of Israel.

Moses told the people all the LORD had said to him and the people responded by saying, **"All the words which the LORD has said we will do"** (Ex. 24:3). Moses wrote down all that the Lord had told him, then rose early in the morning and built an altar at the foot of the mountain, and twelve pillars representing the twelve tribes of Israel, and had young men offer burnt offerings and peace offerings of oxen to the Lord. Moses put half the blood from the animals in basins, and the other half he sprinkled on the altar.

Then he took the Book of the Covenant, all that he had written down of the words of the Lord, and read it to the people. Again, they said, **"All that the LORD has said we will do, and be obedient"** (v.7). Then Moses took the blood from the basins and sprinkled it on the people, saying, **"This is the blood of the covenant which the LORD has made with you according to all these words"** (v.8). So again, this covenant was ratified by blood.

Exodus 31 describes the sign of the covenant, which is the Sabbath. The Lord said to Moses, **"Surely My Sabbaths you shall keep, for it is a sign between Me and you throughout your generations, that you may know that I am the LORD who sanctifies you. You shall keep the Sabbath, therefore, for it is holy to you** (v. 13-14a). Verses 16 and 17 make it clear this is for all the people throughout all generations: **Therefore the children of Israel shall keep the Sabbath, to observe the Sabbath throughout their generations as a perpetual covenant. It is a sign between Me and the children of Israel forever; for in six days the LORD made the heavens and the earth, and on the seventh day He rested and was refreshed."**

Deuteronomy 28 begins with promised blessings if the people obey all the Lord's commandments, and the promise that if they do so **"the LORD your God will set you high above all nations of the earth"** (v.1). It then goes on to list the curses of disobedience, which list is much longer than the list of blessings. As believers washed in the Blood of the Lamb we can be thankful that Jesus has **"redeemed us from the curse of the law, having become a curse for us"** (Gal. 3:13).

In the Mosaic Covenant God promised deliverance of His people from the bondage of Egypt to the land earlier promised to Abraham. After God rescued them and brought them to Mount Sinai, He told Moses to tell the children of Israel, **"Now, therefore, if you will indeed obey My voice and keep My covenant, then** *you shall be a special treasure to Me above all people;* **for all the earth is Mine. And** *you shall be to Me a kingdom of priests and a holy nation"* (Ex. 19:5-6, emphasis mine). The Lord gave Moses the Law for His people, recognized as their Constitution, which the people promised to obey, and this covenant was then ratified by the blood of the sacrificed oxen and sprinkled on the people. The sign of the covenant is the Sabbath. Thus the nation of Israel was born.

As we saw in the previous covenants God made, they were essentially a promise, and God did not specifically require a commitment. Here, however, He says "**if** you will obey ... **then** you will be a special treasure to Me." God wanted to create a special people, a people who would seek Him and love Him, listen to Him, and trust Him. He wanted to teach them to praise Him, to see His holiness and His trustworthiness. He wanted to create a people from whom would come the Savior of the world. He wanted to create a people who would be a light to the nations.

Consequently He gave the people His Law, which showed them how to live, eventually carving out a family line through which His Son would be born. This took time and much effort. The people were often disobedient, and instead of reaching their Promised Land in a relatively short time, they wandered around in the wilderness for forty years.

Besides the giving of the Law, the LORD also established His Feasts. The 23rd chapter of Leviticus describes the LORD'S Feasts in

The Mosaic Covenant

detail, which His people were called to observe. We will examine the Feasts in a later chapter.

While in the wilderness, as the people were learning God's ways, Moses was told to build a Tabernacle, a place where God Himself would come and meet with His people. He was to build it according to very detailed specifications, and the furnishings inside the Tabernacle were also crafted according to minute detail. Each item and its color and material had significance, but those details are outside the scope of this current writing.

First they had to reach the land to which God was leading them. As well, they had to battle the people living in the land, and take that which was promised to them.

God knows the end from the beginning, and He knew that the whole world would need a Savior. He knew that He would have to send His Son in the flesh to pay the penalty for the sins of mankind, and not just for His own called-out people. God is love, and His love extends not only to the Jewish people, but to all peoples. As we shall see in a later chapter, although Jesus was born as the Savior of the world, some of the Jewish people, primarily the Jewish leaders of the day, the Pharisees and the Saducees, took offense at the idea that this poor Galilean Rabbi could be the long-promised Messiah, although many of the common people believed in Him. Jesus called out a band of twelve men to become His disciples, and He taught them God's ways. He sent them out to preach and teach, how to pray and how to heal, and they gathered many followers.

However later, the resurrected Jesus called on Saul, later called Paul, who, in his own words was "a Pharisee, the son of a Pharisee," to preach the gospel to the Gentiles, after he had witnessed Steven's death and, wreaking havoc on the believers, was on his way to Damascus to search for believers he could round up and bring to Jerusalem to be judged.

Jesus called Paul to preach to the Gentiles, to share the love of God with them and offer them the salvation bought by Jesus' blood shed on the cross. To say that was a turning point in Paul's life is an understatement. He became zealous for the Gospel, and the Book of Acts describes his preaching and his travels throughout the known world. As well, most of the epistles, or letters of the New Testament were penned by Paul, teaching much doctrine, including that of the Gentile believers being "grafted in" to the Jewish olive tree in the eleventh chapter of his letter to the Romans.

Chapter 4
The Davidic Covenant

SAMUEL ANOINTS DAVID AS KING when David is still a young lad. David doesn't become king until after Saul's death, first as King of Judah, and later over all of Israel. With his enemies defeated, David brings the Ark of the Covenant to Jerusalem, wanting to build a permanent house for it. However, through the prophet Nathan, the LORD said that He would make David a house.

> "When your days are fulfilled and you rest with your fathers, I will set up your seed after you, who will come from your body, and I will establish his kingdom. He shall build a house for My name, and I will establish the throne of his kingdom forever. I will be his Father, and he shall be My son. If he commits iniquity, I will chasten him with the rod of men and with the blows of the sons of men. But My mercy shall not depart from him, as I took it from Saul, whom I removed from before you. And your house and your kingdom shall be established forever before you. Your throne shall be established forever" (2 Sam. 7: 12-16).

In this passage the Lord is referring not only to David's natural son Solomon but also to God's own Son Jesus, also referred to as the "Son of David," whose throne would last forever. This promise will ultimately fulfill when Messiah Jesus returns and He rules and reigns from Jerusalem.

In the latter part of Solomon's life his many wives turned his heart away from the Lord and he followed other gods. The Lord became angry with him.

> "Because you have done this, and have not kept My covenant and My statutes, which I have commanded you, I will surely tear the kingdom away from you and give it to your servant. Nevertheless I will not do it in your days, for the sake of your father David; I will tear it out of the hand of your son. However I will not tear away the whole kingdom; I will give one tribe to your son for the sake of My servant David, and for the sake of Jerusalem which I have chosen" (1 Kings 11:11-13).

Through the prophet Ahijah the Shilonite, Jeroboam, an Ephraimite, son of Nebat, was graphically shown how the Lord was going to take the ten northern tribes away from Solomon and give them to him. Ahijah took hold of the new garment he wore and tore it into twelve pieces.

> And he said to Jeroboam, "Take for yourself ten pieces, for thus says the Lord, the God of Israel: "Behold, I will tear the kingdom out of the hand of Solomon and will give ten tribes to you (but he shall have one tribe for the sake of My servant David, and for the sake of Jerusalem, the city which I have chosen out of all the tribes of Israel)" (1 Kings 11:31-32).

The two pieces remaining were for Solomon's son Rehoboam after Solomon's death. Notice in the verse above the references to two pieces of the garment and one tribe. This "one tribe" represented the tribes of Judah and Benjamin, but as Benjamin assimilated into Judah the two were often considered as "one tribe" and simply referred to as Judah.

The Davidic Covenant

Recall how the LORD spoke to David through the prophet Nathan, **"And your house and your kingdom shall be established forever before you. Your throne shall be established forever"** (2 Sam. 7:16).

In spite of David's sin with Bathsheba, and having Uriah, her husband, killed after she told David she was with child (2 Sa. 10:5) and he desired to marry her, David was 'a man after God's own heart'. Recall that when the LORD told Samuel to anoint David king as a young lad, He said to Samuel, **"For the LORD does not see as man sees; for man looks at the outward appearance, but the LORD looks at the heart"** (1 Sam. 16:7b).

David had a heart for God, although he was not perfect. Listen to him as he yearns for the presence of the LORD:

> One thing I have desired of the Lord,
> That will I seek;
> That I may dwell in the house of the Lord
> All the days of my life,
> To behold the beauty of the Lord,
> And to inquire in His temple. (Ps. 27:4)
>
> Hear, O Lord, when I cry with my voice!
> Have mercy also upon me, and answer me.
> When You said, "Seek My face,"
> My heart said to You, "Your face, Lord, I will seek. (Ps. 27:8)

Psalm 47 tells us in verses 8 and 9a:

> God reigns over the nations'
> God sits on His holy throne.
> The princes of the people have gathered together,
> The people of the God of Abraham.

Psalm 89 refers to David's throne being eternal:

> I have made a covenant with My chosen,
> I have sworn to My servant David;
> Your seed I will establish forever,
> And build up your throne to all generations. (v.3-4)

It speaks also of the qualities of God's throne:

> Righteousness and justice are the foundation of Your throne;
> Mercy and truth go before Your face. (v.14)

This psalm continues in verses 20-21:

> I have found My servant David;
> With My holy oil I have anointed him,
> With whom my hand shall be established;
> Also My arm shall strengthen him.

Verse 27 refers to God's Son Jesus, for He was resurrected from the dead, and ascended into heaven. He is also referred to as the King of kings in Rev. 19:16, which fits with this idea of the 'highest of the kings of the earth':

> Also I will make him My firstborn,
> The highest of the kings of the earth.

The New Covenant

JEREMIAH SPOKE OF A NEW COVENANT in chapter 31, verses 31-33, **"Behold, the days are coming," says the LORD, "when I will make a new covenant with** *the house of Israel and the house of Judah* **- not according to the covenant I made with their fathers in the day that I took them by the hand to lead them out of the land of Egypt, My covenant which they broke, though I was a husband**

to them," says the LORD. "But this is the covenant that I will make with *the house of Israel* after those days," says the LORD, "I will put my law in their minds, and write it on their hearts; and I will be their God, and they shall be My people" (emphasis mine). He goes on in verse 34, "**For I will forgive their iniquity, and their sin I will remember no more.**"

As Christians, we tend to think of these verses about the New Covenant as applying only to us, but notice who God is talking about – the house of Israel and the house of Judah. They broke the Mosaic Covenant through their disobedience and spent 40 years wandering around in the wilderness. They vexed Him sorely, and even though they did not, as a whole, recognize their Messiah when He came to earth, God promises that He will put His law in their minds, and write it on their hearts; He will forgive their iniquity, and not remember their sin. Although we may not presently see the completion of this promise, there has been a presence of Jewish believers in their Messiah in the world, ever since the days of Paul. Until the rise of Messianic Judaism, Jewish believers in their Messiah were called 'Hebrew Christians' and were part of Christian churches throughout the world.

The New Covenant is one that touches and changes the mind and the heart. Paul writes in Romans 2:25-29, "**For circumcision is indeed profitable if you keep the law; but if you are a breaker of the law, your circumcision has become uncircumcision. Therefore, if an uncircumcised man keeps the righteous requirements of the law, will not his uncircumcision be counted as circumcision? And will not the physically uncircumcised, if he fulfills the law, judge you who, *even* with *your* written *code* and circumcision, *are* a transgressor of the law? For he is not a Jew who *is one* outwardly, nor is circumcision that which is outward in the flesh; but he is a Jew who is one inwardly; and circumcision is that of the heart, in the Spirit, not in the letter; whose praise is not from men but from God.**"

Grafted In the Jewish Olive Tree

As an aside, I recall the very first time I read the verse stating that "he is a Jew who is one inwardly" and something resonated within me because I had always "felt" Jewish. That is not what Paul meant when he wrote those words, but they resonate within me just the same. In the verses above, Paul is saying that physical circumcision, in and of itself does not satisfy God's righteousness, but rather what is in our hearts. A Jewish man can be circumcised in the flesh, but if He does not believe God's word, he is not saved. If we believe God's word, His promises, and follow His commands, and since the time of Jesus' birth receive Him as our Savior and Lord, we - Jew or Gentile - become part of God's family. As we shall see in a later chapter, Gentiles who believe in the Jewish Messiah as the Son of God, our Savior and Redeemer, essentially become part of the Jewish olive tree. I have met many Gentile believers who recognize the Jewish roots of our faith, and many 'feel' this same connection, as though, somewhere in our family's history, perhaps there was Jewish blood.

In the New Covenant Jesus gave a new commandment.

> "A new commandment I give to you, that you love one another; as I have loved you, that you also love one another. By this all will know that you are My disciples, if you have love for one another."
> John 13:34-35

The love of Jesus changes us, draws us, transforms us from the way we were before we knew Him to what He wants us to become. Love is the test of discipleship. This kind of love is not a "feeling," but rather a response to His love – a decision, a commitment, an obedience. This is what He requires of us as His disciples.

Paul says in Galatians 2:20-21, "**I have been crucified with Christ; it is no longer I who live, but Christ lives in me; and the *life* which I now live in the flesh I live by faith in the Son of God, who loved me and gave Himself for me. I do not set aside the** grace of God; for if righteousness *comes* through the law, then Christ died in vain."

I began this section with Jeremiah's words of promise of a new covenant with the house of Israel and the house of Judah, that God would put His law in their minds and write it on their hearts. This promise is fulfilled, at least in part, through the ministry of Jesus and later of His disciples.

In Acts we read of the Day of Pentecost, when the Holy Spirit was poured out upon the disciples and Peter spoke, his words cutting to the heart of the people, who asked, **"What shall we do?"** (Acts 2:37) Peter answered and said, **"Repent, and let every one of you be baptized in the name of Jesus Christ for the remission of sins; and you shall receive the gift of the Holy Spirit. For the promise is to you and to your children, and to all who are afar off, as many as the Lord our God will call"** (v. 38-39). About three thousand people join their number that one day.

As Christians, we often, in our ignorance, assume that because the Jewish authorities, consisting of the chief priests, the scribes and the Pharisees did not recognize Jesus as the Messiah, that the Jewish people collectively did not recognize Him or follow Him. However, crowds of Jewish people followed Him to listen to Him, and He healed many of them. Matthew 4:25 tells us that **Great multitudes followed Him – from Galilee, and from Decapolis, Jerusalem, Judea, and beyond the Jordan.** The Gospels indicate many individuals by name who sought after the Lord and believed in Him, as well as multitudes who believed in Him. Many of these He healed.

The following is a partial list of names and references:

Matthew the tax collector – Matt. 9:9

The woman with an issue of blood – Matt. 9:20

The two blind men – Matt. 9 31

The blind and the lame – Matt. 21:14

The demon-possessed blind and mute person healed – Matt. 12:22. (Verse 23 tells us: And all the multitudes were amazed and said, "Could this be the Son of David?")

Two blind men near Jericho – Matt. 20:29-34

Multitudes spreading branches from the trees and crying out, "Hosanna to the Son of David! Blessed is He who comes in the name of the Lord! Hosanna in the highest!" And when He had come into Jerusalem, all the city was moved, saying, "Who is this?" So the multitudes said, "This is Jesus, the prophet from Nazareth of Galilee." - Matt. 21:8-11.

The paralytic and his friends in Capernaum – Mark 2:1-5, 11-12

A great multitude followed Him **from Galilee ... and from Judea and Jerusalem and Idumea and beyond the Jordan; and those from Tyre and Sidon, a great multitude** - Mark 3:7b – 8

Jairus, leader of the synagogue – Mark 5:22-23

The woman with the flow of blood – Mark 5:25-34. Verses 27- 28 tell us: **When she heard about Jesus, she came behind Him in the crowd and touched His garment. For she said, "If only I may touch His clothes, I shall be made well."** The fringes on Jesus' prayer shawl, or tallit, were often referred to as "wings." This is what this woman wanted to touch so she could be healed, for she obviously clung to the promise in Mal. 4:2: **But to you who fear My name the Sun of Righteousness shall arise with healing in His wings.**

Blind Bartimaeus – Mark 10:47

In Galilee – Luke 4:15 – **And He taught in their synagogues, being glorified by all.**

People witnessing the raising of the widow of Nain's son from death – Luke 7:16-17

Zaccheus, a chief tax collector – Luke 19:3

The Davidic Covenant

Nicodemus, a Pharisee – John 3:1-2

Samaritan woman, and telling others – John 4:28-30

There are several verses in the book of Acts indicating Jewish people joining their number:

Acts 4:4 - many of those who heard the word believed; and the number of the men came to be about five thousand.

Acts 5:14 – And believers were increasingly added to the Lord, multitudes of both men and women.

Acts 6:7 - Then the word of God spread, and the number of the disciples multiplied greatly in Jerusalem, and a great many of the priests were obedient to the faith.

Acts 21:20 – And when they heard it, they glorified the LORD. And they said to him: "You see, brother, how many myriads of Jews there are who have believed, and they are all zealous for the law:"

Several of the above references use words like "multitudes" and "myriads." These words do not indicate just a few, but very many. This Jewish response to the gospel continued for perhaps a couple hundred years, and at the same time the gospel is taken to the Gentiles, begun through the ministry of Paul, Barnabas and others.

However, there came a time in history when Christians essentially separated themselves from the Jews, especially as persecution of them became more and more rampant. As a result, for hundreds of years Jewish people do not hear the gospel, and many of those who did become 'Hebrew Christians' became so under great duress - "Be baptized or die!"

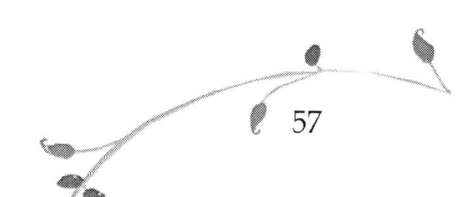

In more recent centuries the Church became mostly Gentile. Christians hear 'Replacement Theology' - that the Church had replaced the Jews in God's heart. As we shall see later, that is a complete lie!

We, as Christians have the responsibility to share the gospel, not only to our Gentile friends and acquaintances, but to Jewish people as well. We will delve into this subject in more detail in a later chapter.

The New Jerusalem

PERHAPS WE DON'T VIEW the promise of the new Jerusalem as a covenant; however, it is a promise. In the book of Revelation, John describes a new heaven and a new earth in Chapter 21, after all the judgments of the previous chapters. In verse 2 he writes, "**Then I, John, saw the Holy City, New Jerusalem, coming down out of heaven from God, prepared as a bride adorned for her husband.**" Verses 3 and 4 continue, "**And I heard a loud voice from heaven saying, 'Behold, the tabernacle of God is with men, and He will dwell with them, and they shall be His people. God Himself will be with them and be their God. And God will wipe away every tear from their eyes; there shall be no more death, nor sorrow, nor crying. There shall be no more pain, for the former things have passed away.'**"

John then goes on to describe the new city of Jerusalem descending out of heaven, with a great high wall and twelve gates, three on each side, with the names of the twelve tribes of Israel written on them, which signify those to whom the old covenant was made. As well, the wall of the city had twelve foundations, on which were written the names of the twelve apostles, signifying those to whom the new covenant was given. Together they represent the people of God who will dwell in the new city of Jerusalem, which is a perfect cube, signifying perfection.

There was no temple in this New Jerusalem, as John tells us in Rev. 21:22, for God Himself and the Lamb are its temple. As well, there was no need of a sun or a moon, for God's glory illuminates it.

John hears Jesus saying, in Rev. 22:12, **"Behold, I am coming quickly, and My reward is with Me, to give to every one according to his work. I am the Alpha and the Omega, the Beginning and the End, the First and the Last."**

Although the Church has not termed the New Jerusalem as a covenant, God does present this promise, along with the conditions which we must adhere to if we want to see this promise for us. Verse 14, **"Blessed are those who do His commandments, that they may have the right to the tree of life, and may enter through the gates into the city."**

This is what the future holds in store for those of us who know the Lord Jesus, the Son of God, and have been washed clean by His blood. And we shall be with the Lord forever!

I would venture to suggest, in view of the fact that the number seven is God's number of perfection, that along with the following:

1) The Adamic Covenant
2) The Noahic Covenant
3) The Abrahamic Covenant (including the Covenant of the Land)
4) The Mosaic Covenant
5) The Davidic Covenant
6) The New Covenant

.... that we could add The New Jerusalem as the 7th Covenant promise from God.

In this chapter we have looked at the past, as well as ahead to the future. In the next chapter we are going to examine the early days of the New Covenant, the early church.

PART 2

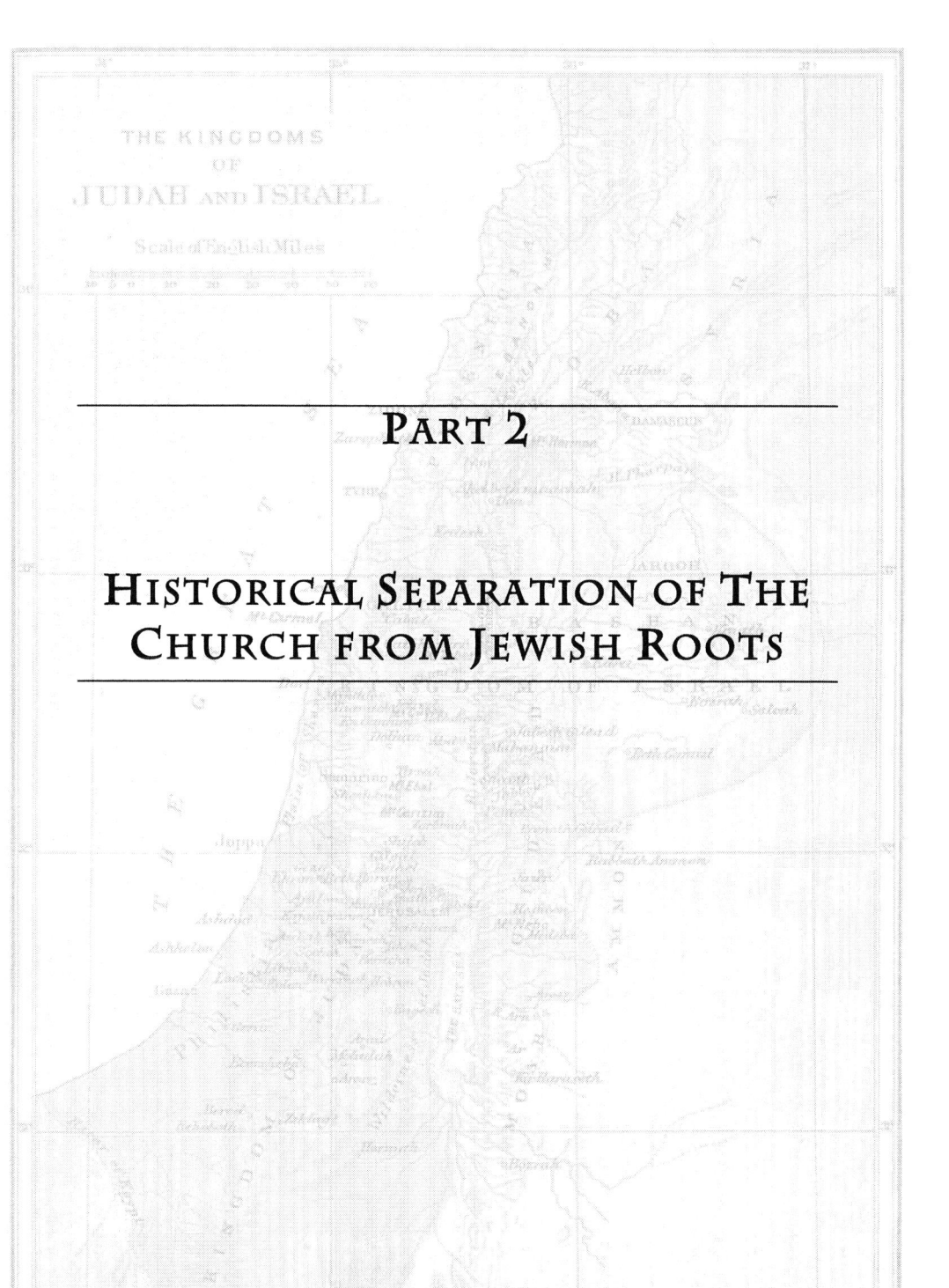

HISTORICAL SEPARATION OF THE CHURCH FROM JEWISH ROOTS

Chapter 5
The Early Church

MANY IN THE CHURCH TODAY are hungry for MORE! We tire of the "same old, same old" and desire for God to move among us. We have heard of the revivals throughout history, and we want to taste it, to experience it. We long for a touch from God. We want to see His power. We desire to see His glory. We long for miracles, signs and wonders, like we read about in the book of Acts. We want to SEE healings when we pray for the sick. We long to see blind eyes opened, and the lame walking, and yes, even the dead raised to life.

These things took place in the early church as a matter of course. They were *expected*. Do we really expect miracles today when we pray for someone? Perhaps we have a thing or two to learn from the early church.

MIRACLES, SIGNS AND WONDERS

A GREAT MANY HEALINGS and other miracles took place in the early days of the church through Peter and the apostles, and later through Paul. In Lydda, a man named Aeneas is healed of paralysis (Acts 9:34). In Joppa, Peter prayed for a woman who had died named Tabitha, who came back to life (Acts 9:40). He was miraculously brought out of prison by an angel (Acts 12:6-8). As well, Paul commanded a spirit of divination to leave a girl who made money for her masters through fortune-telling (Acts 16:18). Because of this, Paul and Silas were put in jail, but as they were praying and singing hymns, an earthquake shook the foundations and the doors were opened and their chains were loosed (Acts 16:25, 26). Even when they laid handkerchiefs on the bodies of the sick healings and deliverance occurred (Acts 19:12-13). The power of God worked through them.

Over the centuries the church lost this power of God as it separated itself from its Jewish roots and became institutionalized. Thankfully in more recent years we have seen a resurgence of God's miracle-working power being returned in greater and greater measure. This seems to happen particularly in the eastern hemisphere. If, perhaps, the west is too modern and advanced to believe in the power of God it is certainly our loss!

THE EARLY CHURCH

PAUL SAYS IN 1 COR. 14:26 – 31, **"Whenever you come together, each of you has a psalm, has a teaching, has a tongue, has a revelation, has an interpretation. Let all things be done for edification. If anyone speaks in a tongue, let there be two or at the most three, each in turn, and let one interpret. But if there is no interpreter, let him keep silent in church, and let him speak to himself and to God. Let two or three prophets speak, and let the others judge. But if anything is revealed to another who sits by, let the first keep silent. For you can all prophesy one by one, that all may learn and all may be encouraged."**

This certainly doesn't sound like many church services today, which are more like that of "performance/audience" than of participation. So what did the early church gatherings look like? Dr. Robert D. Heidler, in his book "The Messianic Church Arising,"

The Early Church

gives us a picture of what it might have been like. He bases his description on the New Testament as well as on other early Christian literature. It is very different from anything we have ever experienced. The "imaginary" church he describes is in Rome in A.D. 95:

"The church we are going to visit is a house church. The early church operated on two levels: the house church and the congregation. Even if the church grew to 20 or 30,000 members, its primary unit would still be the house church. From time to time the house churches would also agree to congregate in a larger group (the congregation). This often took place outdoors or in a rented auditorium. In Jerusalem, they met in the temple courts.

The time is Saturday evening. By Jewish reckoning, the first day of the week began at sundown on Saturday. The church meets in the evening because many of the people have to work during the day. We arrive at the door of a typical Roman house and are warmly welcomed by the host.

Let me warn you before you go in to be prepared for a serious case of "culture shock." What you are about to witness is not church life as you have known it.

As we walk through the door, you look across the entrance into a large open courtyard of the home. There appears to be some kind of party going on. Some of the people are playing flutes, lyres, and tambourines, while others are singing, dancing, and clapping their hands.

You immediately look around to make sure you came into the right house! As you listen to the words, however, you realize that this is the right place, for the words of the songs are words of praise to Jesus! These people are overflowing with joy because they have come to know the living God.

What you are witnessing is the way the early church praised God. This type of worship is foreign to much of the church today, but from the biblical and historical records, this is what the worship in the early church was like. It was a free and joyful celebration, with a great deal of singing and dancing.

Most church services would begin with the people getting in a ring (or several concentric rings) and dancing Jewish-style ring dances (like the Hora)

So here we are in a large courtyard. There is a great deal of singing, dancing, and rejoicing in the Lord. As the songs slow down a little, many people get down on their knees before the Lord. Most are lifting up hands to Him. A tremendous sense of the Lord's presence fills the courtyard.

During the church's praise and worship, there are spontaneous shouts of praise. Some shout, "Amen!" to voice their agreement with what others have said. As we enter into the worship, we are overwhelmed by the love and acceptance of the people."[1]

"After much singing and dancing, food is brought out. People find their seats and prepare for the meal. We are surprised to see people eating a meal in the middle of a church service, but this is described by Paul in 1 Corinthians, as well as by Jude and Peter. This shared weekly meal is called the "love feast" or Agape.

To begin the meal, the woman of the house lights the candles, saying a special prayer of thanksgiving. Then one of the leaders stands with a cup, blesses the Lord, and passes it around so each one can drink from it. He then picks up a loaf of bread and offers thanks. It also is passed from person to person. This is the Lord's Supper in its original context.

The meal is a joyful time centered on devotion to the Lord. As they eat, the believers talk about the things of God, share testimonies, recite and discuss Scripture, and sing praises to the Lord. You are impressed that, while very few have personal copies of any biblical books, most of those present appear to have large portions of the Bible memorized.

During the meal, one of the leaders stands and reads a letter they received that week from an apostle named Junia.

The Early Church

Junia was not one of the original twelve apostles, but by this time there were many apostles in the church.

As you hear the letter read, you are surprised to learn that Junia is a woman! (In Romans 16 Paul describes a woman named Junia as "outstanding among the apostles.")

The leaders of this house church had written to Junia some weeks earlier to seek advice on some issues, and in her letter, Junia carefully addressed each of their questions. It is clear that all present hold Junia in high regard, for they all pay careful attention as her letter is read.

After the meal ends, worship continues until, at some point, a change begins to take place. There is a subtle shift in the atmosphere. The air seems to thicken. A tangible sense of the Presence of God comes and rests in the place. First Corinthians chapter five describes it this way, "When you are assembled in the name of the Lord Jesus ... and the power of our Lord Jesus is present..."

As those assembled sense the Presence of God, some fall to the ground in worship. Others stop and are silent, welcoming the Lord's Presence.

As the Presence of God rests in their midst, ministry begins to take place..... A woman... gives a word of knowledge for healing. A man raises his hand and people cluster around to pray for him. He is instantly healed.

Someone else stands up and reads a passage of Scripture. Another man, a teacher, gives an explanation of the passage.. A woman stands and gives a beautiful prophetic song. Many are so touched by its beauty and anointing they begin to weep.

Prophetic words are given. There are tongues and interpretation. Through it all, they continue to move in and out of worship. This scenario is clearly described in 1 Corinthians 14:23-32.

This is how the early church met and ministered. At one point a man introduces a family who have been sitting quietly near the back of the crowd. They are his neighbors. You can tell by the look on their faces that this is their first time here, and they are not sure they are in the right place.

The man says they have come tonight because their 12-year-old daughter has contracted an illness that has left her totally blind. They have come for the church to pray for her. Those with the gift of healing come and stand with the elders as they anoint the little girl with oil and pray. Suddenly the little girl begins to cry. With tears running down her cheeks, she cries out, "I can see! I can see!"

The mother crouches down and hugs her daughter, and within four or five minutes the entire family is saved, giving their hearts to Jesus.

A prophetic word is given revealing the secrets of someone's heart. That person comes forward and says, "I don't know Jesus but I know God is here. I want to know Him."

Ministry continues. This is where much of the evangelism in the church took place... through the miraculous power of God working in the midst of His people."[2]

I wanted to share with you the entire picture of Dr. Heidler's description of what the early church was like. Isn't it a beautiful picture? This sounds more like the type of thing Paul spoke about in the above scripture verse: a psalm, a teaching, a revelation. Wouldn't it be wonderful to meet together in such an intimate setting to worship and fellowship? Wouldn't it be wonderful to see the power of God at work with such immediate results? Wouldn't it be wonderful to take part in evangelism so natural?

How I long for that day!

THE GOSPEL TAKEN TO THE GENTILES

SINCE THE TIME DESCRIBED in the last section, many detrimental changes have taken place in the church. Translation of the Gospels

The Early Church

and the letters resulted in much of the Jewish idiom and thought being replaced by Greek influences. According to Daniel Gruber in his book, "The Separation of Church and Faith Vol. 1, Copernicus and the Jews," even Greeks did not like the Greek translation because it contained peculiarities in the grammar and vocabulary that were not found in ordinary Greek.

The first followers of Jesus were Jews, and preaching occurred in synagogues and the countryside to the Jewish people. Although some of the Jewish leaders of the day did not believe Him, many Jews believed that this Jewish Rabbi was the long-awaited Messiah. It was not until Peter received the vision and was told to go to Cornelius' house that the gospel was preached to Gentiles, and they realized that **"God had also granted to the Gentiles repentance to life"** (Acts 11:18).

The early church was built on Hebraic roots, with Yeshua, Jesus' Hebrew name, (meaning "salvation") as its foundation stone. Their Scriptures promised a coming Messiah, and these men and women recognized Him as such. In fact, it was considered one of several Jewish sects, along with the Sadducees, Pharisees, and Essenes. It was the old religion become new, because the Messiah they had long been waiting for had come. Followers of Jesus were called "Nazarenes." I would like to note here that the original Hebrew word translated from the Greek *ecclesia* as "church" was *kahila,* and means "assembly."

It was only after Paul had his Damascus Road experience and began preaching to the Gentiles that the church began to get significant numbers of Gentile members. It wasn't until the eleventh chapter of Acts that believers in Antioch were called Christians. A footnote in The Spirit Filled Life Bible on Acts 11:26 suggests that the term "Christian" was "most likely a derisive name given to the early followers of Christ...not unlike a believer today being called a 'Jesus-person' in an uncomplimentary way."[3] I recall in the 1970s when there was a revival happening and many were coming to the Lord, they were often referred to as "Jesus freaks," which certainly was not complimentary.

After these changes, from being primarily Jewish to including so many Gentiles, the Judaizers began giving Paul trouble, for they taught that Gentiles must be circumcised according to the custom of Moses in order to be saved (see Acts 15:1).

THE JERUSALEM DECREE

AS A RESULT OF THE DISSENSION, Paul, Barnabus and others went up to Jerusalem to meet with the leaders there to settle this question. They discovered that some of the believing Pharisees also thought that Gentiles should be circumcised and that they should keep the law of Moses. The Judaizers and the believing Pharisees thought that Gentiles should become Jews first, in order to be Messianic.

After much discussion, Peter stood up and reminded them how God had commanded him to preach to the Gentiles at Cornelius' house, and the Holy Spirit came upon them just as He had at Pentecost to the Jewish believers, making no distinction between the Jews and the Gentiles. Paul and Barnabus then spoke, describing the wonderful miracles that were being done among the Gentiles.

Finally James spoke, and reminded them of Amos' words of prophecy concerning **"the Gentiles who are called by My name"** (Amos 9: 11-12), and told them that Gentiles who are turning to God should not be troubled with the Law of Moses, in particular circumcision, and a decree was drawn up saying the Gentile believers should **"abstain from things polluted by idols, from sexual immorality, from things strangled, and from blood"** (Acts 15:20).

Thus the Jerusalem Decree was drafted (see Acts 15:24-29).

It is interesting to note that this first council of the church was made up of Jewish believers, and the question dealt with whether a person had to become a Jew in order to be saved. Paul later wrote that **"there is neither Jew nor Greek** (Gentile)... **slave nor free... male nor female... for (we) are all one in Christ Jesus'** (Gal. 3:28). In the fourth century, after the church had become mostly Gentile and "Romanized," a Jew who believed in Jesus as the Messiah was required to become "Christian" and give up his Jewish traditions.

Regarding the "four necessary things" that James spoke of, do we, as believers, obey these commands? Or do we look at the first one - to abstain from things offered to idols - and think, "This doesn't apply in today's world," and just skip over the rest? What about things strangled? What about blood? How do we know how our meat is prepared? How should a believer view these missives today? It was important enough to mention these things twice in nine verses. If the outcome of the Jerusalem Council was essentially these commands for Gentile believers, perhaps we should be paying more attention to them. Food for thought...

The point I am stressing is that the earliest assembly was made up of Messianic Jews, who believed that Yeshua (Jesus) was their long-awaited Messiah. Believing that Jesus was who He claimed to be did not make them non-Jews. Yeshua, after all, was Jewish. In fact, they continued to meet on the Sabbath, in the synagogues, for several centuries.

Later the Church was cut off and separated from her Jewish roots, and replaced with a "Romanized" version of Christianity, much to our detriment. For although Luther and his Reformation did break away from the church in Rome, many early influences remain to this day. We shall examine these in a later chapter.

Chapter 6
The Roman Influence

THE PREVIOUS CHAPTER SPOKE of the spread of the Gospel to the Gentiles, the difficulties that were encountered, and finally, the Jerusalem Decree which spelled out the requirements of the Gentile believers with regard to Jewish life and law. This growth was wrought through persecution by the religious Jews towards believing Jews, who were imprisoned and put to death for their faith.

However, by Acts Chapter 12 Herod began to harass believers as well, and **"killed James the brother of John with the sword"** (verse 2), and put Peter into prison. He died a violent death at the hand of an angel a short time later, who struck him for not giving glory to God, and he was eaten by worms (v.23). His death occurred in AD 44.

The church continued to grow and spread through Paul's missionary journeys.

PERSECUTION OF CHRISTIANS

PERSECUTION OF CHRISTIANS began with Nero in 64 AD after Rome burned. Scholars believe that Nero himself set the fires. He needed a scapegoat, someone to blame, so he blamed the Christians. Chaim Potok, in his book "Wanderings," quotes Tacitus, "To get rid of the rumor, Nero fastened the guilt and inflicted the most brutal torture on a class hated for their abominations, called Christians by the populace."[1] In the following centuries, Christians continued to be persecuted by Rome, and many were martyred. From 303 to 312 AD the Church suffered its worst persecutions under Roman Emperor Diocletion as well as Galerius, who followed him.

Finally, in 311 AD, Roman Emperor Galerius "made a deathbed statement repenting the persecutions and granting legal recognition to Christians."[2]

Maximus was successor to Galerius. However, Constantine challenged him for the throne. Constantine worshiped the Unconquerable Sun, as had his father before him. The story goes that Constantine had a vision of the words "in hoc signo vinces" on a Christian cross before the battle, and therefore ordered his soldiers to paint a cross on their standards. Maximus' army greatly outnumbered Constantine's, thus he considered his victory a "miracle" and subsequently converted to Christianity. Scholars continue to debate how genuine his conversion to Christianity was, as his baptism did not occur until he was on his deathbed years later:

> "Soon after the Feast of Easter 337, Constantine fell seriously ill. [218] He left Constantinople for the hot baths near his mother's city of Helenopolis (Altinova), on the southern shores of the Gulf of izmit. There, in a church his mother built in honor of Lucian the Apostle, he prayed, and there he realized that he was dying. Seeking purification, he became a catechumen, and attempted a return to Constantinople, making it only as far as a suburb of Nicomedia. [219] He summoned the bishops, and told them of his hope to be baptized in the River Jordan, where Christ was written to have been baptized. He requested the baptism right away, promising to live a more

Christian life should he live through his illness. The bishops, Eusebius records, "performed the sacred ceremonies according to custom." [220] He chose the Arianizing bishop, Eusebius of Nicomedia, bishop of the "Nicomedia" city where he lay dying, as his baptizer. [221] In postponing his baptism, he followed one custom at the time which postponed baptism until old age or death. [222] It was thought Constantine put off baptism as long as he did so as to be absolved from as much of his sin as possible. [223] Constantine died soon after at a suburban villa called Achyron, on the last day of the fifty-day festival of Pentecost directly following Easter, on 22 May 337." [224] [3]

THE CHURCH UNDER CONSTANTINE

AS VICTOR IN THE BATTLE against Maximus, Constantine became emperor of the Roman Empire. In the year 315 AD he published the Edict of Milan in which he granted religious tolerance to Christians, but Jews were no longer allowed to live in Jerusalem, their Holy City, nor could they share their faith. He wanted to remove the church as far as possible from anything "Jewish."

It was Constantine who called and presided over the first Church Council at Nicaea in 325 AD to combat the heresy of Arianism. As noted in the above quote, Constantine was baptized by the Arianizing bishop Eusebius shortly before his death, so at some point he obviously changed his mind regarding Arianism. He instituted Sunday as a compulsory day of rest. This was due, in part, to give honor to his Sun god, also to distance the church from the Jews. In view of his questionable conversion, it makes one wonder what the leaders of the church were thinking to grant such authority to the Roman Emperor. He certainly was not baptized at this time, as we saw above.

At this same Council of Nicea it was ruled, regarding Passover:

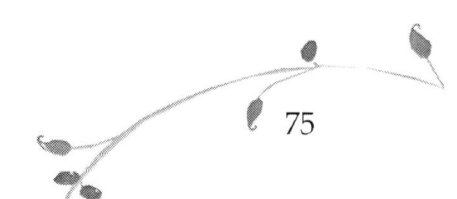

> "For it is unbecoming beyond measure that on this holiest of festivals we should follow the custom of the Jews. Henceforth let us have nothing in common with this odious people ... We ought not, therefore, to have anything in common with the Jews ... our worship follows a ... more convenient course ... we desire dearest brethren, to separate ourselves from the detestable company of the Jews ... How, then, could we follow these Jews, who are almost certainly blinded."[4]

Also in the fourth century the Church of Constantinople mandated the following:

> "I renounce all customs, rites, legalisms, unleavened breads and feasts of lambs of the Hebrews, sacrifices, prayers, aspersions, purifications, sanctifications and propitiations, and fasts, and new moons, and Sabbaths, and superstitions, and hymns and chants and observances and synagogues, and the food and drink of the Hebrews; in one word, I renounce absolutely everything Jewish, every law, rite and custom ..."[5]

Since from that time forward the Church cut itself off from anything Jewish, how were they able to understand God's Word? Consequent preaching and teaching became corrupted from the truth and gave rise to Replacement Theology, which still affects the church today. We are missing out on the Jewish understanding of the Scriptures, which were written by Jewish people, with the exception of Luke's Gospel and the Book of Acts, and he was in all likelihood a proselyte to the Jewish faith. There is a depth of understanding available that we cannot fathom without taking Jewish thought, idioms and customs into account. I have heard it said that we should read God's Word with "Jewish eyes"; perhaps with a Jewish heart as well.

Throughout history much of the truth of the Gospel vanishes. The Dark Ages were dark in a spiritual sense. The Church had lost its meaning and purpose, joining itself to paganism and to the state. The Middle Ages saw pomp and ceremony in Rome as befitted kings and royalty. Erasmus of Rotterdam, arriving in Rome for the first time, appalled the pomp and ceremony surrounding the pope, and thought it more fitting for a king than for the head of God's church.

PAGAN INFLUENCES

WE CELEBRATE CHRISTMAS on December 25 as the birth of our Lord, but we know that isn't really the date He was born. Serious Bible scholars and Messianic Jews agree that Jesus was not born on December 25th, but more likely during the Feast of Tabernacles in the fall. Have you ever stopped to think why we celebrate on this day? Where did this date come from? In fact, it was chosen to coincide with the pagan festival of Saturnalia which celebrated the birth of Tammuz, the son of Semiramis, the widow of Nimrod, (see Gen. 10:6-12) whose kingdom began in Babel. I will speak more about this in the next chapter. Constantine didn't want to upset the pagans by making too many changes, and he also desired a greater influx of pagans into the church, so he took a pagan festival and "Christianized" it, calling it Christmas, to celebrate Jesus' birth.

He changed the celebration of Passover to Easter which in reality celebrated the fertility goddess Asherah or Astarte, who supposedly came from the gods in a giant egg. The Bible warns us in many references about this female counterpart to Baal (see Judges 3:7; 1 Kings 18:19). Josiah, in 2 Kings 23:4, ordered all the articles that were made for Baal and Asherah to be burned, as he restored true worship to God.

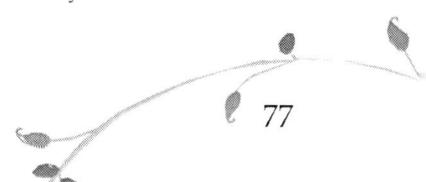

These ancient Easter occult celebrations began with a service at sunrise to honor the sun god, and included sex ceremonies as part of their fertility rites, as well as egg hunts and the bunny rabbit, of which the latter remain part of Easter to this day. What has all this to do with Christ's resurrection from the dead? Yet even today, 2000 years later, many in the church seem oblivious to the paganism evident even in this celebration, and if not oblivious, consider it too unimportant to consider its ramifications. I often wonder what God thinks. Just because we have "always done it that way" doesn't necessarily make it right.

In the next chapter we will consider the root of these pagan influences.

"*It is finished*"

JOHN'S GOSPEL TELLS US that Jesus said, **"It is finished!"** and then gave up His spirit (John 19:30). He had finished the work that His Father had given Him to do. He had come to enact the New Covenant that had been promised many years before, **"But this is the covenant that I will make with the house of Israel after those days, says the LORD: I will put My law in their minds, and write it on their hearts; and I will be their God, and they shall be My people"** (Jeremiah 31:33). In His obedience to His Father, Jesus paid the ultimate price as the ultimate sacrifice for the sins of mankind. He was the sacrificial Lamb of God, sacrificed at that last Passover of His life on earth.

Jesus changed the requirements from keeping the letter of the law, as in the Old Mosaic Covenant, to keeping the spirit of the law, which is faith. Paul tells us in Romans 2:29, "**... but he is a Jew who is one inwardly; and circumcision is that of the heart, in the Spirit, not in the letter; whose praise is not from men but from God.**"

Chapter 7
Paganism In The Church

AFTER THE CHURCH JOINED WITH Constantine the Roman Emperor, she became infiltrated with pagan ideas and severed herself from her Jewish roots. She became, at that point, the Roman Catholic Church, and remained so until the time of Martin Luther in the sixteenth century.

Throughout those many centuries the Church moved away from the first-century model the apostles initiated as they sought the Holy Spirit. In so doing, they agreed to mix their beliefs with pagan practices and dates. The Bible tells us what God thought of such mixtures. It provoked Him to anger.

What the Bible Says

IN CHAPTER 7 OF THE BOOK of Jeremiah God is angry because **"The children gather wood, the fathers kindle the fire, and the women knead dough, to make cakes for the queen of heaven; and they pour out drink offerings to other gods, that they may provoke Me to anger"** (verse 18). When I was growing up in the Roman Catholic Church, Mary, the mother of Jesus, was referred to as the "Queen of Heaven." In May of each year there was a ceremony to crown a statue of Mary with a garland of flowers. As a child, through to high school, I participated in these ceremonies. Yes, we are to honor the mother of Jesus and to call her blessed. But are we to call her the "Queen of heaven?"

Who is this "queen of heaven" referred to in the above Scripture verse? In Ezekiel 8 the Lord took Ezekiel in the spirit to the temple in Jerusalem. In verse 5 the Lord points to the image of jealousy at the entrance north of the altar gate, saying, **"Son of man, lift your eyes now toward the north." So I lifted my eyes toward the north, and there, north of the altar gate, was this image of jealousy in the entrance.** What is an image of jealousy? In the Ten Commandments we are told, **"You shall have no other gods before Me. You shall not make for yourself a carved image – any likeness of anything that is in heaven above, or that is in the earth beneath, or that is in the water under the earth; you shall not bow down to them nor serve them. For I, the LORD your God, am a jealous God, visiting the iniquity of the fathers upon the children to the third and fourth generations of those who hate Me, but showing mercy to thousands, to those who love Me and keep My commandments"** (Ex. 20:3-6).

An image of jealousy, then, is any image, although this particular one is likely the image of Asherah, who is also called Ashtarte or Ashtoreth, the fertility goddess and the "queen of heaven," spoken of in 2 Kings 21:7 when Manasseh placed a carved image of her in the temple. Manasseh was Israel's most wicked king, reviving idol worship and desecrating the sacred things of the Lord. He even sacrificed his son to Molech. When Josiah became king he restored true worship; he cleansed the temple of **"all the articles that were made for Baal, for Asherah, and for all the host of heaven"** (2 Kings 23:4).

Ezekiel 8:14 speaks about the women "weeping for Tammuz" when the Lord showed him all the abominations that were taking place in the temple. According to Babylonian legend, after Nimrod's death he ascended into heaven and became the sun god.

The rays of the sun then impregnated his widow Semiramis, and Tammuz was miraculously born during the winter solstice. According to legend, as an adult he was gored by a wild boar. The women wept over his death.

ROOTS OF PAGANISM

OBVIOUSLY THEN, PAGANISM GOES back a long way. Where and how did it originate? Chapter 10 of Genesis describes the nations that descended from Noah and his sons Shem, Ham and Japheth after the flood. One of the sons of Ham was Cush. Verses 8 and 9 tell us, **"Cush begot Nimrod; he began to be a mighty one on the earth. He was a mighty hunter before the LORD; therefore it is said, "Like Nimrod the mighty hunter before the LORD."** The Bible goes on to tell us that the beginning of his kingdom was Babel... in the land of Shinar. He then went to Assyria and built Nineveh.

We are all familiar with the story of the Tower of Babel. These descendents of Cush, through Nimrod, wanted to make a name for themselves by building a tower so high it would reach the heavens. Until that time the whole earth had one language, but after the tower was built, God confused their language so they could no longer understand one another, and scattered them over the face of the earth.

God said in Genesis 1:26 – **"Let Us make man in Our image,"** signifying the Godhead. The Church has used the term" Trinity" for centuries to signify the Father, Son and Holy Spirit. I recently came across the term "Tri-Unity" as a more fitting word to describe the Godhead. As there is only one God, perhaps it is a better word to use.

The ancient world also recognized a "trinity" of sorts indicating this primeval doctrine. In ancient Babylon they had the goddess mother, Semiramis and her son Tammuz. Worship of "Mother and

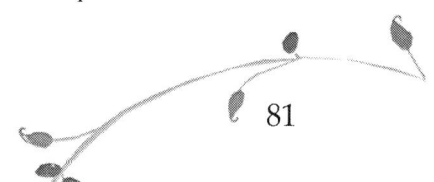

Child" spread throughout the known world, having different names in different countries.

The following chart shows the names of the mother and son throughout the ancient world:

Area	Mother	Son
Babylon	Semiramis	Tammuz
Egypt	Isis	Osiris
India	Isi	Iswara
Asia	Cybele	Deoius
Pagan Rome	Fortuna	Jupiter-puer
Greece	Ceres	Babe at her breast
Greece	Irene, goddess of Peace	Plutus

Semiramis, the origin of the "goddess," derived all her glory from her son Tammuz. We can see how the Roman church received its idea of honoring Mary holding Jesus in her arms, a common statue in Roman Catholic churches, at least in former days.

As noted above, the women of Israel were weeping for Tammuz. The following explanation does get complicated for western ears, but please bear with me. In mythology, Tammuz is also known as Bacchus, the "Lamented One." In classical history this "lamented one" seems to have been the husband of Semiramis, and whose name, Ninus, literally signified the son. It sounds confusing that Ninus is sometimes called the husband, and sometimes the son of Semiramis. Semiramis was worshipped as Rhea, the great "goddess-mother" with her husband/son Ninus, also known as Tammuz. The confusion of husband/son relationship was not confined to Babylon, and the worship of this "mother and son" was diffused throughout the ancient world, as signified in the table

82

above. In Egypt, Osiris was also represented as both husband and son of his mother Isis, and bore as a title of honor the name "Husband of the Mother" or Kamut.

The title "Madonna" often used in the Roman Catholic Church as a name for Mary, the mother of Jesus, derives from the Greek female divinity Beltis, which, in English, means "My Lady." In Latin, formerly used throughout the church and making a recent comeback in some areas, this term becomes "Mea Domina," and shortened to become "Madonna."

The Egyptian god named Hermes, also called Mercury or Cush, is said to be a synonym for "son of Ham." He is the recognized author of pagan rites, and "interpreter of the gods," as he was responsible for dividing the speech of men at Babel. Hermes, then, "son of Ham," must be Nimrod.

Another name given to the father of Ninus, or Nimrod, was Belus or Bel. The Greek "Belus" represented the Chaldean *Baal* and *Bel*, two names having different meanings. *Baal* signified "The Lord," while *Bel* meant "The Confounder." Ninus, or Nimrod, this son of Cush, was the first mortal to be "deified" as "Father of the gods." The Baals are mentioned many times in the Scriptures as deities of Canaanite polytheism who ensnared the Israelites. (Adapted from The Two Babylons or The Papal Worship, © 1916 Rev. Alexander Hislop, First American Edition 1943, 2nd American Edition 1959; Published in America by Loizeaux Brothers Inc.)

CHRISTMAS

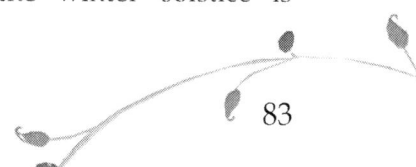

IN THE PRECEDING PAGES I mentioned Tammuz, both in the context of being the son of Semiramis, and in the heart of God as an abomination when the women were weeping for him in Ezekiel chapter 8. December 25th was chosen by Constantine as the date to celebrate the birth of Christ, although the winter solstice is generally closer to the 21st of December. Why was the 25th chosen? Although opinions vary, one stands out which may be valid:

> "... that the early Church, in moving all its celebrations away from Judaism without denying its followers the holidays they had come to enjoy, took the date of Hanukkah, the Feast of Dedication, and "Romanized" it. Hanukkah occurs on the 25th day of the Hebrew month of Kislev, which occurs approximately in December."[1]

According to Babylonian legend, Shem cut Nimrod into pieces, and Nimrod ascended into the heavens and became the sun god, the rays of which impregnated Semiramis, resulting in the birth of Tammuz at the winter solstice. Another pagan legend, this one from the Persians, states that followers of Mithra believed the winter solstice was the birth of the sun, and these beliefs were widespread throughout the Roman Empire.

Frazier, in *The Golden Bough* (page 471), states without hesitation:

> "The largest pagan religious cult which fostered the celebration of December 25th as a holiday throughout the Roman and Greek worlds was the pagan sun worship – Mithraism." He adds, "This winter festival was called 'the Nativity' – the 'nativity' of the sun."[2]

Since this festival was called the "Nativity of the Sun," it is easy to see the change for Christians being made to the "Nativity of the Son".

It is interesting to note that in astronomy, the sun reaches its lowest zenith on December 21st and is considered "dead" for three days before reversing and rising. In other words, the hours of sunlight wane as we approach December 21, and after a lull of three days, the hours of sunshine begin once again to increase. Although this is a purely physical and scientific observation of

God's design, I find it interesting that Jesus died and was buried three days before rising, albeit at a different time of the year.

According to Alexander Hyslop in "The Two Babylons,"

> "Long before the fourth century, and long before the Christian era itself, a festival was celebrated among the heathen, at that precise time of the year, in honor of the birth of the son of the Babylonian queen of heaven; and it may fairly be presumed that, in order to conciliate the heathen, and to swell the number of the nominal adherents of Christianity, the same festival was adopted by the Roman Church, giving it only the name of Christ. This tendency on the part of Christians to meet Paganism halfway was very early developed; and we find Tertullian, even in his day, about the year 230, bitterly lamenting the inconsistency of the disciples of Christ in this respect, and contrasting it with the strict fidelity of the Pagans to their own superstition."[3]

As stated above, both the word Christmas and its trappings have its roots in paganism, a celebration of the sun god at the winter solstice when the days become longer, called Saturnalia.

Christmas Traditions

I would like to look at the traditions we have adopted as part of the celebration of Christmas. I am not suggesting that Christians should depart from all these practices, but I do think we should be aware of their roots:

Christmas Tree and Gifts

According to pagan legends, Nimrod would visit the evergreen tree and leave gifts. During the Saturnalia people would give gifts to one another. Hislop gives us insight here as well:

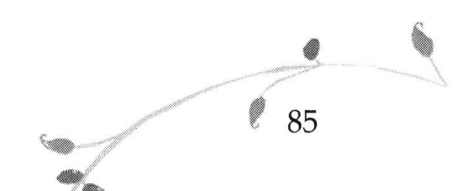

"The Christmas tree, now so common among us, was equally common in Pagan Rome and Pagan Egypt. In Egypt that tree was the palm tree; in Rome it was the fir; the palm tree denoting the Pagan messiah, as Baal-Tamar, the fir referring to him as Baal Berith. The mother of Adonis, the sun-god and great mediatorial divinity, was mystically said to have been changed into a tree, and when in that state to have brought forth her divine son. If the mother was a tree, the son must have been recognized as 'Man the branch.' And this entirely accounts for the putting of the Yule Log into the fire on Christmas Eve, and the appearance of the Christmas tree the next morning."[4]

The Yule Log

The Yule Log mentioned above has traditionally held more importance in England than in North America. However, in paganism it represents the dead Nimrod, deified as the sun-god but killed by his enemies; the Christmas tree represents the dead god returned to life.

Jeremiah 10:2-4 even refers to a decorated tree, **"Thus says the LORD: 'Do not learn the way of the Gentiles; Do not be dismayed at the signs of heaven. For the Gentiles are dismayed at them, For the customs of the peoples are futile; For one cuts a tree from the forest, the work of the hands of the workman, with the axe. They decorate it with silver and gold; they fasten it with nails and hammers so that it will not topple.'"**

Santa Claus

Santa Claus is a very prevalent and important part of the celebration of Christmas in North America. Every town and city holds its annual Santa Claus Parade, and children wait with bated breath for his arrival sometime between Christmas Eve and Christmas morning.

The Roman Influence

Some stories of Santa Claus relate to **St. Nicholas** of Myra, in Lycia, part of modern-day Turkey. According to the page on Saint Nicholas on Wikipedia, he was also known as Nicholas the Wonderworker because of the many miracles attributed to his intercession. As well, he had a reputation for secretly giving gifts of tucking coins into the shoes of children who set them out for him. Consequently, he became the model for our more modern Santa Claus, whose English name comes from the German Sankt Niklaus.

The Dutch story embraces St. Nicholas' help for three young maidens whose father could not afford a proper dowry for them, thereby dooming them to remain unmarried. Due to lack of suitable employment with which to support themselves, they would very likely need to resort to prostitution. Nicholas, on hearing about this plight, wanted to help the father of these girls. However, he did not want to humiliate the man by helping him publicly, so he went to the man's house at night and threw three purses filled with gold coins through the window. According to the Wikipedia article, there are several variations of this transaction. Many European countries have their own variations of stories and celebrations of this saint.

In North America the origin of Santa goes back to the Dutch. According to the website www.stnicholascenter.org:

> "After the American Revolution, New Yorkers remembered with pride the colony's nearly-forgotten Dutch roots. John Pintard, influential patriot and antiquarian, who founded the New York Historical Society in 1804, promoted St. Nicholas as patron saint of both society and city. In January 1809, Washington Irving joined the society and on St. Nicholas Day that year he published the satirical fiction, *Knickerbocker's History of New York*, with numerous references to a jolly St. Nicholas character. This was not a saintly bishop, rather an elfin Dutch burgher with a clay pipe. These delightful flights of imagination are the origin of the New Amsterdam St. Nicholas

legends: that the first Dutch emigrant ship had a figurehead of St. Nicholas; that St. Nicholas Day was observed in the colony; that the first church was dedicated to him; and that St. Nicholas comes down chimneys to bring gifts. Irving's work was regarded as the "first notable work of *imagination* in the New World."

The New York Historical Society held its first St. Nicholas anniversary dinner on December 6, 1810. John Pintard commissioned artist Alexander Anderson to create the first American image of Nicholas for the occasion. Nicholas was shown in a gift-giving role with children's treats in stockings hanging at a fireplace. The accompanying poem ends, "Saint Nicholas, my dear good friend! To serve you ever was my end, If you will, now, me something give, I'll serve you ever while I live."

The present-day Santa Claus in North America today is largely the patented brainchild of CocaCola, developed as a marketing tool, and has become very successful as such. Advertisements largely focus on children, but because Christmas has become such a great commercial holiday, there are advertisements for all members of the family.

In fostering this idea of Santa Claus to our children, although it is fun and the children get excited, perhaps we should examine the implication in the idea that "**Santa knows** when you're naughty and nice." This attribute of "knowing all" belongs to God alone. He alone is omniscient. I can't help wonder what our heavenly Father thinks as we attribute it to a mythical character. As well, Santa's ability to deliver gifts to children all over the world in one night is magical to say the least.. In the Bible magic is related to sorcery. Is this something we should be teaching our children?

EASTER

ANOTHER PAGAN LEGEND has it that Tammuz was gored by a wild boar when he was 40 years old. Consequently, 40 days were set aside each year to mourn for him. This legend draws together the celebration of his birth at the winter solstice, December 25th, with the 40 days of mourning for his death, one day for each year of his life. Throughout these 40 days people would deny worldly pleasures, just as the Catholic Church, and later others, adopted the Forty days of Lent, where congregants were to do the same. I recall as a child having to give up something for Lent, as well as going to Mass every morning, trudging through the cold and snow.

As with Christmas, the celebration of Easter is a result of Christianity being proclaimed by Rome as the religion of the Roman Empire, changing the old pagan observances into Christian celebrations. Although Christians today are celebrating the resurrection of Christ from the grave, it is mixed with ancient pagan symbols. The word Easter comes from the Anglo-Saxon word Ostara or Eastre, the name of a pagan goddess of spring. In Babylon, she was called Ishtar, the goddess of fertility. In the spring when the earth again turned green and new growth sprouted, the pagans would hold great festivals celebrating symbols of fertility like the egg and the rabbit.

As noted above, Semiramis, in pagan lore, was the "queen of heaven." After her death the "gods" sent her back to earth as the spring fertility goddess Ashstarte (Easter). According to the story

> "she emerged from a giant egg that landed in the Euphrates river at sunrise on the "sun" day after the vernal equinox. To proclaim her divine authority, she changed a bird into an egg laying rabbit. As the cult developed, the priests of Easter would impregnate young virgins on the altar of the goddess of fertility at sunrise on Easter Sunday. A year later the priests of Easter would sacrifice those three-month-old babies on the altar at the front of the sanctuary and dye Easter eggs in the blood of the sacrificed infants. The forty days of Lent – or weeping for Tammuz, starts the Easter fertility season. The festivities culminate on Easter Sunday, when the priests of Easter

slaughtered the "wild boar that killed Tammuz" and the entire congregation would eat the "ham" on Easter Sunday. In later years "Good Friday," the day that the Philistines sacrificed to Dagon, the Philistine fish god, also became an integral part of the Easter pageantry."[5]

As you can see, many of our customs today, the dyeing of eggs, the Easter Bunny, and eating the Easter ham are very closely connected to these pagan customs. Regarding "Good Friday" I recall as a child we had to eat fish on Fridays, which was the custom in the Catholic Church at that time. However, how the church ever came up with the idea that Jesus was crucified on "Good Friday" is beyond my comprehension. This issue is addressed in the next chapter.

In Deuteronomy, God tells the Israelites, "**When the LORD your God cuts off from before you the nations which you go to dispossess, and you displace them and dwell in their land, take heed to yourself that you are not ensnared to follow them, after they are destroyed from before you, and that you do not inquire after their gods, saying, 'How did these nations serve their gods? I also will do likewise.' "You shall not worship the LORD your God in that way; for every abomination to the LORD which He hates they have done to their gods; for they burn even their sons and daughters in the fire to their gods. Whatever I command you, be careful to observe it; you shall not add to it nor take away from it."** (Deuteronomy 12:29-32) As God warned the Israelites, He also warns us today.

In a later chapter I will show how our celebrations of the birth of Christ and His resurrection from the dead are related to the Feasts of the Lord as recorded in the 23rd chapter of Leviticus.

WHAT ABOUT HALLOWEEN?

A QUESTION OFTEN ASKED by Christians is whether they should celebrate Halloween. In fact, in recent years churches often host a "harvest festival" to give Christian children an alternative to the traditional ways of celebrating on this night. What are the roots of this particular celebration, both in and outside of the church?

The Christian Church kept the Jewish tradition of marking a "holy day" (contracted to form the word "holiday") for the twenty-four hours beginning at sundown and ending at sundown the following day. It also divided the year into commemorative events, eventually resulting in what became known as "The Church Calendar".

Halloween, a contraction for "Hallows Eve" or "Holy Eve," originally referred to the evening before All Saints' Day, November 1, a day to remember believers of the past who were often persecuted, tortured, or even chose death rather than renounce Christ. The Book of Hebrews encourages us to remember those who with great faith have gone before us.

However, the date for this day of remembrance was chosen specifically to correspond to an ancient Celtic religious holiday called Samhain which celebrated "the end of the harvest, the beginning of winter, and death."[6]

In conjuction with this celebration the pagans believed that:

> "the spirits of those who died during the previous year could not go to their "final resting place" until they were properly prepared with possessions, wealth, food, and drink (either for themselves or to pay the god who ruled the next world). Until then, their spirits wandered where they had lived and died. A common Samhain tradition was to placate the spirits and send them off on a one-way trip to the nether world by "treating" them. If a spirit was not "treated" well, it would "trick," or

haunt, those who had neglected preparing it for leaving this world." [7]

The Druids, the Celtic priests, believed in reincarnation. Samhain was the Lord of the Dead. It was believed that on Halloween he gathered together the souls of the evil dead and cast them into the bodies of animals. According to a wiccan website[8] it is one of two "spirit-nights" of the year, a time when "laws of time and space are temporarily suspended and the Thin Veil between the worlds is lifted,"[9] making it easy to communicate with the dead.

> "Turnips were hollowed out and carved to look like protective spirits, for this was the night of magic and chaos. The Wee Folk became very active, pulling pranks on unsuspecting humans. Traveling after dark was not advised. People dressed in white (like ghosts), wore disguises made of straw, or dressed as the opposite gender in order to fool the Nature spirits.... Bonfires were built and stones were marked with people's names. Then they were thrown into the fire, to be retrieved in the morning. The condition of the retrieved stone foretold of that person's fortune for the coming year."[10]

Halloween today is directly related to this pagan festival. God's Word tells us in Leviticus 19:26b: **nor shall you practice divination or soothsaying.** What we are allowing our children to celebrate is a feast day which honors Satan.

> There shall not be found among you anyone who makes his son or his daughter pass through the fire, or one who practices witchcraft, or a soothsayer, or one who interprets omens, or a sorcerer, or one who conjures spells, or a medium, or a spiritist, or one who calls up the dead. For all who do these things are an abomination to the LORD, and

because of these abominations the LORD your God drives them out from before you. Deuteronomy 18:10-12

There is much in the world today which glorifies these things that God warns us about, among them the Harry Potter books and movies. These are not harmless entertaining stories, but open the door to the occult, indoctrinating young readers into the basic principles of witchcraft. We need to protect our children from such things. Fortune-telling, mediums, palm-reading, and New Age techniques, such as Transcendental Meditation, Yoga, and the use of crystals should all be off-limits to God's people.

There is even such a thing today called "Christian Yoga," which is questionable, as well as the practice of Christians using acupuncture and other ancient Chinese techniques. I confess I have used acupuncture myself, much to my regret. I might add that it did not help me. Thankfully, we have a forgiving Father! I believe it is important to renounce these practices and ask His forgiveness. The use of such things are ploys of the enemy of our souls.

In this chapter we have looked at paganism in the Church, beginning with the Catholic Church under Constantine, which continued for centuries. It wasn't until about a thousand years later that a man was burned at the stake for his protest against many of the practices of the Roman Catholic hierarchy. In the next chapter we will examine the reformation in the church and the protests leading up to it.

Chapter 8
Protestantism

THERE ARE CENTURIES OF HISTORY, both inside and outside the Church, which contributed to the Reformation, but are beyond the scope of this book. However, a little-known fact is that it was the Moravians who first protested against the Roman Catholic Church, sixty years before Luther nailed his famous thesis to the door of the church at Wittenberg.

THE MORAVIANS

FOLLOWERS OF JOHN HUS, a university professor and a rector, became known as the Unity of the Brethren in 1457. This is not to be confused with other "Brethren" denominations, as there is no connection. Hus was burned at the stake as a martyr in 1415, sixty years before Luther began his reformation, for leading a protest against many of the practices of the Roman Catholic clergy and hierarchy.

Due to persecution, his followers were forced to meet secretly, and a group of them eventually left Moravia and Bohemia, which later became known as the Czech Republic, and settled in Saxony where Count Nicholas von Zinzendorf gave them refuge on his estate. Here they formed a community called Herrnhut (which means "protected by the Lord"). Thus the establishment of the Moravian Church. Herrnhut is still in existence today.

The group reorganized in 1727, and they began a 24-hour "prayer watch" which continued for over a hundred years. According to an article written by James Goll on his Encounters Network website[1], twenty-four men and twenty-four women covenanted to pray one hour each day in scheduled prayer. Others joined them. According to historian A. J. Lewis, "For over 100 years, the members of the Moravian church all shared in the "hourly intercession." At home and abroad, on land and sea, this prayer watch ascended unceasingly to the Lord."[2] Count Zinzendorf was instrumental in giving these believers the vision of taking the gospel to other parts of the world, and 65 years after the prayer vigil began, the Moravian community had sent out 300 missionaries.

A Moravian settlement was established in the United States in 1735. In 1742 a congregation settled the town of Bethlehem, Pennsylvania, which remains today as the church headquarters. They gained many converts from the Pennsylvania German population. As more settlers arrived from Europe, they branched out to North Carolina. English-speaking settlers also joined their ranks, and the Hope Moravian Church was founded in 1780.

From 1752 to 1771 Moravian missions set up in Labrador. Nain, Labrador became their headquarters, and from there they established ten stations, half of which are still in operation today.[3] In the late 1800s they nurtured the spiritual needs of Moravian refugees of German ancestry who were settling in western Canada.

Their spread has continued in North America since the end of the second world war, to southern California, as well the Midwest in the US, and to Alberta in Canada, where there are many congregations.

The basic motto of the Moravian Church in North America is "In essentials, unity; in nonessentials, liberty; and in all things, love."[4]

THE "REFORMATION"

DURING THE MIDDLE AGES the Roman Catholic Church began construction of St. Peter's Basilica. As this was a costly venture, the Church, of course, needed resources.

Consequently, they added to their list of requirements for the faithful. At that time these requirements included doing penance – which consisted of prayer and fasting – making pilgrimages, and serving in the military during the Crusades. Donations of money in addition to their regular offerings was a new requirement which had to do with their new doctrine regarding Purgatory.

One can't help but wonder, if the doctrine is based on truth from God's word, why it took a thousand years for them to realize it.

This doctrine, described below, formulated at the Councils of Florence (1439 A.D.) and Trent (three sessions between 1545 and 1563 A.D.).

According to item #1030 in the Catechism of the Catholic Church:

> All who die in God's grace and friendship, but still imperfectly purified, are indeed assured of their eternal salvation; but after death they undergo purification, to achieve the holiness necessary to enter the joy of heaven.[5]

Item #1031 continues:

> The Church gives the name Purgatory to this final purification of the elect, which is entirely different from the punishment of the damned. The Church formulated her doctrine of faith on Purgatory especially at the Councils of Florence and Trent. The tradition of the Church, by reference to certain texts of Scripture, speaks of a cleansing fire:

> As for certain lesser faults, we must believe that, before the Final Judgment, there is a purifying fire. He who is truth says that whoever utters blasphemy against the Holy Spirit will be pardoned neither in this age nor in the age to come. From this sentence we understand that certain offenses can be forgiven in this age, but certain others in the age to come. (St. Gregory the Great, Dial. 4, 39:PL 77, 396; cf. Mt.12:31)[6]

As a consequence of this doctrine of Purgatory, and the need for additional money in their coffers, the Church played on the peoples' fears of this "refinement by fire" in purgatory by selling "indulgences." An indulgence was considered to be a spiritual pardon. Again I quote from the Catechism of the Catholic Church, Item #1471:

> An indulgence is a remission before God of the temporal punishment due to sins whose guilt has already been forgiven, which the faithful Christian who is duly disposed gains under certain prescribed conditions through the action of the Church which, as the minister of redemption, dispenses and applies with authority the treasury of the satisfaction of Christ and the saints.
>
> An indulgence is partial or plenary according as it removes either part or all of the temporal punishment due to sin (Indulgentairum doctrina, Norm 2; cf. Norm 3). Indulgences may be applied to the living or the dead.[7]

The idea was that with enough "indulgences" applied, a person could escape the torment of purgatory and go straight to heaven. According to an article written by Charles Kimball[8] these indulgences sold for a price by agents chosen by the pope for their persuasiveness, and it became quite a business. These "salesmen"

hawked their wares like any other traveling salesman, complete with a "hellfire and damnation" sermon to convince those within earshot that this was the way both for them and their dearly departed to avoid suffering in purgatory. Martin Luther, an Augustinian monk from Wittenburg, was part of the crowd one day.

A Struggling Monk

Luther considered himself a good monk, doing all he was required to do. However, he still felt unworthy, in spite of his efforts to win God's favor. In 1512 he had a "moment of clarity" while reading Romans 1:17 – **The just shall live by faith.** This freed him from trying to *earn* the favor of the Lord, with the new understanding that God wasn't in heaven keeping a tally sheet based on his good or bad works. He finally understood that all that was required was to believe in Christ's finished work on the cross and to accept it by faith. This, of course, was at odds with much of the doctrine he had learned in the Catholic Church regarding rewards of doing enough penance, saying enough prayers, going on enough pilgrimages, and buying enough indulgences. He now saw these in a different light altogether, more as permits to commit sin rather than as ways to become holy[9].

The Start of Something Big

It was on October 31, 1517 that Luther nailed his ninety-five thesis to the door of the Wittenberg castle church, thus instigating a change in the face of the church forever. The sale of indulgences was only one of the many issues that Luther wanted to discuss with the hierarchy of the Church. Written in Latin, the accepted language for discussion on such topics, the majority of people were unable to read them. However, news quickly spread, as a great number of German people were fed up with the church preying on the fears of the people and making money through the sale of indulgences.

It wasn't long before the news reached the Archbishop, who sent a copy of the thesis to the pope, Leo X. Consequently, Luther's challenge to papal authority spread throughout western Europe. He was ordered to Rome, but refused to go, as he feared a death penalty. Instead, he agreed to meet a representative of the pope, a cardinal, in Augsberg. The two met three times, but each argumentative meeting resulted in a stalemate. Luther questioned whether the pope was, indeed, God's representative on earth!

Luther was eventually considered a heretic by the Church, and was excommunicated in 1520, which was the year he published many books and pamphlets. He used these writings to promote the authority of the Bible, and they eventually became the fundamentals of Protestantism. Contrary to the unwritten rule that subjects such as theology, philosophy and science should be written in Latin, he began to write in German, and promoted the use of the language of the people.

His most revolutionary concept was "the priesthood of all believers."[10] Therefore, he allowed all clergy to marry, as he was cognizant of the fact that many priests and monks had great difficulty keeping their vow of chastity and recognized that not everyone can remain celibate. He also abandoned religious holidays and saints' days.

Before long, the Church, through Emperor Charles V, retaliated with the Diet of Worms, where Luther was to appear before 150 princes, and delegates. He was asked if he would recant all he had written, and he gave his most important speech:

> "Since your serene majesty and your lordships request a simple answer, I shall give it, with no strings and no catches. Unless I am convicted by the testimony of Scripture or plain reason (for I believe neither in pope nor councils alone, since it is agreed

that they have often erred and contradicted themselves), I am bound by the Scriptures I have quoted, and my conscience is captive to the Word of God. I neither can nor will revoke anything, for it is neither safe nor honest to act against one's conscience. Here I take my stand, I can do no other."[11]

The emperor declared Luther an outlaw, but before he could pass the Edict of Worms, Luther went into hiding, where he remained until 1522, when he returned to Wittenberg.

THE GROWTH OF LUTHERANISM AND OFFSHOOTS

BY 1540 A THIRD OF GERMANY and all of Scandinavia had converted to Lutheranism. As well, it had made a dent in Poland, Bohemia and Moravia (today's Czech Republic), Hungary, and Transylvania.

In the city-state of Zurich under the leadership of Ulrich Zwingli (1484-1531) Luther's new movement flourished. "Zwingli had risen through the ranks of the Catholic church until appointed 'People's Priest' in 1519, the most powerful ecclesiastical position in the city."[12] However, by this time he fully agreed with Luther's reform program and had begun to implement changes accordingly. In 1523, the city of Zurich officially adopted the reforms Zwingli had put into place, and from there the Protestant revolution swept across Switzerland.

Zwingli's theology was simple, based on a single principle, "if the Old or New Testament did not say something explicitly and literally, then no Christian should believe or practice it. This was the basis of his critique of indulgences. In 1522, for instance, Zwingli mounted a protest against the fast at Lent, a standard Catholic practice. His argument: the New Testament says absolutely nothing about fasting at Lent so the practice is inherently unchristian."[13]

Consequently, if a practice was not specifically called for in the Scriptures, it was abolished. Those practices that were, however, mentioned in Scripture were to be kept. This literal understanding of the Scriptures became the basis for the Puritans in England and their colonies in America.

Zwingli and Luther disagreed in one major area, the Eucharist. In this, Luther continued to agree with the Catholic Church, that the bread and wine not only *represented* the body and blood of Christ, but actually became spiritually *transformed* into the body and blood of Christ.

> "At the heart of the dispute was the nature of Jesus Christ himself. For Luther, what made the spiritual transformation of the Eucharist into the physical body and blood of Christ was the dual nature of Christ: as both God and human, Christ was both spiritual and physical, God and human being. Zwinglian Protestantism, as well as its spiritual inheritors (the majority of Protestant churches), overwhelmingly stressed the divine nature of Christ. Jesus Christ was the divine; the Catholic insistence on the human nature of Christ was an incorrect and dangerous reading of the Christ event in history. Therefore, any implicit suggestion in the practice of the Eucharist that Christ was human must be rejected."[14]

Zwingli also took the second commandment literally, and consequently did away with all crucifixes, statues, chalices, censers and clerical vestments.[15] He even did away with music during services, because he could find no references authorizing it. Perhaps he should have looked at the Psalms!

Other Groups Emerge

With the break from the Catholic Church by Luther, followed by Zwingli and the rise of Puritanism, it was only a matter of time before others took a stand on some matter of doctrine.

Conrad Grebel, a follower of Zwingli, decided that infant baptism or forced baptisms were invalid, and required everyone who joined his church to be re-baptized, to ensure it was done correctly. Thus the **Anabaptists** came on the scene. They also taught that no Christian should be in government, since the state is sinful. Persecution drove them out of Zurich, scattering them across Germany.

During an uprising, Luther called for a massacre of the rebels, and thousands of peasants were killed. A few Anabaptists survived, but because of the bad reputation resulting from the uprising, they wanted to change their name.

A small number of them got together in the Netherlands under the leadership of Menno Simons, who taught about the need for a pure church, with adult baptism, the authority of the Bible, separation from politics, as well as from people of other faiths, and a total commitment to peace. Today their descendants are known by different names in differing parts of the world: the "Brethren" in Switzerland and south Germany; Mennonites in the Netherlands and north Germany; and Hutterites (after another leader) in the Czech Republic. All three groups have members in the United States and Canada. The Amish community in the US is an offshoot of the Brethren, begun by Jacob Ammann from Switzerland.[16]

Calvinism

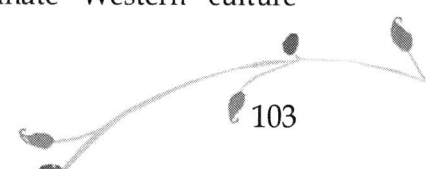

John Calvin (1509-64), rather than attacking dogma in an existing branch of the Church, emphasized personal responsibility. "Perhaps even more so than Martin Luther, Calvin created the patterns and thought that would dominate Western culture throughout the modern period. American culture, in particular, is thoroughly Calvinist in some form or another; at the heart of the way Americans think and act, you'll find this fierce and imposing reformer."[17]

In comparison with Luther, who stressed God's mercy and grace, Calvin concentrated on Jehovah, Master of the universe. He disagreed with both Luther and the Catholic Church on the means of salvation and introduced the concept of predestination. Accordingly, God chose who would be saved, and who would not. As man has no way of knowing for sure, he preached a righteous lifestyle. He drew up a new code of law in Geneva, based mostly on the Bible, which was enforced by a group known as the Consistory, or Presbytery, made up of five pastors and twelve elders. The faithful were policed by this group, and called to account. "Criminal offenses included missing church, laughing during services, wearing bright colors, dancing, playing cards, and swearing."[18] Offenders were excommunicated in the sense that they could not partake of the Lord's table, nor associate with citizens, although they were still expected to listen to sermons. In extreme cases they used torture, and even had heretics burned at the stake.

Calvinism had little effect in established Lutheran areas, "but to the persecuted Huguenots, the embattled Dutch, and the rebel Scots, God spoke with Calvin's voice."[19]

THE PRESBYTERIAN CHURCH IN SCOTLAND

A CONVERT TO CALVINISM, John Knox studied in Switzerland and returned to his native Scotland, where he was asked by the nobility to head a council called "The Lords of the Congregation of Jesus Christ."[20] Thus a Reformation was brought to Scotland, but not without violence and rioting. Mary Queen of Scots called in French soldiers, and the Lords of the Congregation brought in troops sent by England's new Queen, Elizabeth I. When the dust settled, the reformers came out on top, "and the largest Parliament in Scotland's history convened to replace Catholicism with a new state religion."[21] As a consequence, Knox established Calvinism in Scotland, which became known as the Presbyterian Church. Knox wrote the "Confession of Faith" in 1560, a "Book of Discipline" in 1561, and a liturgy called the "Book of Common Order" in 1564.[22]

THE ANGLICAN CHURCH IN ENGLAND

DURING THE MIDDLE AGES England produced a number of reformers, as her relationship with Rome was tenuous at best. Wycliffe, rebelling against Rome, was the first person to translate the Scriptures from Latin into English. As well, humanism helped to prepare the way for Protestantism.

Although Luther's writings had reached England, the break with the Catholic Church in that country was more political than it was religious. The Holy Roman Emperor, Charles V, at that time virtually held the pope captive after invading Rome. At the same time, King Henry VIII wanted to divorce his wife Catherine because she had not given him a son as an heir to the throne. This meant seeking a special dispensation from the pope to annul his marriage. Henry wanted to marry Anne Boleyn, who was a lady-in-waiting to the queen. Of course, the pope refused.

Henry promptly fired his closest adviser, Cardinal Wolsey, the Lord Chancellor of England who had been carrying on the negotiations with the pope, and replaced him with Thomas Cranmer and Thomas Cromwell, both of whom were sympathetic to Luther's teachings. They suggested to Henry that if he did not receive an annulment from the pope, he should split from the Roman Catholic church, and become head of the English Church. That way Henry could grant his own annulment.

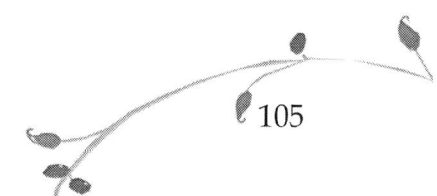

After several years of parliamentary debate, a law passed that placed the clergy under Henry's control. Thus he divorced Catherine and married Ann Boleyn. In 1534 Parliament prohibited all contributions by both clergy and lay people to the Roman Church. Another law passed stating that no foreign power had the right to interfere in England's affairs, thus granting Henry complete control over church appointments. The Act of Succession declared Henry as the ultimate head of the Church of England, which became known as the Anglican or Episcopal Church.

However, few changes were made either in doctrine or practice. "The Book of Common Prayer" and the "Forty-Two Articles" were written by Thomas Crammer while Henry was still alive, and these books became central to the Anglican Church, becoming the official books under Henry's successor, Edward VI.

The Church in England suffered throughout tumultuous decades of teeter-tottering back and forth between Catholicism and Protestantism, depending on who was on the throne. Through the reigns of Edward VI (Protestant) and Mary (Catholic), laws changed. When Elizabeth took the throne, she worked out a compromise, retaining much from the Catholic Church, but at the same time proclaiming moderate ideas of Calvinism, and keeping the Queen as head of the church.

THE HUGUENOTS

THE REFORMATION BEGUN in Germany spread rapidly throughout France. However, these Protestant believers eventually became more Calvinist than Lutheran. Many members of the French nobility and social middle-class practiced the new "Reformed religion," based on a belief in salvation through individual faith without the need for the intercession of a church hierarchy. As well, they believed in an individual's right to interpret scriptures for themselves. This placed these French Protestants in direct theological conflict with both the Catholic Church and the King of France in the theocratic system which prevailed at that time. Followers of this new Protestantism were soon accused of heresy against the Catholic government and the established religion of France. A General Edict, issued in 1536, urged extermination of these heretics (Huguenots).

Nevertheless, Protestantism continued to spread and grow, and about 1555 the first Huguenot church was founded in a home in Paris based upon the teachings of John Calvin. The number and influence of the French Reformers (Huguenots) continued to increase after this event, leading to an escalation in hostility and conflict between the Catholic Church/State and the Huguenots. Finally, in 1562, some 1200 Huguenots were slain at Vassey, France, thus igniting the French Wars of Religion which would devastate France for the next thirty-five years."[23]

"The exact origin of the word *Huguenot* is unknown, but many consider it to be a combination of Flemish and German. Protestants who met to study the Bible in secret were called *Huis Genooten*, meaning "house fellows." They were also referred to as *Eid Genossen*, or "oath fellows" meaning persons bound by an oath."[24]

PART 3

DEFINITION OF GOD'S CUSTOMS AND JEWISH CUSTOMS

Chapter 9
Back To God's Word

PAGANISM INTRODUCED INTO the Church through Constantine effectively cut the church from its Jewish roots in the process.

As a consequence, we have an understanding of God's word which is not entirely correct, which is much to our detriment, as well as a detriment to the Jewish people.

The early believers were considered to be simply another sect of Judaism, along with the Pharisees, Saducees, and Essenes. However, all of that changed as more and more gentiles heard the Gospel, and particularly, as we have seen, when it was essentially taken over by the Romans.

Being so removed from our Jewish roots we often look at the Old Testament more as history than as having impact on our lives today. That is unfortunate, as there is much richness to garner if we read the Old Testament "with Jewish eyes." We tend to navigate toward the Psalms for praise and comfort, and Proverbs for wisdom for our own lives, but we often skim over portions regarding God's dealings with His chosen people throughout their desert wanderings, assuming that it only pertained to the Jewish people, but has no real importance to us as Christians today. However, what the LORD taught His people as they wandered in the wilderness is valuable to Christians today.

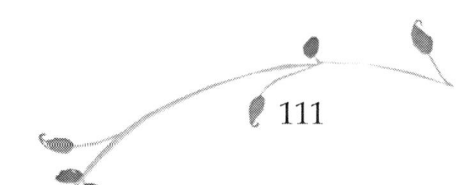

The Church Fathers have chosen to stress some aspects of the Old Testament, while omitting others. For example, they stressed the Ten Commandments, while they 'reinvented' some of the Feasts to melt in with pagan festivals. In the process, the Church has lost not only the knowledge of how each of the feasts have to do with the promise of the coming Messiah, but also its connection to the Jewish people. As a consequence, both Christians and Jews have lost.

In the following chapters I hope to impart to the reader a sense of excitement as we explore the Feasts of the LORD. They are not the "Jewish Feasts", to be ignored by the Church. In Leviticus Chapter 23:1-2 it says:

> And the LORD spoke to Moses, saying, "Speak to the children of Israel, and say to them: 'The feasts of the LORD, which you shall proclaim to be holy convocations, these are My feasts.'"

We shall see as we explore each of these Feasts that Jesus, the Jewish Messiah, is the ultimate fulfillment of each of the feasts. The first feast is the Sabbath of the LORD, the seventh day of the week. In today's vernacular, this is Saturday. It is to be a day of rest and holy convocation, as are all the Feasts.

Next are the Feasts of Passover and Unleavened Bread on the 14th and 15th of the first month of the Jewish calendar, Nisan, which commemorate the 'passing over' of Jewish homes in Egypt by the Angel of Death when he saw the blood on the doorposts and lintels of their homes, but the firstborn of man and beast in Egypt died by God's hand.

The Feast of Firstfruits was to commemorate the reaping of the first harvest in the land to which God was leading them. They were to offer a wave offering before the LORD at this time of the spring harvest, a time of thanksgiving.

During the Feast of Weeks, seven weeks later, they were to offer a new grain offering to the LORD, as well as other offerings, including both a sin and a peace offering. We know this feast as Pentecost, which takes its name from the Latin word for fifty, as it was celebrated fifty days after Firstfruits.

In the seventh month they were told to celebrate the Feast of Trumpets, celebrated by the blowing of trumpets in various manners, each one signifying a different meaning.

The final Feast of the LORD was the Feast of Tabernacles, also in the seventh month, which was to be celebrated for seven days, which was a memorial to their days in the wilderness, when they dwelled in tents.

These were all to be days of rest, where no customary work was to be done.

Unfortunately, throughout history, we have lost touch with how we can honor God by being aware of and even celebrating these feasts. In subsequent chapters we will examine them in more detail, as well as see how Jesus ultimately fulfills each one.

Chapter 10
The Feasts Of The Lord

IN THIS AND FOLLOWING CHAPTERS, I want to delve into the Lord's Feasts which He laid out for us in the Book of Leviticus.

As we will see, these feasts were significant not only to the Jewish people thousands of years ago, but have meaning for Christians today as well.

WHY SHOULD CHRISTIANS BE AWARE OF THE FEASTS?

THESE ARE NOT "JEWISH" FEASTS, although religious Jews keep them. They are called "The Feasts of the Lord" in Leviticus. The exciting part about it is that Jesus fulfills each of these feasts!

Sabbath	Jesus is our Sabbath rest.
Passover (Pesach)	Jesus is our Passover Lamb who was slain for our sins.
Firstfruits	Jesus is the Firstfruits of those who have died, and is risen.
Pentecost (Shavuot)	Jesus sent the Holy Spirit after His ascension into heaven.
Trumpets (Rosh Hashana)	Jesus will return when the last trumpet sounds, as King of kings and Lord of lords.

Atonement (Yom Kippur)	Jesus made complete atonement for our sins.
Tabernacles (Sukkot)	Jesus tabernacled with us on earth for 33 years, and will tabernacle with us again!
Feast of Dedication (Hanukkah)	Jesus is the Light of the world.

Jesus is all in all. He is present in every feast! That is reason to celebrate! All the Lord's special days have two distinct Hebrew words applied to them: **mo'ed** – which means "appointment," and **mikrah** which means a "rehearsal." They are all appointments the Lord keeps, and they are all rehearsals for the Day of the Lord.

> And the LORD spoke to Moses, saying, "Speak to the children of Israel, and say to them: "The feasts of the LORD, which you shall proclaim to be holy convocations, these are My feasts."
> Leviticus 23:1

Many times when I have spoken to Christians regarding the feasts, the response is, "You mean the Jewish feasts?" As you will note in the above verse, the Lord says, "These are **My** feasts." It is unfortunate that so many Christians think of them as belonging only to the Jewish people, and not to all of God's people. There is much richness to glean from them.

Our Lord and Savior, Jesus Christ, is the fulfillment of each of these feasts. They are a celebration of what God has done in the past, shown in the Spring Feasts, as well as what He will do in the future, as shown through the Fall feasts. Our God is an unchanging God. Malachi 3:6 tells us, **"For I am the LORD, I do not change."**

Let us examine each of these feasts as set out in Leviticus 23 and discover how they apply to Christians today.

The Sabbath (Lev. 23:3)

"Six days shall work be done, but the seventh day is a Sabbath of solemn rest, a holy convocation. You shall do no work on it; it is the Sabbath of the Lord in all your dwellings."

This pronouncement of the Sabbath as the first of the Feasts of the Lord echoes Gen. 2:3, **"Then God blessed the seventh day, and sanctified it, because in it He rested from all His work which God had created and made."** As well, it is included as one of the Ten Commandments in Ex. 20:8, **"Remember the Sabbath day, to keep it holy."** As Christians, we cannot deny that God has blessed, sanctified, and made holy the seventh day of the week. These are just three examples of what God's word says.

Yet, as Christians, we don't heed this word. Instead, we have accepted, unquestioningly, the changes made through history. When was this "holy day" changed from the seventh day to the first? As we saw in a previous chapter, it was the Roman Emperor Constantine who changed the day after he became emperor. Rather than cause a furor among the pagan majority of his empire by changing their day of worship of the Sun god to Saturday, he synchronized the day for both Christians and pagans to worship on Sunday. Many claim that keeping Sunday as our day of worship is a memorial of the Resurrection of Christ from the dead (cf. Luke 24:1). Where has God authorized this change? A question we should perhaps ask ourselves is, *"Was the Sabbath and the other Feasts just for the Jews?"*

Jesus said in Mark 2:27-28, **"The Sabbath was made for man, and not man for the Sabbath. Therefore the Son of Man is also the Lord of the Sabbath."** If Jesus Himself is the Lord of the Sabbath, and He is our Savior and Lord, how can we suggest that the Sabbath is only for the Jews?

> "He is the image of the invisible God, the firstborn over all creation. For by Him all things were created that are in heaven and that are on earth, visible and invisible, whether thrones or dominions or principalities or powers. All things were created through Him and for Him. And He is before all things, and in Him all things consist." Colossians 1:15-17

Under Mosaic Law there were strict regulations regarding the Sabbath, and it is these observances only that were to be kept until Jesus came and began to preach the Kingdom of God. As the Gospels make clear, the Pharisees had added many restrictions in the extreme regarding exactly how a person was to keep the Law of Moses, thereby placing a burden on them. These extreme restrictions of "doing" without engaging the heart were the things Jesus spoke against, not about keeping the Sabbath. He Himself kept the Sabbath.

The Sabbath is the first example of the Biblical pattern of seven, which is God's sacred number. He rested on the seventh day. Therefore the Sabbath is a celebration of God's complete and beautiful creation of the world out of nothing, a celebration of His omnipotence. This model of God working for six days and resting on the seventh indicates to us that we also need a day of rest after our labors. This need for rest is obvious in today's fast-paced society with all its stress, and the assumed need of so many to be connected to their work 24/7.

In the Old Covenant times, the Sabbath became perverted, and strict commands regarding the keeping of the Sabbath became overbearing and far from what God had intended. In Isaiah 58:13-14a he addresses what our holy God requires: calling the Sabbath a delight, not doing our own pleasures, or speaking our own words, but honouring Him.

Jesus confronted the rulers in His day regarding their outward ceremonial restrictions in observing the Sabbath while their hearts were not pure towards God, and indicated His compassion for the sick by healing on the Sabbath. He did not, however, say that He intended to do away with this day of rest. The writer of the Book of Hebrews says in chapter 4, verses 9-10, "**There remains therefore a rest for the people of God, for he who has entered His rest has himself also ceased from his works as God did from His.**" David H. Stern, in his Complete Jewish Bible, comments in his introduction the book of Hebrews was "A Letter to a Group of Messianic Jews"[1] and translates these verses as, "**So there remains a Shabbat-keeping for God's people. For the one who has entered God's rest has also rested from his own works, as God did from his.**"[2]

The early church under the apostles continued to worship at the temple in Jerusalem. After the outpouring of the Holy Spirit they "**continued steadfastly in the apostles doctrine and fellowship, in the breaking of bread, and in prayers**" (Acts 2:42).

Jesus rose from the grave sometime after sundown on Saturday and before sunrise on Sunday morning. Each of the writers of the gospels tells of the empty tomb, and of how He appeared to Mary Magdalene in the early morning on the first day of the week, and at evening appeared to the disciples. These instances, however, do not tell us just when the shift was made from the seventh day of the week to the first as the day of worship. Chuck Missler, in his article entitled "Christians and the Sabbath: The Seventh Day" wrote,

> "The writings of a number of the early church fathers in the 2nd and 3rd centuries support the tradition of Sunday worship. However, the views of the early church after the book of Acts is, in some views, an unreliable basis to establish doctrine."[3]

Today Messianic congregations, often consisting of both Jews and Gentiles, generally meet together on Saturday mornings, often with an "Oneg" following, a time of eating a meal together and having fellowship with one another. In the next chapter we will examine the Spring feasts.

Chapter 11
The Spring Feasts

THE LORD'S FEASTS IN THE BIBLE are generally divided, with the exception of the Sabbath, into the Spring Feasts of Passover (Pesach), Unleavened Bread and Firstfruits, followed by Weeks (Pentecost or Shavuot) and the Fall Feasts of Trumpets, Day of Atonement, and Tabernacles.

PASSOVER AND UNLEAVENED BREAD (LEV. 23:4-8)

> "On the fourteenth day of the first month at twilight is the LORD'S Passover. And on the fifteenth day of the same month is the Feast of Unleavened Bread to the LORD; seven days you must eat unleavened bread. On the first day you shall have a holy convocation; you shall do no customary work on it. But you shall offer an offering made by fire to the LORD for seven days. The seventh day shall be a holy convocation; you shall do no customary work on it." (Lev. 23:5-8)

THE FIRST MONTH IN THE JEWISH calendar is the month of Abib which corresponds to our March-April. The name of Abib was later changed to Nisan during the Babylonian captivity. As with several of the feasts, Passover has an agriculture basis, and represented the beginning of the barley harvest. The origin of this Feast takes us back to the Book of Exodus, when God instructed Moses to prepare the Israelites to leave Egypt.

> "Therefore say to the children of Israel: 'I *am* the LORD; I will bring you out from under the burdens of the Egyptians, I will rescue you from their bondage, and I will redeem you with an outstretched arm and with great judgments. I will take you as My people, and I will be your God. Then you shall know that I *am* the LORD your God who brings you out from under the burdens of the Egyptians. And I will bring you into the land which I swore to give to Abraham, Isaac, and Jacob; and I will give it to you *as* a heritage: I *am* the LORD.'" (Ex. 6:6-8)

This was an announcement of new beginnings for the Israelites. After being brutally treated as slaves for four hundred years by the Egyptians, God was going to lead them out of Egypt and bring them into the land that He had promised to their forefathers.

> [The Lord told Moses,] "Speak to all the congregation of Israel, saying: 'On the tenth of this month every man shall take for himself a lamb, according to the house of *his* father, a lamb for a household. And if the household is too small for the lamb, let him and his neighbor next to his house take *it* according to the number of the persons; according to each man's need you shall make your count for the lamb. Your lamb shall be without blemish, a male of the first year. You may take *it* from the sheep or from the goats. Now you shall keep it until the fourteenth day of the same month. Then the whole assembly of the congregation of Israel shall kill it at twilight. And they shall take *some* of the blood and put *it* on

The Spring Feasts

the two doorposts and on the lintel of the houses where they eat it.'"

What, we may ask, does this have to do with us today? Very much indeed! The events of this first Passover, when the Angel of Death "passed over" those homes having the blood on the lintels and doorposts, were but a foreshadow of things to come when Jesus, the Lamb of God without blemish, shed His blood so that whoever applied His blood to the doorposts and lintels of their hearts would be saved from an eternal death. Jesus has delivered those covered by His blood from the bondage of sin and has paid the penalty for their sins.

Why were they told to take the lamb on the tenth of the month and keep it until the fourteenth? From the 10th to the 14th the lamb was inspected for blemishes, as it was to be without blemish. In the first century, the High Priest chose a lamb on the 10th and it was tied in the Temple area in public view so it could be inspected for blemishes. This was a joyous time in Israel, a remembrance of their deliverance from Egypt, their birth as a nation.

Jesus rode into Jerusalem on a colt on the 10th of Abib/Nisan, and multitudes of people praised Him, saying, **"Blessed is the King who comes in the name of the LORD! Peace in heaven and glory in the highest!"** (Luke 19:38) In the following days, Jesus wept over the city of Jerusalem, because He knew that Israel's enemies would trample and destroy the city. He wept because His people did not recognize the time of their visitation. He cleansed the temple, driving out those who bought and sold. He was teaching daily in the temple, and was questioned by the chief priests and scribes, who asked Him by whose or what authority He was doing these things. They probed Him, trying to trip Him up, asking Him if it was lawful to pay taxes to Caesar, asking about marriage in the resurrection. He answered their questions with authority. He predicted the destruction of the temple, and told them what would happen at the end of the age. So Jesus, too, was being inspected by the ruling authorities during these days.

Jesus told Peter and John to go and prepare the Passover meal (v. 8) and He and His disciples celebrated the Passover meal together, where Jesus instituted the Lord's Supper, what we today call "Communion." This was their Passover meal. After the supper Jesus went to the Garden of Gethsemane where He asked His Father to take this cup from Him, but added, **"Nevertheless, not My will but Yours be done."** He was arrested, mocked and beaten, faced the Sanhedrin, handed over to Pilate, then Herod, who sent Him back to Pilate. And He was crucified, shedding His blood for the sins of the world.

MEANING OF PASSOVER

IN THE TIME OF THE ORIGINAL Passover, as the people applied the blood from the lambs on their doorposts and lintels, the Angel of Death passed over their houses, and their firstborn were not killed. As a result of this final act of God on the Egyptians, Pharoah finally let Moses and his people go. It was a deliverance, a release from the bondage they had known for 400 years.

Today Passover has a special meaning for believers as well. As we apply the Blood of the Lamb of God to the doorposts and lintels of our hearts, we too are delivered - from sin, and become part of the family of God.

Messianic Believers today continue to hold a Passover Seder, where the original story of the release from the bondage in Egypt is recounted, as well as a sharing together of Jesus' last meal with His apostles. This joins together the significance of this time from both the Old Covenant Scriptures and the New. Sometimes it includes the washing of the feet, which is a moving, humbling and personal experience. The evening concludes with a celebration of music and dance. I have attended several of these wonderful celebrations.

THE CHURCH'S CELEBRATION OF "EASTER"

WE ARE TOLD THAT JESUS was crucified on Good Friday and that He rose from the grave on Easter Sunday. When I first became a believer and began to read the Gospels it puzzled me when I read what Jesus Himself said in Matt. 12:40, "**For as Jonah was three days and three nights in the belly of the great fish, so will the Son of Man be three days and three nights in the heart of the earth.**" If He was crucified and buried on Friday evening and rose from the dead on Sunday, that would make the above verse incorrect, and we know that Jesus would not tell a lie. How do we explain this inconsistency? If Jesus was in the heart of the earth for three days and three nights, it would have been impossible for Him to have been buried on Friday and arise from the grave on Sunday, as that would indicate He was in the earth the two nights of Friday and Saturday, and only one day, being the Saturday.

Keep in mind how the Jewish people reckon a day, from sundown to sundown. The following information which I found on the internet[1] explains how Jesus' words in Matt. 12:40 are true.

The following chart shows the times and dates of the New Moon when it first appears in the sky from the years 26 A.D. to 34 A.D. The date of Passover is determined by the first sighting of the moon on the 14th day of Nisan on the Jewish calendar. Recall that the Jewish people determine the beginning of a new day at sundown. This harkens back to Genesis, when God began His creation. Genesis 1:5 tells us: **God called the light Day, and the darkness He called Night. So the evening and the morning were the first day.**

This concept is foreign to us, as we think of a new day beginning in the morning when we arise, or specifically after midnight,

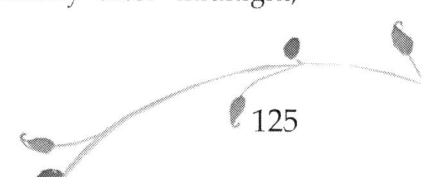

GRAFTED *IN* THE JEWISH OLIVE TREE

according to our clocks. However, this is not how God called day and night. For Him, and for the Jewish people, 'day' is determined by the first sighting of the moon in the evening, at sundown.

As we saw earlier, Passover begins on the 14th of Nisan on the Jewish calendar. The following chart shows the time of the first sighting of the moon for several years around the time period that Jesus was crucified, for both the Gregorian calendar, which we use today, and the Jewish calendar showing the date of Passover, the 14th of Nisan.

Passover dates 26-34 A.D.

The following astronomical data in the first three columns on the next page were obtained from the U.S. Naval Observatory Astronomical Applications Department. The pertinent file may be accessed on the Internet at http://aa.usno.navy.mil/data/docs/SpringPhenom.html.

Note: The times of day given in the second and third columns have been adjusted +2 hours from U.S. Naval Observatory figures to account for the difference between Jerusalem Israel and Greenwich England (universal) time.

It should also be noted that the first evening of a visible crescent moon (column 4) always occurs only minutes after sundown, which is at the very beginning of a new day on the Hebrew calendar. This Hebrew day correlates to the following day on our Gregorian calendar as noted in the chart below (column 5). Column 6 is Passover dates for the given years.

* Midnight at the end of the given day.

** Conjunction occurs too late in the day for crescent to be seen the next evening.

*** Conjunction occurred *on* date of Equinox actually preceding

126

The Spring Feasts

it by 4 hours. But as noted above, it is the <u>visible</u> crescent that established the 1st of Nisan which occurred on the 2nd evening *after* Equinox.

Year	Vernal Equinox	Astronomical New Moon Conjunction	First evening of visible crescent	Date of the first of Nisan	14th day of Nisan (Passover)
		(On date, or first after vernal Equinox)	(Gregorian calendar. Midnight to midnight)	(Beginning at sundown the evening before...)	(Beginning at sundown the evening before...)
26 A.D.	Fri. Mar. 22, 0*	Sat. Apr. 6, 7 a.m.	Sun. Apr. 7	Mon. Apr. 8	Sun. Apr. 21
27 A.D.	Sun. Mar. 23, 6 a.m.	Wed. Mar.26, 7 p.m.	Fri. Mar. 28	Sat. Mar. 29	Fri. Apr. 11
28 A.D.	Mon. Mar. 22 noon	Tues. Apr. 13 2 p.m.	Wed. Apr. 14	Thurs. Apr. 15	Wed. Apr. 28
29 A.D.	Tues. Mar. 22 6 p.m.	Sat. Apr. 2 7 p.m.**	Mon. Apr. 4	Tues. Apr. 5	Mon. Apr. 18
30 A.D.	Wed. Mar. 2,0*	Wed. Mar. 22, 8 p.m.	Fri. Mar. 24	Sat. Mar. 25	Fri. Apr. 7
31 A.D.	**Fri. Mar. 23 5 a.m.**	**Tues. Apr. 10 2 p.m.**	**<u>Wed. Apr. 11</u>**	**<u>Thurs. Apr. 12</u>**	**<u>Wed. Apr. 25</u>**
32 A.D.	Sat. Mar. 22 11 a.m.	Sat. Mar. 29 10 p.m.**	Mon. Mar. 31	Tues. Apr. 1	Mon. Apr. 14
33 A.D.	Sun. Mar. 22 5 p.m.	Fri. Apr. 17 9 p.m.**	Sun. Apr. 19	Mon. Apr. 20	Sun. May 3

Year	Vernal Equinox	Astronomical New Moon Conjunction	First evening of visible crescent	Date of the first of Nisan	14th day of Nisan (Passover)
34 A.D.	Mon. Mar. 22 11 p.m.	Wed. Apr. 7 2 p.m.	Thurs. Apr. 8	Fri. Apr. 9	Thurs. Apr. 22

Take note that a Passover on Wednesday is the only day of the week that works with all Biblical accounts of the crucifixion. Yahshua was in the grave "three days and three nights" Matthew 12:40. From Wednesday just before sunset to Saturday just before sunset is three days and three nights. The fact the day following Yahshua's crucifixion was a Sabbath (Mark 15:42, Luke 23:52-54, & John 19:31) does not prove He was crucified on a Friday. According to the Law of Moses, the day following Passover (which is also the first day of the Feast of Unleavened Bread) is also, always a Sabbath day of rest to be observed like the 7th day weekly Sabbath no matter what day of the week it falls on. (See Leviticus 23:4-8, Numbers 28:16-18, and take special notice of John 19:31 again. The Sabbath immediately following Yahshua's crucifixion was no ordinary Sabbath.)

Understanding that it was a Wednesday Passover and crucifixion also solves apparent conflicts in the Gospel records. In Luke 23:55,56 it says that women (Mary Magdalene and Mary the mother of James) went and prepared anointing spices and oils BEFORE the Sabbath. In Mark 16:1 it says that they bought them AFTER the Sabbath! The answer lies in the fact there are two different Sabbaths referred to here. The women both bought and prepared the spices on the same day. The day of the week was Friday. When Mark says they bought the spices AFTER the Sabbath, the Sabbath he is referring to was the special Thursday Sabbath ...the first day of unleavened bread that followed the day of

Passover. When Luke says they prepared the spices and then rested the Sabbath, the Sabbath he is referring to is Saturday ...the weekly Sabbath.

There is also proof found in Matthew 28:1 there were two Sabbaths. Most Bible translations render this word "Sabbath" in the singular because translators, believing the traditional Friday crucifixion scenario, couldn't make any sense of the fact that Greek manuscripts all render this word in the plural. This fact can be verified by anyone with a Greek interlinear translation or Greek lexicon. Matthew 28:1 therefore should read, "Now after the SABBATHS as the first day of the week began to dawn..." Therefore, for all the records to add up it must be concluded that Yahshua was crucified on a Wednesday.] (end of quote)

Jesus' name in Hebrew is "Yahshua" (containing the Father's Name, "Yah" or Yahweh) and often today is pronounced "Yeshua." It means "God saves."

We see from the above account that even very difficult passages from God's Word can be explained. At our Passover Seder last year, the Messianic Rabbi further explained the timing regarding the crucifixion. Because Passover is one of the feasts when all Jewish males are to go up to Jerusalem, there would have been extra thousands of people in the city at that time. In order for the priests to sacrifice all these extra lambs it was necessary to spread it out over a two-day period, as it would be impossible to accomplish it all in one day. Consequently, the residents of Jerusalem brought their lambs to be sacrificed the day before Passover, which would have been a Tuesday that year.

Jesus and His disciples would have held their Passover supper Tuesday evening, which likely lasted several hours, after which Jesus went to the Garden of Gethsemane along with Peter, James, and John to pray. After praying for a period of time, He came to His disciples and found them sleeping, and asked them, **"What? Could you not watch with Me one hour?"** (Matt. 26:40). He went a distance and prayed again, and again found them sleeping. He went and prayed a third time, after which Judas and many with clubs and swords came to arrest Him.

He was first taken before the Sanhedrin who put Him on trial. Early in the morning He was led before Pilate, after which He was mocked and scourged and crowned with thorns. Then they led Him away to be crucified. It is still Wednesday forenoon.

The Scriptures don't indicate the exact time He was crucified, but they do tell us the skies darkened all over the land from the sixth to the ninth hour, which would have been from noon until 3 PM, when He called out to His Father, and then yielded up His spirit.

We see, then, that He was buried Wednesday evening, and would have been in the grave Wednesday, Thursday, and Friday nights; and Thursday, Friday and Saturday days – three days and three nights, as the Scriptures tell us.

Feast of Unleavened Bread (Lev. 23:4-8)

THERE ARE THREE FEASTS CELEBRATED within eight days which together make up the Passover season. Because the Feast of Unleavened Bread begins on the day after Passover, preparations are begun well in advance. God instructed the children of Israel in Ex. 12:15-17 to remove all leaven from their houses and eat only unleavened bread during this time. This was taken seriously, because they were warned that whoever ate leavened bread would be cut off from Israel. Leaven is yeast, or the ingredient in bread which makes it rise.

In the New Testament, Paul tells us in 1 Cor. 5:8 that we are to **"keep the feast, not with old leaven, nor with the leaven of malice and wickedness, but with the unleavened *bread* of sincerity and truth."** Verse 7 tells us **"Therefore purge out the old leaven, that**

you may be a new lump, since you truly are unleavened. For indeed Christ, our Passover, was sacrificed for us."

Leaven in the Bible represents sin. Just as the Israelites were instructed to clean the leaven from their houses, which is still done today among the Orthodox and Messianic Jews, so today it has a spiritual application for us as believers: We are to clean out our "houses," search our hearts for any sin that may remain there. The term "spring housecleaning" not only applies to the physical dwellings in which we live, but also to the dwelling where the Holy Spirit lives within us.

God's feasts were given to His people as an "everlasting ordinance" (Ex. 12:14). Because we Gentile believers have been grafted in to the Jewish Olive Tree (Rom. 11:17-25), these Feasts of the Lord apply to us as well. We can see how the physical reality of the Old Covenant is a picture or foreshadowing of the spiritual reality in the New Covenant.

THE FEAST OF FIRSTFRUITS (LEV. 23:9-14)

> And the LORD spoke to Moses, saying, "Speak to the children of Israel, and say to them: 'When you come into the land which I give to you, and reap its harvest, then you shall bring a sheaf of the firstfruits of your harvest to the priest. He shall wave the sheaf before the LORD, to be accepted on your behalf; on the day after the Sabbath the priest shall wave it. And you shall offer on that day, when you wave the sheaf, a male lamb of the first year, without blemish, as a burnt offering to the LORD. Its grain offering *shall be* two-tenths *of an ephah* of fine flour mixed with oil, an offering made by fire to the LORD, for a sweet aroma; and its drink offering *shall be* of wine, one-fourth of a hin. You shall eat neither bread nor parched grain nor fresh grain until the

same day that you have brought an offering to your God; *it shall be* a statute forever throughout your generations in all your dwellings.'"

JOHN 20:17 TELLS US, when Jesus appeared to Mary Magdalene in the garden after He had risen from the grave that Jesus said to her, **"Do not cling to Me, for I have not yet ascended to My Father; but go to My brethren and say to them, 'I am ascending to My Father and your Father, and to My God and your God.'"** In the New Testament, Jesus is the firstfruits of the harvest. Before He allowed Mary to cling to Him, Jesus had to present Himself to His Father as the Firstfruits. Paul tells us in 1 Cor. 15:20, **"But now Christ is risen from the dead, *and* has become the firstfruits of those who have fallen asleep."** Again in verse 23 Paul tells us, **"But each one in his own order: Christ the firstfruits, afterward those *who are* Christ's at His coming."**

PASSOVER AS CELEBRATED THEN AND NOW

THE WORD "PASSOVER," taken from the Hebrew word "pesach," means to "skip over (or spare); used only technically of the Jewish Passover; passover (offering)," according to The New Strong's Exhaustive Concordance of the Bible.[2] Exodus Chapter 12 describes the way in which the Passover meal was to be observed, roasting the lamb, and eaten with unleavened bread and bitter herbs.

Much of the tradition for this celebration developed before the first century, as we can see from the gospel accounts when Jesus celebrated this feast with His disciples. The gospels of Matthew and Mark mention dipping the hand in the dish of bitter herbs. All three synoptic gospels mention the bread and the wine, although Luke mentions the wine twice.

The Spring Feasts

Since the gospel accounts, rabbis have added other elements to the meal, including green vegetables, a roasted egg, *kharoset*, a mixture of cut up apples and cinnamon, and four cups of wine. Later in history, rabbis added a fifth cup, called the Cup of Elijah, expressing hope that Elijah will come and drink from the cup, and announce the Messiah has come, according to Malachi 4:5.

Today the feasts of Passover and Unleavened Bread are celebrated with a meal on the first day, and the feast of Unleavened Bread continues for seven days. The order of service for this meal is called the Seder, which is often contained in a booklet called a Haggadah. This booklet also contains the blessings and a commentary so that everyone present can follow along. This is wonderful for Christians who are able to join with Messianic Jews for this special celebration.

There is a depth of meaning to Passover which many Christians are sadly unaware. Paul wrote in 1 Corinthians 5:7b, **"For indeed Christ, our Passover, was sacrificed for us."** He goes on to say in verse 8, **"Therefore let us keep the feast, not with the old leaven, nor with the leaven of malice and wickedness, but with the unleavened bread of sincerity and truth."** I encourage you, if a Messianic Passover celebration is available in your community, to attend and take part. It is a very rewarding experience.

THE FEAST OF WEEKS - ALSO CALLED PENTECOST OR SHAVUOT (LEV. 23:15-22)

"And you shall count for yourselves from the day after the Sabbath, from the day that you brought the sheaf of the wave offering: seven Sabbaths shall be completed. Count fifty days to the day after the seventh Sabbath; then you shall offer a new grain offering to the LORD. You shall bring from your dwellings two wave *loaves* of two-tenths *of*

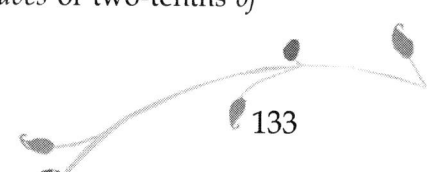

GRAFTED IN THE JEWISH OLIVE TREE

an ephah. They shall be of fine flour; they shall be baked with leaven. *They are* the firstfruits to the LORD. And you shall offer with the bread seven lambs of the first year, without blemish, one young bull, and two rams. They shall be *as* a burnt offering to the LORD, with their grain offering and their drink offerings, an offering made by fire for a sweet aroma to the LORD. Then you shall sacrifice one kid of the goats as a sin offering, and two male lambs of the first year as a sacrifice of a peace offering. The priest shall wave them with the bread of the firstfruits *as* a wave offering before the LORD, with the two lambs. They shall be holy to the LORD for the priest. And you shall proclaim on the same day *that* it is a holy convocation to you. You shall do no customary work *on it. It shall be* a statute forever in all your dwellings throughout your generations. When you reap the harvest of your land, you shall not wholly reap the corners of your field when you reap, nor shall you gather any gleaning from your harvest. You shall leave them for the poor and for the stranger: I *am* the LORD your God."

HISTORICALLY THIS FEAST was observed as an agricultural feast, marking the end of the barley harvest and the beginning of the wheat harvest. In Judaism it is called Shavuot, and in Christianity it is called Pentecost, taken from the Greek word for "fifty." Counting the days from the third day of Passover, the day after the Sabbath, which is the Feast of Firstfruits, until Pentecost is called "Counting the Omer" and connects Passover to Pentecost. The primary activity on this feast was presenting a wave offering of thanksgiving to the Lord consisting of two loaves of bread made with leaven. This offering was to be made with seven male lambs, a young bull and two rams as a burnt offering, as well as a sin offering of a male goat. The wave offering of thanksgiving signified their dependence on God for the harvest. Shavuot, or Pentecost, is one of the three feasts that all males were to appear before the Lord, at the place of the Lord's choosing. The other two are the Feast of Unleavened Bread and the Feast of Tabernacles (Deut. 16:16).

Besides the agricultural aspect, the Feast of Weeks or Pentecost also signifies the process of freedom which began with the Exodus from Egypt at Passover. It is believed it was at this time that the handing down of the Law on Mount Sinai took place; consequently it is an observance of the giving of the Torah. After the temple in Jerusalem was razed in 70 A.D, this feast lost much of its agricultural meaning, and instead came to be primarily celebrated as the time the Law was given by God to Israel.

In the giving of the Law at Mount Sinai, God made a covenant with the people, and made them His special people. He said to them, "**Now therefore, if you will indeed obey My voice and keep My covenant, then you shall be a special treasure to Me above all people: for all the earth is Mine.**" (Ex. 19:5)

According to Messianic Jewish thought:

> Jewish tradition teaches that Passover is when God promised to marry Israel, while Shavuot is the time when God entered into the marriage covenant with them. The seven weeks between Passover and Shavuot symbolize the seven days a bride-to-be counts in preparation for the consummation of her marriage.
>
> Exodus 19 describes the giving of the law to Israel. In fact, this law represents the time when God entered into and proposed His marriage covenant to Israel. The covenant of the law is parallel to the Ketubah. A Ketubah is a written marriage contract between husband and wife whereby they agree to the terms and obligations outlined in their relationship. Ex. 19:6-8, when God entered into this covenant of marriage with Israel, there were great manifestations of His presence to demonstrate His commitment to his covenant.3

This "marriage covenant" mentioned above is offered to all who will believe. Jesus said, **"This cup is the new covenant in My blood, which is shed for you."** (Luke 22:20) Our act of betrothal is when we accept Jesus as our Messiah, our Lord, our Savior. Jesus is our Bridegroom.

> And Jesus said to them, "Can the friends of the bridegroom mourn as long as the bridegroom is with them? But the days will come when the bridegroom will be taken away from them, and then they will fast." (Matt. 9:15)

He promised us that He would send the Spirit, **"However, when He, the Spirit of truth, has come, He will guide you into all truth; for He will not speak on His own authority, but whatever He hears He will speak; and He will tell you things to come"** (John 16:13).

Pentecost is the time when the Holy Spirit was poured out upon the believers, and after Peter's sermon, about three thousand were added to their number that day.

> "When the Day of Pentecost had fully come, they were all with one accord in one place. And suddenly there came a sound from heaven, as of a rushing mighty wind, and it filled the whole house where they were sitting. Then there appeared to them divided tongues, as of fire, and *one* sat upon each of them. And they were all filled with the Holy Spirit and began to speak with other tongues, as the Spirit gave them utterance." (Acts 2:1-4)

Ephesians 1:13-14 tells us, **"In Him you also trusted, after you heard the word of truth, the gospel of your salvation; in whom** also, having believed, you were sealed with the Holy Spirit of promise, who is the guarantee of our inheritance until the redemption of the purchased possession, to the praise of His glory.

In the next section we shall examine the Fall Feasts, and their significance for us today.

Chapter 12
The Fall Feasts

The Feast of Trumpets – Yom Teruah (Lev. 23:23-25)

(The Day of the Blowing the Ram's Horn)

Then the LORD spoke to Moses, saying, "Speak to the children of Israel, saying: 'In the seventh month, on the first *day* of the month, you shall have a Sabbath-rest, a memorial of blowing of trumpets, a holy convocation. You shall do no customary work *on it*; and you shall offer an offering made by fire to the LORD.'" (Lev. 23:23-25)

(Numbers 29:1-6 explains how this feast was to be carried out.)

ROSH HASHANAH IS ANOTHER NAME for this feast, and is traditionally regarded as the first day of creation. As the Sabbath, the day God rested from His works, was the seventh day at creation, so this feast is celebrated on the first and second days of the seventh month of Tishri. In Hebrew Rosh Hashanah means *the head of the year*, and applies to the observance of the civil new year. It marks the beginning of the ten days of penitence leading up to Yom Kippur, the Day of Atonement, and is therefore a time of self-examination and of seeking God. The Feast of Trumpets and the Day of Atonement are the two holiest days of the Jewish year. The ten days between these two feasts are referred to as The Days of Awe and are considered to be High Holy Days. These feasts, unlike the others, do not celebrate a historical event, but are, rather, days of introspection for spiritual growth.

As the observance of the Head of the Year or the Jewish New Year, people wish each other "LaShannah Tova," meaning *a good year*, with the hope that their names will be found in the Book of Life. In Messianic congregations, the greeting is "L'shana tovah ki nichtavnu," which means "Happy New Year for we are inscribed!"

The Feast of Trumpets celebrates the birth of the world at creation, and celebrates God's royalty. The blowing of the shofar announces God's Kingship and rule. Rosh Hashanah introduces the holiest month on the Jewish calendar.

However, this holiday is one of mixed emotions. It is joyous because of the celebration of the new year, but somber because it begins a time of reflection of one's life, and is the day leading into the Ten Days of Awe which culminate at Yom Kippur.

The blowing of the shofar is a call to repentance. According to tradition, the Book of Life is opened on Rosh Hashanah. The righteous are sealed in the Book for the coming year, and the unrighteous are removed. They believe the fate of Jewish people is set during the Ten Days of Awe and determined on Yom Kippur. Consequently, the mood during these ten days is introspective and somber, and reminds us of the mood that will be prevalent in the world before the Messiah returns. This is the reason that many believe the return of Messiah Jesus will take place during the Fall Feasts.

The shofar is blown a number of times and with a variety of sounds in synagogues, both Orthodox and Messianic, during the

Rosh Hashanah service. There are four different sounds from the shofar on this feast:
- Tekiah – one blast, which is a pure, unbroken sound, a call to search our hearts, repent of our evil ways, and seek forgiveness
- Shevarim – three blasts, a broken, staccato sound, signifying sorrow for the wrongs we've done and a desire to change
- Teruah – nine blasts of a wave-like sound of alarm, calling us to stand by the banner of God (which is love)
- Tekiah Gedolah – a prolonged unbroken sound – a final invitation to sincerely repent

The shofar itself is a cleaned out ram's horn of various sizes, from small to large, and is twisted, reminding people of their twisted condition. It is also bent, which indicates that in humility we must bend our hearts toward God.

An interesting aspect in the blowing of the shofar is a call to remember Abraham's willingness to sacrifice Isaac, and how God used a substitute – the ram He provided – in place of Isaac. This speaks to us of the substitutionary sacrifice of Jesus for us.

Earlier I had mentioned that Passover was the time when God promised to marry Israel, and that Pentecost was the time when He entered into the marriage covenant with them. The Feast of Trumpets points to the actual wedding!

THE DAY OF ATONEMENT (YOM KIPPUR) (LEV. 23:26-32)

> And the LORD spoke to Moses, saying: "Also the tenth day of this seventh month shall be the Day of Atonement. It shall be a holy convocation for you; you shall afflict your souls, and offer an offering made by fire to the LORD. And you shall do no work on that same day, for it is the Day of Atonement, to make atonement for you before the LORD your God. For any person

who is not afflicted in soul on that same day shall be cut off from his people. And any person who does any work on that same day, that person I will destroy from among his people. You shall do no manner of work; it shall be a statute forever throughout your generations in all your dwellings. It shall be to you a sabbath of solemn rest, and you shall afflict your souls; on the ninth day of the month at evening, from evening to evening, you shall celebrate your sabbath."

YOM KIPPUR IS THE HOLIEST DAY on the Jewish calendar, the 10th of Tishri. It is a fast day rather than a feast day, a day of confession and prayer. This is the day when the High Priest entered the Holy of Holies to make atonement for the nation by the sacrifice of an animal. It is said that a bell was tied to the hem of his garment, and a rope to his ankle, so if God did not accept his sacrifice and struck him dead, he could be pulled out of the Most Holy Place. It is also called the "Day of Redemption" because through the shed blood of the sacrifice forgiveness is obtained.

Barney Kasdan, in his book "God's Appointed Times" describes the ceremony of the two goats, as laid out in Lev. 16:

> "One goat, called *Chatat* was to be slain as a blood sacrifice to symbolically cover the sins of Israel. The other goat, called *Azazel*, or Scapegoat, would be brought before the priest. The priest would lay his hands on the head of the goat as he confessed the sins of the people. But instead of slaying this animal in the traditional fashion, the goat would be set free in the wilderness symbolically taking the sins of the nation out from their midst."[8]

This is a foreshadow of what would take place in the New Covenant, when Jesus shed His blood as a sacrifice for the sins of mankind for all who would receive it. He too was buried outside the gate of the city.

The Fall Feasts

We can see then the theme of repentance beginning at Rosh Hashanah, the Feast of Trumpets, culminates on Yom Kippur, the Day of Atonement, with the offering of a vicarious sacrifice for the sins of the people.

I came across an interesting phenomenon regarding this scapegoat bearing the sins of the nation. Before it was taken out into the wilderness, a red sash was tied around its horns. A priest would then take it to the wilderness, but would not release it until a sign from God was given: the red sash would turn white, signifying that God accepted their sacrifice, and their sins forgiven.

However, the year that Jesus died as an atonement for man's sins, the sash remained red. For the first time in their history, the sash did not turn white. Of course, with hindsight, and with knowing the truth, we would wonder why the priests at that time would not realize that Jesus was Who He said He was! The Talmud, the Jewish book expounding the Law, states:

Forty years before the Temple was destroyed, the lot never came into the right hand, **the red wool did not become white,** the western light did not burn, and the gates of the Temple opened of themselves, till the time that R. Johanan b. Zakkai rebuked them, saying, "Temple, Temple, why alarmest thou us? We know that thou art destined to be destroyed. For of thee hath prophesied Zechariah ben Iddo [Zech. xi. 1], "Open thy doors, O Lebanon, and the fire shall eat thy cedars."[9] (emphasis mine)

The Temple was destroyed in A.D. 70 by the Romans. Forty years prior to that Jesus died on the cross, shedding His blood as the perfect sacrifice for sin. For those forty years the red sash no longer turned white, as it previously had, which would have signified that their sacrifice had been accepted and their sins were forgiven! Instead, it indicated that their sacrifice was no longer acceptable to God. The writer of the Book of Hebrews states in Heb. 9:12 – **He did not enter by means of the blood of goats and**

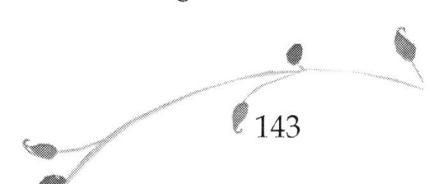

calves, but He entered the Most Holy Place once for all by His own blood, having obtained eternal redemption.

Prophetically, then, we can see the Day of Atonement in the Old Covenant, with the sacrifice of the blood of bulls and goats was a shadow of the ultimate sacrifice of Jesus, the perfect High Priest shedding His blood, for it is also written: **Without the shedding of blood there is no remission** (Heb. 9:22) of sin.

There is further prophetic meaning in the Fall Feasts. As the theme of repentance is associated with Rosh Hashanah, Zechariah spoke of a future day when Israel will look in repentance on the One they have pierced in Zech. 12:10, "**And I will pour on the house of David and on the inhabitants of Jerusalem the Spirit of grace and supplication; then they will look on Me whom they have pierced. Yes, they will mourn for Him as one mourns for *his* only *son*, and grieve for Him as one grieves for a firstborn.**" Just as Yom Kippur follows Rosh Hashanah, so regeneration follows repentance.

Paul speaks of this promise to the Jewish people in Rom. 11:25-27, "**For I do not desire, brethren, that you should be ignorant of this mystery, lest you should be wise in your own opinion, that blindness in part has happened to Israel until the fullness of the Gentiles has come in. And so all Israel will be saved, as it is written:**

"The Deliverer will come out of Zion,
And He will turn away ungodliness from Jacob;
For this is My covenant with them,
When I take away their sins."

This, then, is the ultimate fulfillment of Yom Kippur, when the Jewish people are regenerated! This regeneration has already begun, with the "Jesus Freaks" of the 70s culminating in the Messianic Movement, which has resulted in tens of thousands of

Jews today believing that Yeshua (Jesus) is their Messiah! And the numbers continue to grow!

THE FEAST OF TABERNACLES (SUKKOT) (LEV. 23:33-44)

> Then the LORD spoke to Moses, saying, "Speak to the children of Israel, saying: 'The fifteenth day of this seventh month shall be the Feast of Tabernacles for seven days to the LORD. On the first day there shall be a holy convocation. You shall do no customary work on it. For seven days you shall offer an offering made by fire to the LORD. On the eighth day you shall have a holy convocation, and you shall offer an offering made by fire to the LORD. It is a sacred assembly, and you shall do no customary work on it.
> 'These are the feasts of the LORD which you shall proclaim to be holy convocations, to offer an offering made by fire to the LORD, a burnt offering and a grain offering, a sacrifice and drink offerings, everything on its day — besides the Sabbaths of the LORD, besides your gifts, besides all your vows, and besides all your freewill offerings which you give to the LORD.
> 'Also on the fifteenth day of the seventh month, when you have gathered in the fruit of the land, you shall keep the feast of the LORD for seven days; on the first day there shall be a Sabbath-rest, and on the eighth day a Sabbath-rest. And you shall take for yourselves on the first day the fruit of beautiful trees, branches of palm trees, the boughs of leafy trees, and willows of the brook; and you shall rejoice before the LORD your God for seven days. You shall keep it as a feast to the LORD for seven days in the year. It shall be a statute forever in your generations. You shall celebrate it in the seventh month. You shall dwell in booths for seven days. All who are native Israelites shall dwell in booths, that your generations may know that I made the children of Israel dwell in booths when I

brought them out of the land of Egypt: I am the LORD your God.'" So Moses declared to the children of Israel the feasts of the LORD. (Lev. 23:33-44)

THE FEAST OF TABERNACLES BEGINS on the 15th of Tishri, the seventh month, which corresponds to October in our calendar and continues for eight days, beginning and ending with a holy convocation. The people are commanded to dwell in booths or tents, as a reminder of the Israelites dwelling in booths when they came out of Egypt on their way to the Promised Land.

Today the Jewish people make booths, tabernacles or "sukkahs" to dwell in during this feast. They are a temporary dwelling, often made of canvas, with branches for the roof so they can see the stars on a clear night, reminding them that their time on earth is temporary, and that their ultimate dwelling place is to be with God. In colder climates the people generally don't sleep in these shelters, but often have their meals in them.

In Temple times, seventy bulls were sacrificed throughout the week, representing the number of nations in the world, according to the Babylonian Talmud.[10] Thus their prayer and sacrifices were for the world, and a demonstration that God's desire was to dwell with humanity.

Some years ago while doing a word study on the word "tabernacle," I discovered that in both the Old and New Covenants the word signifies "a dwelling place." The Hebrew in the Old Covenant uses the following words:

- **ohel** translated as covering, dwelling, dwelling place, home, tabernacle, (some examples are Gen. 4:20, 1 Sam. 17:54, Ps. 91:10, and is designated as "tent of meeting" in Ex. 33:7-11 and "tent of testimony" in Num. 9:15)

The Fall Feasts

- **mish-kan** translated as dwelling, habitation, tabernacle, tent, (some examples are Job 18:21, Ps. 87:2, Ps. 45:6). The predominant use of mish-kan is of the Lord's Tabernacle, and is the place where God resided in Old Covenant times

- **sukkah** translated as booth, cottage, pavilion, tabernacle, tent (examples are Jonah 4:5, Job 27:18, Is. 4:6). In Amos 9:11 God promised that He would build again the Tabernacle of David that was fallen down, which is considered a Messianic prophecy.

In the Greek, in the New Covenant, the following words are used:

- **skene** – representing a tent or cloth hut, translated as habitation, tabernacle; the Mosaic Tabernacle, the Tabernacle of Witness (Acts 7:44, Heb. 8:5, 9:1, 8:21); tent of meeting, tabernacle of the congregation, the outer court (Heb. 9:2, 6); the inner sanctuary (Heb. 9:3); the heavenly prototype, the true Tabernacle (Heb. 8:2; 9:2, 3, 6, 8, 11 and 21).

- **skenopegia** is translated as a hut or temporary residence and specifically suggests the human body as the abode of the Holy Spirit. It is the word used in reference to the Feast of Tabernacles in John 7:2. The Hebrew word **Sukkah** becomes **Skenopegia** in Greek.

- **skeenos** – again, a hut or temporary residence, figuratively as the human body being a temporary dwelling-place of the Holy Spirit; tabernacle (2 Cor. 5:1, 4)

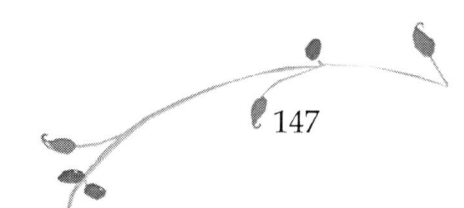

- **skeenoo** – to tent or encamp, to reside or dwell. *The Word was made flesh and dwelt* (lit. tabernacled) *among us.* (John 1:14). *The Lamb shall dwell* (lit. tabernacle) *with them.* (Rev. 7:15)

(The above information was taken from a computer program of Strong's Definitions)

In old Hebrew culture, the date of birth of a person was not considered important; rather, they took note of the date on which a person died, because the state of one's soul at death was what was important. Perhaps that is why the Scriptures do not spell out for us exactly when Jesus was born, although we know when He died.

As I mentioned in a previous chapter, after the Church was Romanized, it was decided that Christ's birth would be celebrated on December 25th to correspond to their pagan traditions to honor Tammuz. As I was doing the above word study the thought hit me like a lightning bolt that Jesus was born during the Feast of Tabernacles. The Apostle John's words echoed in my mind, **"The Word was made flesh and dwelt among us."** (John 1:14) He was made flesh – was born, and dwelt – tabernacled – among us. Rev. 21:3 tells us that **"Behold, the tabernacle of God is with men, and He will dwell with them, and they shall be His people. God Himself will be with them and be their God."**

Ultimately, Jesus will dwell with us again when He returns and sets up His kingdom. Jesus was born on this earth and lived and dwelt among His people for 33 years. The prophet Isaiah prophesied about the coming Messiah, **"Behold, the virgin shall conceive and bear a Son, and shall call His name Immanuel."** (Is. 7:14). *Immanuel* means "God with us." I am not alone in my belief that Jesus was born at this time. Many Messianic Jews also believe that Yeshua was born during the Feast of Tabernacles.

Galen Peterson in his book "The Everlasting Tradition" suggests that Luke's gospel gives us a clue as to the time of Messiah's birth. In Luke chapter 1 the angel Gabriel appears to a priest named

The Fall Feasts

Zacharias who was carrying out his duties in the temple, and tells him he and his wife Elizabeth were going to have a son in their old age. We know the story of how Zacharias was struck dumb because he didn't believe what he was being told.

1 Chronicles 24 states that the priests were divided according to the schedule of their service (v.3) into 24 groups, 16 from the house of Eleazar and 8 from that of Ithamar. The duties were assigned by the casting of lots (v.5), and Abijah's was the 8th lot (v. 10), to which Zacharias belonged.

A footnote in the Spirit Filled Life Bible says the priests were divided into 24 groups, each group being responsible for the temple sacrifices for 2 weeks each year. The Nelson Study Bible notes that, since there were sixteen family divisions from Eleazar and eight from Ithamar, that the duties were assigned by casting lots. The NIV Study Bible also mentions in its footnote that service was likely in two-week shifts once a year as found in New Testament times. Eerdmans Handbook to the Bible also suggests two-week shifts.

The first two shifts, then, would have been for the month of Nisan, the first month according to God's calendar. Abijah's shift, being the eighth lot, would have taken place in the month of Tammuz. The following chart shows the months of the Hebrew calendar with the corresponding timeframe of our calendar:

Nisan	March-April
Iyar	April-May
Sivan	May-June
Tamuz	**June-July**
Av	July-August
Elul	August-September
Tishrei	September-October
Cheshvan	October-November
Kislev	November-December
Tevet	December-January
Shvat	January-February

Adar   February-March

Consequently, Zacharias would have been serving in the temple in the month of Tamuz (June-July) when the angel Gabriel told him he would have a son.

The following chart shows the chronology:

Mid-June During Zacharias' term of service, Gabriel revealed to him that he was about to father a son when he returned home to his wife Elizabeth, who had been barren until that time (vv. 8-13).

Early to mid-July As promised, Elizabeth became pregnant (vv. 23-24).

Late December In the sixth month of Elizabeth's pregnancy, Gabriel appeared again, this time to her relative Miriam (known in the English as Mary). Miriam received the news from Gabriel that she was about to conceive, through the miracle of the Holy Spirit, and give birth to Messiah (vv. 26-38).

Late December to   Miriam conceives Yeshua.
early January

Early January Miriam went to visit Elizabeth, who was then nearly six months pregnant (vv. 39-45).

Early April   After a three-month visit, Miriam left for home (v. 56).

Early to mid-April Elizabeth reached full-term and gave birth to her son John (v. 57).

Late September to early October Nine months after conception, Miriam gave birth to Yeshua in the town of Bethlehem (Luke 2:1-7).[11]

The above chart shows a biblically correct interpretation of the timing of Jesus' birth, which is totally contrary to the tradition rooted in paganism which has been handed down to us. How can we continue to propagate a lie?

During Jesus' ministry He went up to Jerusalem for the Feast of Tabernacles (John 7:10) and began to teach in the temple. Many believed in Him, but the authorities wanted to take Him (John 7:32). They did not understand Him.

The last day of the feast was called *Hoshana Rabba,* The Great Hosanna. This is when a priest went to the Pool of Siloam and filled a golden pitcher with water, and then returned to the Temple. Jesus cried out, **"If anyone thirsts, let him come to Me and drink. He who believes in Me, as the Scripture has said, out of his heart will flow rivers of living water"** (John 7:37b-38), indicating the future pouring out of the Holy Spirit. So we can see that Jesus kept the Feast of Tabernacles.

THE JEWISH WEDDING AND JESUS OUR BRIDEGROOM

IN A TRADITIONAL JEWISH WEDDING, there is a prescribed chain of events to be followed. I have compared this with the New Covenant expressions that Jesus is our bridegroom, and His followers are His bride, which I italicize. The following verses are all taken from the NIV:

GRAFTED IN THE JEWISH OLIVE TREE

- The bridegroom or an agent of the groom's father went in search of a bride. For example, Abraham sent his servant to find a bride for Isaac. Often, a bride would consent without meeting the groom, as Rebekah did, and went with Abraham's servant (see Gen. 24). Or, if the young man himself chose a young woman to marry, he prepared a contract or covenant to present to her and her father in her home. A very important part of this contract was the price, which was to be paid to the young woman's father in exchange for permission to marry his daughter.

   Jesus came to earth, the home of His bride and presented His marriage contract, which is the New Covenant that provides for the forgiveness of sins for those who believe.

- A price would be established for the bride, whatever the groom had to offer. The price both the father and the bridegroom agreed upon was called a mohar. A scribe would draw up a marriage contract called a ketubah, which set out the bride price, her rights, and the groom's promises to his bride.

   Jesus paid the price of His bride with His life and the shedding of His blood. Hebrews 9:15 makes it clear that He died as the price of the New Covenant: **...Christ is the mediator of a new covenant, that those who are called may receive the promised eternal inheritance – now that He has died as a ransom to set them free from the sins committed under the first covenant.** *The marriage contract, the New Covenant, is described* **in Jer.31:31-34, "The time is coming," declares the LORD, "when I will make a new covenant with the house of Israel and the house of Judah. It will not be like the covenant I made with their forefathers when I took them by the hand to lead them out of Egypt, because they broke my covenant, though I was a husband to them," declares the LORD. "This is the covenant I will make with the house of**

152

The Fall Feasts

Israel after that time," declares the LORD. *"I will put my law in their minds and write it on their hearts. I will be their God, and they will be my people ...... they will all know me, from the least of them to the greatest," declares the* LORD. *"For I will forgive their wickedness and will remember their sins no more."*

- If the bride's father agreed to the price, the young man would pour a glass of wine for the young woman. If she drank the wine, it would indicate her acceptance of the proposal. The bride and groom were then betrothed, legally bound together, but not yet married. Good examples of this stage are Mary and Joseph. During this time the bride and bridegroom would each be preparing for the wedding, and would not see each other.

    Jesus poured wine for His disciples on the night before He died. **Matt. 26:27-29:** *Then he took the cup, gave thanks and offered it to them saying, "This is the blood of the covenant, which is poured out for many for the forgiveness of sins. I tell you, I will not drink of this fruit of the vine from now on until that day when I drink it anew with you in my Father's kingdom."*

- The groom would present his bride with gifts. Unlike today, it was not an engagement ring, but could have been almost anything the groom had to give. These gifts were intended to show his appreciation for her, as well as to help her remember him during the long betrothal period, which was typically 1-2 years.

    Jesus also gave us gifts: the gift of the Holy Spirit, as well as the gift of His peace. **1 John 4:13** *We know that we live in him and he in us, because he has given us of his Spirit. Jesus described this gift in John 14:26-27, "But the Counselor, the Holy Spirit, whom the Father will send in my name, will teach you all things and will* *remind you of everything I have said to you. Peace I leave with you, my peace I give you. I do not give as the world gives. Do not let your hearts be troubled and do not be afraid."*

- Before the groom left her, he would say to his betrothed, "**I go to prepare a place for you. If I go, I will return again to you**."

    *Jesus said this to His disciples. In **John 14:2-3** Jesus said, "**In My Father's house are many rooms; if it were not so, I would have told you. I am going there to prepare a place for you. And if I go to prepare a place for you, I will come back and take you to be with Me that you also may be where I am.**"*

- The groom would go to his father's house to begin to prepare a wedding chamber for the honeymoon, typically in his father's house, and according to his father's specifications. It had to be a beautiful place to bring his bride. This is where he and his bride would spend seven days. The young man could go for his bride only when his father approved.

    Likewise, Jesus can only come back for His Bride when His Father gives the word. In Matthew 24 Jesus describes the Great Tribulation, and His return. In verse 36 He says, **"But of that day and hour no one knows, not even the angels of heaven, but My Father only."**

- Meanwhile, the bride would prepare herself. She was consecrated and set apart, bought with a price, and waiting for her groom. A mikvah, or cleansing bath, was prepared for her to be purified for her wedding. Mikvah is the same word used for baptism. If she went out she wore a veil, so others would know she was betrothed. She would pamper herself to make herself beautiful for her husband. She wanted to be ready, and she had no idea when her groom would come for her. Often she would

The Fall Feasts

keep a lamp burning in the window and keep extra oil on hand, because she wanted to be ready day and night. Her sisters or bridesmaids would also be waiting, keeping their lamps trimmed in anticipation for the late night festivities.

> *This reminds us of the parable of the wise and foolish virgins in the Matt. 25:1-13. We also, as God's people, are now consecrated and set apart, waiting for the return of our Bridegroom. We should be spending this time preparing ourselves for Jesus' return so we will be ready when He comes.*

- A wedding date was not set. The groom could not go to his bride until his father approved of his preparations. So if asked about a date, he could only reply, "No one knows except my father."

> *We also do not know when Jesus will return. He said in* **Mark 13:32-33, "No one knows about the day or hour, not even the angels in heaven, nor the Son, but only the Father. Be on guard! Be alert!. You do not know when that time will come ..."**

- When his father was satisfied that everything was ready, he would allow his son to go and get his bride. The bridegroom would come like a thief in the night, with a shout and the sound of a shofar to let his bride know he was coming, so she could gather her belongings to take with her to the wedding chamber. The bridegroom would then present his marriage contract to the bride's father, and take her to his father's house, where his father would place the bride's hand into his son's hand. This was called the "presentation," and it was at that moment when she became his wife.

The sounds would also attract his friends and relatives, and they would come. A close friend would stand outside the door of the wedding chamber, and when the marriage was consummated, the bridegroom would tell his friend through the door. He would then announce it to the other guests that had gathered, and they would celebrate for seven days until the bride and bridegroom emerged from the wedding chamber.

Ancient Jewish eschatology taught that a seven year "time of trouble" would come upon the earth before the coming of the Messiah. During this time of trouble, the righteous would be resurrected and would enter the wedding chamber where they would be protected from the time of trouble. Indeed, Daniel spoke of a 7-year covenant which will bring desolation (Dan. 9:27). Today we refer to that time as the tribulation. Jesus spoke of this time in **Matt. 24.**

- After the seven days spent in the wedding chamber, the bridegroom would introduce his bride to his friends and all who had gathered at the sound of the trumpet and they would celebrate the marriage feast.

    Likewise, Jesus and His bride will celebrate with the Marriage Supper of the Lamb. **Then I heard what sounded like a great multitude, like the roar of rushing waters and like loud peals of thunder, shouting, "Hallelujah! For our Lord God Almighty reigns. Let us rejoice and be glad and give him glory! For the wedding of the Lamb has come, and his bride has made herself ready. Fine linen, bright and clean, was given her to wear."** *(Fine linen stands for the righteous acts of the saints.)* **Then the angel said to me, "Write: Blessed are those who are invited to the wedding supper of the Lamb!" (Rev. 19:6-9)**

- After the marriage supper, the bride and bridegroom would leave the groom's father's house where the groom had built the wedding chamber. They would go to their own home, which the bridegroom had prepared.

> *In the same way, after the Marriage Supper of the Lamb, Jesus and His bride will depart for their new home,* **"Then I saw a new heaven and a new earth, for the first heaven and the first earth had passed away, and there was no longer any sea. I saw the Holy City, the new Jerusalem, coming down out of heaven from God, prepared as a bride beautifully dressed for her husband. And I heard a loud voice from the throne saying, "Now the dwelling of God is with men, and he will live with them. They will be his people, and God himself will be with them and be their God. He will wipe every tear from their eyes...One of the angels who had the seven bowls full of the last seven plagues came and said to me, "Come, I will show you the bride, the wife of the Lamb." And he carried me away in the Spirit to a mountain great and high, and showed me the Holy City, Jerusalem, coming down out of heaven from God ... Rev. 21:1-4.**

From the pattern of the ancient wedding practices, we see that, like the bridegroom of ancient times, Jesus came to the home of His bride for the betrothal, made a covenant with His bride and sealed it with a glass of wine, paid the bride price with His life and sent His bride gifts of the Holy Spirit. We, the betrothed (the Church) currently await the return of our Bridegroom to take us to the wedding chamber when we meet the Lord in the air.. We will then celebrate the Marriage Supper of the Lamb and depart with our Bridegroom for our new home, the new Jerusalem.

Paul tells us in 2 Cor. 11:2: **For I am jealous for you with a godly jealousy. For I have betrothed you to one husband, that I may present you as a chaste virgin to Christ.** The details of the ancient Jewish wedding are so reminiscent of what God is preparing for us! The Feast of Trumpets is a prophetic look at the return of our Bridegroom! And when Jesus returns at that last trump, we will share in the Marriage Supper of the Lamb! We are His betrothed. He is our Bridegroom, and He is preparing a place for us! Our heavenly Father accepted Jesus' sacrifice, His blood shed for our redemption, and we, as believers, accepted Jesus, our Bridegroom, and His great love for us. The Bible – the Word of God – is our marriage contract, for every promise Jesus made to us is contained therein.

The Fall Feasts, then, are a time of spiritual renewal, a time to dig deeper into the heart of God, a time to humble ourselves before the Lord, asking Him for His vision for our lives with a greater desire to reach the lost. It is a time to repent, to right any wrongs in our relationships with others, and to strengthen the bonds with the special people God has put in our lives. It is a time of preparation for our coming Bridegroom!

Chapter 13
Other Feasts and Special Days

THE FEAST OF DEDICATION (HANUKKAH OR CHANUKAH)

ALTHOUGH THIS FEAST IS NOT MENTIONED along with the others in the book of Leviticus, as the reason for it had not yet taken place, it is mentioned in the Gospel of John, (10:22-23) – "**Now it was the Feast of Dedication in Jerusalem, and it was winter. And Jesus walked in the temple in Solomon's porch.**" Its story took place in the midst of the 400 "silent years" between the Tanakh, the original Scriptures, and the Messianic Writings of Jesus' ministry.

The purpose of this feast was the remembrance of the cleansing and rededication of the temple after Antiochus Epiphanes had desecrated it. In order to understand what happened, we have to go back in history to the time of the Greek Empire which ruled much of the known world from 331 –167 B.C. under Alexander the Great.

After Alexander's death his empire was divided and ruled by four of his generals. Two of the areas were Syria, ruled by the

Seleucids, and Egypt, ruled by the Ptolemies. These two generals were constantly at war, and Israel was caught in the middle.

By the second century B.C. the Syrians under Antiochus, who had chosen the title "Epiphanes" (which means "God manifest"), controlled Jerusalem and the surrounding area. He wanted to make everyone Hellenistic – Greek in all ways, and become their "lord." 1 Maccabees 1:41-43 tells us:

> Antiochus now issued a decree that all nations in his empire should abandon their own customs and become one people. All the Gentiles and even many of the Israelites submitted to this decree. They adopted the official pagan religion, offered sacrifices to idols, and no longer observed the Sabbath.[12]

According to Josephus[13], after the death of the High Priest Onias, his brother was to take his place. However, Antiochus didn't like him and instead put his younger brother in as High Priest, causing a rift among the people. Some of them went to Antiochus, telling him they no longer wanted to follow the Jewish way of living, but rather they desired to follow the king's laws and the ways of the Greeks. They asked him to build them a gymnasium in Jerusalem. According to Josephus, many Jewish mothers did not circumcise their male babies so that they would be able to go into the gymnasiums and not be mocked, as the games were carried out naked. Those mothers who did circumcise their sons were put to death, as well as their families.

In the year 167 BC, in the month of Kislev, according to Josephus, Antiochus

> "...left the temple bare, and took away the golden candlesticks, and the golden altar [of incense], and table [of shewbread], and the altar [of burnt offering]; and did not abstain from even the veils, which were made of fine linen and scarlet. He also emptied it of its secret treasures, and left nothing at all

remaining; and by this means cast the Jews into great lamentation, for he forbade them to offer those daily sacrifices which they used to offer God, according to the law.... And when the king had built an idol altar upon God's Altar, he slew swine upon it, and so offered a sacrifice neither according to the law, nor the Jewish religious worship in that country."[14]

Many Jewish people accepted this new way of life, turning away from their old beliefs and customs. Schools taught Hellenist rationalism and many parents no longer circumcised their sons. It was becoming a hedonistic society instead of a Biblical one.

However, not all Jews were happy with the situation. Some refused to bow down to this new "god," some were killed for not doing so. A revolt began to foment against the Syrians, led by a priest named Mattathias and his five sons. After Mattathias' death his son Judah took over leadership of this group. They soon began calling themselves The Maccabees. According to Galen Peterson, some scholars say this name comes from the word makkabet, which means "hammer," while others suggest that it comes from the first Hebrew letters of the words "Who is like Thee, O Mighty Lord?" from the Psalm 89:8.[15]

Judas Maccabee built a great army, and prayed to God for assistance before each battle. They fought and prevailed against their enemies. Josephus continues:

"When, therefore, the generals of Antiochus's armies had been beaten so often, Judas assembled the people together, and told them, that after these many victories which God had given them, they ought to go up to Jerusalem, and purify the temple, and offer appointed sacrifices. But as soon as he, with the whole multitude, was come to Jerusalem, and found the temple deserted, and its gates burnt down, and plants growing in the temple of their own accord, on account of its desertion, he and those that were with him began to lament, and were quite confounded at the sight of the temple......When therefore he had carefully purged it, and had brought in new vessels, the candlestick, the table [of shewbread], and the altar [of incense], which were made of gold, he hung up the veils at the gates, and added doors to them. He also took down the altar [of burnt offering], and built a new one of stones that he gathered, and not of such as were hewn with iron tools."[16]

On the 25th of Kislev they rededicated the Temple to the Lord – the same day of the month that their worship had been profaned three years earlier. They celebrated this restoration of the temple sacrifices for eight days, and called it the Festival of Lights or Hanukkah.

According to tradition, Judas and his men could find only one flask of oil which had the High Priest's seal on it, which indicated its approval for use in the Temple menorah. Miraculously, however, this one day's supply of oil lasted the complete eight days. Since then, Jews have been celebrating this miracle of oil at the rededication of the Temple at Hanukkah, using an 8-branched menorah or candalabra called a Hanukkiah.

Today, Jewish people celebrate this festival with candles, giving gifts and *gelt*, which is money. They often use the foil-wrapped chocolate "coins" as gelt in a dreidl game that is played. They also have special foods for the occasion, particularly *latkes*, which are potato pancakes served with sour cream or apple sauce, as well as jelly donuts which are fried in oil, drawing their attention to the oil that God miraculously supplied for eight days.

The Hebrew word - *khanak* – from which Hanukkah comes – means to narrow, to discipline, to train up, to focus in on, and often refers to things of God. Consequently, as Hanukkah means dedication, renewal, and consecration, it is a good time to renew our dedication to God. As the Festival of Lights, it reminds us that Jesus is the Light of the world (John 8:12).

OTHER SPECIAL DAYS

The 9th of Av – Tish B"Av

ALTHOUGH THIS IS NOT A FEAST, it is mentioned in the Bible, in Zechariah 8:19 where it refers to **"the fast of the fifth month."**

It is a date believers should be aware of. Av is the fifth month on God's calendar, and corresponds to our July-August. Throughout history many terrible things have happened on this date.

The **9th of Av** is not a *feast*, but rather a *fast*. Initially, it was a time of mourning over the destruction of the Temple of the Lord, Solomon's Temple, which was destroyed in 532 BC by Nebuchadnezzar, King of Babylon (2 Kings 25:9). In 70 AD – the destruction of the second Temple (the Temple of Herod) took place as Jesus had prophesied (Luke 19:43-44; 21:6).

Following is a list of events that have taken place throughout history on the ninth of Av:

1312 BC	Spies return from forty days in Israel with bad reports
421 BC	Destruction of the first Temple under Nebuchadnezzar. Approximately 1 million Jews killed during this Babylonian invasion. Remaining tribes from the southern kingdom exiled to Babylon and Persia.
70 AD	Romans destroyed the Second Temple, under Titus. Two and a half million Jews died as a result of war, famine and disease. Over one million Jews were enslaved by the Romans, some tortured and killed in gladiatorial "games" and other pagan celebrations.

132 AD	Bar Kochba claimed as the Messiah, causing a revolt, with many thousands killed.
133 AD	Romans plough Temple site, and build the pagan city of Aelia Capitolina on the site of Jerusalem.
1095 AD	The First Crusade was declared by Pope Urban the Second. 10,000 Jews were killed in the first month.
1290 AD	Jews were expelled from England, accompanied by pogroms and confiscation of property.
1492 AD	The Inquisition in Spain and Portugal. Jews expelled from the Iberian Peninsula with great loss of property. Families were separated.
1914 AD	Britain and Russia declare war on Germany, beginning First World War. As issues were unresolved, it ultimately led to World War 2 and the Holocaust.
1942 AD	Deportation of Jews from the Warsaw Ghetto to Treblinka concentration camp.
1989 AD	Iraq walked out of talks with Kuwait.
1994 AD	Deadly bombing of the Jewish Community Centre in Buenos Aires, Argentina, killing 86 and wounding 300.

However, in Zechariah 8:19 the Lord says there will come a time when the fast of the fifth month will be a time of cheerful feasts, with joy and gladness. We look forward to that day!

In a later chapter we will look at another special day called Purim, which is a time of feasting rather than fasting.

Part 4

God Establishes Relationship with Gentiles

Chapter 14
The Story Of Ruth

THERE ARE TWO WOMEN IN THE BIBLE, each of whom has an important message for the Church today. Their stories are different in circumstance, but similar in courage and steadfastness. The first is Ruth, whom we shall look at now, and the other is Esther, whom we shall study in the next chapter.

THE STORY OF RUTH

I RECALL WHEN I WAS perhaps nine or ten years old I saw a Biblical movie. Unfortunately, I don't remember the name of the movie, but I do remember one line from it which settled deeply in my heart. That line was, "Where you go I will go. Your people shall be my people, and your God shall be my God."

Many years later, when I began to read the Bible, I found those words in the Book of Ruth. It was a deja vu kind of experience, and again the words resonated deep within me.

It is the story of Naomi and Ruth. It begins when Naomi (which means "pleasantness") and her husband Elimelech (which means "my God is King") left their home town of Bethlehem ("house of bread") along with their two sons Mahlon (meaning "sick") and

Chilion (meaning "pining away") because of a great famine in the land of Israel, and went to the pagan country of Moab.

Over time, Elimelech died and the two sons married. Their wives' names were Orpah and Ruth. Mahlon and his brother Chilion also died, leaving Naomi only with her two daughters-in-law.

Naomi then heard the Lord had visited His people and there was no longer a famine in the land. So she prepared to return to Judah. She told each of her daughters-in-law to return to their mother's house, and find husbands because they were still young. Naomi explained to them that she had no more sons to become their husbands. They were all weeping, and finally Orpah kissed her mother-in-law goodbye, and returned to her people.

However, Ruth would not go back. She said to Naomi, **"Urge me not to leave you or to turn back from following you; for where you go I will go, and where you lodge I will lodge.** *Your people shall be my people* **and your God my God. Where you die, I will die; and there I will be buried. The Lord do so to me, and more also, if anything but death parts me from you."** (Ruth 1:16-17, Amplified Bible, emphasis mine).

Interestingly, both Orpah and Ruth lived up to the meaning of their names. Orpah means "stiffneck" or "one who turns back," and Ruth means "friend".

RUTH AND THE CHURCH

AN INTERESTING FACT is that it is traditional for the Jewish people to read the story of Ruth at the Feast of Shavuot or Pentecost. Messianic Jews understand the significance of this, for that was when the Holy Spirit was poured out and the "church" was born. Ruth is a picture of the Church. She left behind her old life and old gods in Moab, just as we leave behind our old lives and our old

The Story of Ruth

gods, or our old understanding of God. She met Boaz, through gleaning in his fields, just as Naomi planned. In the old Jewish culture, if a husband died without leaving an heir, his widow was to marry his brother, and the first child of that union would, in effect, be his brother's child.

However, Ruth's husband didn't leave a brother for Ruth to marry. In this case, the "kinsman-redeemer," as he was called, would be the next person in the family line. Naomi knew that Boaz was a relative of her dead husband Elimelech, so she made sure that Ruth would meet Boaz, through gleaning grain in his field, and find favor with him.

As it turned out, there was another relative nearer to Elimelech than Boaz, so Boaz presented him with the opportunity to do the part of the kinsman-redeemer, by buying Elimelech's field from Naomi and marrying Ruth to restore the name of the dead husband to his inheritance. However, this relative did not want to buy the field or marry a Moabitess, so he told Boaz to take his right of redemption (Ruth 4:6).

Ruth the Gentile, and Boaz the Jew, marry. This is a "wonderful picture of the type of relationship that should exist between the Gentile Church and the Messianic Jewish Community today."[1] Unfortunately, this is not what we see.

When Naomi and Ruth returned to Bethlehem, Naomi wanted to be called Mara, which means "bitterness," because of her harsh and sad life in Moab. God used Ruth, the Gentile, to restore pleasantness, happiness and redemption to Naomi. I believe in the same way, God wants to use us, the Gentile Church, to restore pleasantness, happiness and redemption to the Jewish people. Paul tells us that we are to preach the gospel "to the Jew first" (see Rom. 1:16), and we are to pray for the peace of Jerusalem (Ps. 122:6) and to be watchmen on her walls (Is. 61:6-7).

There is a great deal of symbolism in this story which we should note. Naomi, a Jewess, represents Israel. Ruth, a Gentile, represents the Church. Boaz, the kinsman-redeemer to Naomi, represents our Messiah. As we read the Book of Ruth, notice that Naomi (the Jew) didn't go directly to Boaz (the Redeemer), but rather her point of contact with him was through Ruth (the Church). Just so, the Jewish people today need us, the Church, to share with them the good news of their Redeemer and Messiah.

On a personal level, just as Ruth needed to meet Naomi's kinsman-redeemer, we also need a Redeemer, and He is Jesus Christ, our Bridegroom. Just as Ruth left her old life, we leave our old lives. What did she say to Naomi? She said, **"...your people will be my people and your God will be my God."** No one would argue with the fact the God of the Christian Church is the God of Abraham, Isaac and Jacob, and His Son Yeshua (Jesus) is our Redeemer. However, there is little or no evidence that we have also adopted Naomi's people as our people. Naomi's people were the Jewish people. Her husband was of the tribe of Judah. Her grandson, through Ruth as well as Boaz, was Obed who was the father of Jesse, the father of David, the ancestor of our Savior and Redeemer Yeshua the Messiah (Jesus Christ).

The Church does not have a Gentile Savior. We have a Jewish Savior, although through Boaz there is some Gentile blood, as Boaz' mother was Rahab, the Gentile harlot who helped the spies that Joshua sent in to spy out Jericho. We read the stories of His people throughout the Old Covenant Scriptures, and we take the lessons that we learn as our own, and that is good, for so they are.

But as Christians, do we feel any connection or responsibility towards the Jewish people today? A few do. A few **pray for the peace of Jerusalem**, which we are commanded to do in Psalm 122:6. A few take to heart God's words to Abraham in Genesis 12:3 – **"And I will bless those who bless you, and I will curse him who curses you, and in you all the families of the earth will be blessed."** If God blesses those who bless the Jewish people, and if He curses those who curse them, does He ignore those who ignore

The Story of Ruth

them? Are we missing some blessings God would like to give us, because we don't bless His people?

We are reminded almost daily in the news that Israel and the Jewish people desperately need our prayers. Do we pray for the peace of Jerusalem? Do we follow what is going on in the Middle East? Are we aware of how surrounded by enemies they are, enemies that want to annihilate them? For the most part, people around the world, even in the church, were silent during the Holocaust, and six million Jews were exterminated. Are we going to stand by and let Iran do it again? Certainly, we can't stay Ahmadinejad's hand. But our God can! Will we ask Him? Will we pray for the peace of Jerusalem and the safety of the Jewish people? If the Church doesn't pray for them, who will? Will we, like Ruth, say **"Your people shall be my people, and your God my God?"**

Isaiah 61:6-7 tells us:

> I have set watchmen on your walls, O Jerusalem;
> They shall never hold their peace day or night.
> You who make mention of the LORD, do not keep silent,
> And give Him no rest till He establishes
> And till He makes Jerusalem a praise in the earth.

Are we willing to be watchmen on the walls of God's holy city? In the next chapter we will see how Esther was not only willing to listen to her watchman relative, Mordecai, but she was willing to put her life on the line as well.

Chapter 15
The Story Of Esther

ESTHER IS A WOMAN THAT GOD USED mightily. Her story is one of intercession and the saving of the Jewish people in Persia.

The Book of Esther is the only book in the Bible that does not mention the Name of God, but His power and sovereignty are clearly evident.

To give some background, the story takes place during the fifth century BC. After the Babylonian captivity, many Jews remained in the area under Persian rule, even though they could have returned to Israel when Ezra returned to rebuild Jerusalem. Persia was ruled at that time by King Ahasuerus, who reigned from Shushan.

Esther, whose Hebrew name is Hadassah, had lost her parents when she was a child, and was brought up by her uncle Mordecai who raised her as his own. Mordecai was the leader of the Jews in the empire, so he had access to the palace and the King's gate.

The King's wife, Vashti, had disobeyed an order of the king and was consequently banished. The king put out a call to find another who would become queen, and Esther had joined other young women in this "beauty contest" at the palace to undergo a time of preparation before they would meet with the king. Mordecai had told her not to disclose that she was Jewish. At the end of this preparation time, Esther was chosen to be queen, as the king found her very pleasing.

The villain in the story is Haman, a descendant of Agag, king of the Amalekites during King Saul's reign. He hated the Jews and sought to destroy them. The king had made him his right-hand man, and therefore all the king's servants bowed and paid homage to him. Mordecai would not pay him homage, which angered Haman. Consequently he sought a way to destroy all the Jews throughout the kingdom. Lots were cast to determine the day when this should be carried out.

Haman then went to the King and said there were people in his kingdom who did not keep the laws of the king, but rather kept their own laws. He suggested that a decree be sent out that they be destroyed. The king agreed, and gave Haman the money he asked for to pay those who would carry out his plans.

When Mordecai heard about this plot he was very grieved, and put on sackcloth. Through Hathach, Esther's attendant, she learned of this plot, and what Mordecai wanted her to do. Mordecai desired Esther to go to the king and plead with him to save her people. Esther responded with a message for Mordecai that anyone who approached the king without being summoned would be put to death unless the king held out his scepter. She also included the fact the king had not summoned her for thirty days.

Upon receiving this message from Esther, Mordecai responded with another, reminding her that she too was Jewish and would not escape this death sentence. He told her that perhaps she had come to be queen "for such a time as this."

Esther responded by asking Mordecai to call on all the Jews in Shushan to fast for her for three days and nights, neither eat or drink, and that she and her maids would do likewise. Then she would go to the king, even though it was against the law, ending her message with the words, "And if I perish, I perish."

As it turned out, after the fast as Esther approached the king, he held out his scepter, and asked for her request. She invited both the king and Haman to a banquet, where again the king asked for her request. In response, she invited them both to another banquet the next day, and told the king she would make her request at that time.

Haman, overjoyed at being thus honored at these banquets, bragged to his friends and family. However, he was still galled that Mordecai would not acknowledge him, and therefore told his friends to build a gallows on which to hang Mordecai.

That night the king, being unable to sleep, asked the book of chronicles be read to him. One entry that interested him was regarding Mordecai, who had saved the king from treachery by two of his doorkeepers. When he discovered that nothing had been done to honor Mordecai for this, he wanted to do something for him. When Haman entered the court, the king asked him what should be done for a man whom the king wanted to honor. Of course, Haman thought the king was referring to himself, and told the king how this honor might be carried out. However, the king responded by telling Haman to do so for Mordecai. He carried out the king's orders, but afterwards went home angry and grieving, and told his wife and friends what he had been told to do. His wife and wise men warned him that if Mordecai is of Jewish descent he would not be able to stand against him, but would fall. At that moment the king's men came to take him to Esther's banquet.

Now Esther was ready to give the king her request. She told the king of the plot against her people to have them annihilated, and asked him to save her and her people. The king became angry and asked who planned such a thing. Esther pointed to Haman and told the king he was the man. As a result, Haman was hanged on the gallows he had built for Mordecai.

The king then honored Mordecai, giving him his signet ring, which he had retrieved from Haman. Because a decree bearing the king's seal could not simply be revoked, Esther implored the king to draw up a new decree so her people would not be annihilated. He responded by telling Esther and Mordecai to write a new decree and seal it with the signet ring he had just given to Mordecai, which bore the king's seal.

So on the twenty-third of Sivan the decree was written and sealed that all the Jews were permitted to protect their lives and belongings, taking whatever measures were necessary, even if it meant killing their adversaries. This decree was delivered to every province in the kingdom, and the Jews gathered together in the provinces on the thirteenth of Adar and killed their adversaries, but did not take any plunder. On the fourteenth of the month they rested, and made it a day of celebration with feasting and gladness. Esther also reminded the king about Haman's ten sons, and asked that they be hanged on the gallows, and the king granted her request.

In Shushan, the capitol, the Jews gathered on both the thirteenth and the fourteenth of the month, and they celebrated on the fifteenth with feasting and giving gifts to one another. Mordecai sent letters to all the Jews throughout the provinces to establish the fourteenth and fifteenth of Adar (February-March) as a time of celebration, a time that their sorrow was turned to joy, so that it should be a time of feasting and giving gifts to one another, as well as to the poor. And they called these days of celebration Purim, after the word *Pur* which means "lots," because the day chosen by Haman to destroy the Jews was determined by lots or lottery.

The Significance of this Story

WHAT DOES THIS MEAN for the Church today? This festival comes and goes each year without any attention from most Christians, who seem oblivious to it. And yet anti-Semitism is very much alive in our world today, as it was in Haman's day. The Church was, for the most part, silent during the Holocaust, and six million Jews were slaughtered. Recently, the present Pope was about to reinstate a bishop who denied the Holocaust even took place, but backed down because of the great public outcry against it. Anti-Semitism is on the rise again throughout the world, with desecrated cemeteries, anti-Jewish graffiti, attacks against synagogues, and protests in the streets of cities all over the world. In fact, according to a Reuters UK report, anti-Semitism is at its highest level since World War II.

As mentioned above, Haman was a descendant of Amalek, who warred against the Jewish people during the time of Moses. We read in Exodus 17:8-16 how Moses told Joshua to take some men and fight with Amalek, while Moses himself would stand on the top of the hill with the rod of God in his hand. As long as he held up his hand, the Israelites prevailed, but when he let down his hand, Amalek prevailed. Moses' arms became too heavy to hold up constantly, so Aaron and Hur supported him so his hands were steady, and Joshua and his army defeated Amalek. Verses 14-16 tells us:

"Then the LORD said to Moses, 'Write this for a memorial in the book and recount it in the hearing of Joshua, that I will utterly blot out the remembrance of Amalek from under heaven.'

"And Moses built an altar and called its name, The-LORD-Is-My-Banner; for he said, 'Because the LORD has sworn: the LORD will have war with Amalek from generation to generation.'"

God told King Saul in 1 Samuel 15 to totally destroy Amalek, but Saul did not do so.

"Samuel also said to Saul, The LORD sent me to anoint you king over His people, over Israel. Now therefore, heed the voice of the words of the LORD. Thus says the LORD of hosts: 'I will punish Amalek for what he did to Israel, how he ambushed him on the way when he came up from Egypt. Now go and attack Amalek, and utterly destroy all that they have, and do not spare them. But kill both man and woman, infant and nursing child, ox and sheep, camel and donkey.'" (v. 1-3)

Saul attacked the Amalekites, but did not do according to all that God told him. Verses 8 and 9 tell us, "**He also took Agag king of the Amalekites alive, and utterly destroyed all the people with the edge of the sword. But Saul and the people spared Agag and the best of the sheep, the oxen, the fatlings, the lambs, and all that was good, and were unwilling to utterly destroy them. But everything despised and worthless, that they utterly destroyed."**

Later Samuel himself killed Agag. The Bible is not clear as to how much time had passed. However, since Haman was a descendant of the Amalekites, Agag must have fathered a child before Samuel killed him.

Psalm 83 also mentions Amalek in verse 7. This psalm is a wonderful prayer for Israel's protection, and very appropriate for today, calling out to God to protect Israel from her enemies. It is interesting that in view of our story of Esther, which took place in Persia, that we seem to have come full circle. Ancient Persia is present-day Iran, and today it is the leader of that country who is bent on eradicating the Jews from the face of the earth. Just as in Haman's day, intercession for the Jewish people foiled Haman's plans, so today there is a great need for intercession to foil the plans of the Iranian leader.

THE ONGOING CONSPIRACY AGAINST ISRAEL AND THE JEWISH PEOPLE

WHY IS THERE SO MUCH HATRED toward the Jewish people? I believe there is a deeper root than what we are able to see in the natural. Ever since satan was told in the Garden of Eden that the Seed of the woman would bruise his head, he has been after God's people. He tried to stop the rise of the Jewish people in Moses' day, both when Moses was a baby and later when he returned to Egypt to save his people and bring them out from under Pharoah's control. He used

Haman against the Jewish exiles in Persia. He used King Herod to have all the baby boys killed after Jesus was born, to try to kill the Messiah. Throughout the centuries since then, satan has used people to do his dirty work. He knows his days are numbered and that he has been defeated, but he keeps on trying. He used the Romans, and he used the Church through the Middle Ages with the Crusades and the Inquisition. More recently he used Hitler to annihilate as many Jews as possible. Even the day after Israel was declared a sovereign state in 1948 she was attacked by the neighboring nations, and has been attacked many times since then. At present satan is using world media to stir up hatred for God's chosen people, and he is using Iran's Ahmadinejad, whose desire is to wipe the Jewish people off the face of the earth.

It is interesting that in view of our story of Esther, which took place in Persia, that we seem to have come full circle.

In the 10th Chapter of Daniel he tells us that he was in mourning for three full weeks (v.2). " **I ate no pleasant food, no meat or wine came into my mouth, nor did I anoint myself at all, till the whole three weeks were fulfilled**" (verse 3). This has come to be known as "The Daniel Fast".

"**Soon a 'man' (an angel) appeared to him and told him that from the first day of his fast and seeking the Lord, his plea had been heard, but that the prince of the kingdom of Persia had held him back from coming to him until Michael came to help him**" (vv. 12-13). This "prince of the kingdom of Persia" is one of the powers and principalities of the evil one which still operates today over Persia, present-day Iran, ruled by a man who wants to push the Jewish people into the sea.

Just as the Jewish people in Esther's day were called to prayer and fasting to be saved from the plans of Haman, so too in our day believers are being called by several present-day "Mordecais" to pray and fast for Israel to be saved from the plans of today's 'Haman'. Perhaps we could follow Daniel's lead for a breakthrough in the heavenly realm, and pray and fast as he did. A good time to do this specifically would be the 21 days prior to the Feast of Purim, which occurs at the end of February or early March on our calendar. However, in this day, as Israel is surrounded by enemies on all sides, prayer for Israel and her people is necessary constantly. May we, as members of the Body of Christ, follow Moses' example and hold up our hands in prayer for the safety and protection of God's chosen people and His land.

As I will show in the next chapter, anti-Semitism is far from dead. In fact, according to reports, it is again on the rise.

Chapter 16
Anti-Semitism Throughout History

HAMAN TRIED TO ELIMINATE ALL the Jews who were living in the Persian kingdom during the time that Esther was queen 2500 years ago. Since that time there have been other 'Hamans' throughout history whose desire has been to eliminate the Jewish people.

News reports today indicate that anti-Semitism is at its highest level since the second world war. With Israel's enemy Iran pursuing nuclear power and often threatening to wipe Israel off the map, we would be wise to take note of the extreme persecution throughout history towards God's chosen people, and the very real danger of today's 'Haman.'

The following shows a timeline of anti-Semitic events that have taken place historically.

ANTIQUITY

175 BC – 165 BC
The Deuterocanonical First and Second *Books of the Maccabees* record that Antiochus Epiphanes sacked Jerusalem and committed atrocities against the Jews and the Jewish religion. As we have already seen, the festival of Hanukkah commemorates the uprising of the Maccabees against his rule.

SECOND CENTURY

VARIOUS GREEK AND ROMAN writers, such as Mnaseas of Patras, Apollonius Molon, Apion and Plutarch, repeated the legend that Jews worship a golden calf, a head, etc. Josephus collected and denied the rumors. [1][2]

19 AD — Roman Emperor Tiberius expelled Jews from Rome. Expulsion is reported by the Roman historical writers Suetonius, Josephus, and Cassius Dio.

37-41 — Thousands of Jews killed by mobs in Alexandria (Egypt), as recounted by Philo of Alexandria in Flaccus.

50 — Jews ordered by Roman Emperor Claudius "not to hold meetings", in the words of Cassius Dio (Roman History, 60.6.6). Claudius later expelled Jews from Rome, according to both Suetonius ("Lives of the Twelve Caesars", Claudius, Section 25.4) and Acts 18:2.

66-73 — Great Jewish Revolt against the Romans was crushed by Vespasian and Titus. Titus refused to accept a wreath of victory, as there is "no merit in vanquishing people forsaken by their own God." (Philostratus, *Vita Apollonii*). The events of this period were recorded in detail by the Jewish-Roman historian Josephus. However, Josephus describes the Jewish revolt as being led by "tyrants," to the detriment of the city, and of Titus as having "moderation" in his escalation of the Siege of Jerusalem (70).

115-117 Thousands of Jews were killed during civil unrest in Egypt, Cyprus, and Cyrenaica, as recounted by Cassius Dio, *History of Rome* (68.31), Eusebius, *Historia Ecclesiastica* (4.2), and papyrii.

c. 119 Roman emperor Hadrian banned circumcision, making Judaism *de facto* illegal.

132-135 Crushing of the Bar Kokhba revolt. According to Cassius Dio, 580,000 Jews were killed. Hadrian ordered the expulsion of Jews from Judea, which was merged with Galilee to form the province Syria Palaestina. Although large Jewish populations remained in Samaria and Galilee, with Tiberias as the headquarters of exiled Jewish patriarchs, this was the beginning of the Jewish diaspora. Hadrian constructed a pagan temple to Jupiter at the site of the Temple in Jerusalem, and built Aelia Capitolina among ruins of Jerusalem.[4]

167 Earliest known accusation of Jewish deicide (the notion that Jews were responsible for the death of Jesus) was made in a sermon *On the Passover* attributed to Melito of Sardis. This accusation has been thought of as the cornerstone of Christian anti-Semitism.

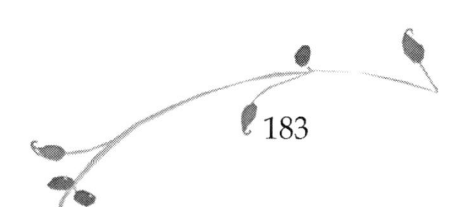

200	Roman Emperor Serverus forbade religious conversions to Judaism.

FOURTH CENTURY

306	The <u>Synod of Elvira</u> banned intermarriage between <u>Christians</u> and <u>Jews</u>. Other social occasions such as eating together were also forbidden.
<u>315</u>-<u>337</u>	Constantine enacted various laws regarding the Jews: they were not allowed to own Christian slaves or to circumcise their slaves. Conversion of Christians to Judaism was outlawed. Congregations for religious services were restricted, but Jews were also allowed to enter the restituted Jerusalem on the anniversary of the Temple's destruction.
<u>325</u>	The First Ecumenical Council of Nicea, called by the Roman Emperor Constantine. The <u>Christian Church</u> separated the calculation of the date of <u>Easter</u> from the Jewish <u>Passover</u>: It was ... *"declared improper to follow the custom of the Jews in the celebration of this holy festival, because, their hands having been stained with crime, the minds of these wretched men are necessarily blinded.... Let us, then, have nothing in common with the Jews, who are our adversaries. ... avoiding all contact with that evil way. ... who, after having compassed the death of the Lord, being out of their minds, are guided not by sound reason, but by an unrestrained passion, wherever their innate madness carries them. ... a people so utterly depraved. ... Therefore, this irregularity must be corrected, in order that we may no more have any thing in common with those parricides and the <u>murderers of our Lord</u>. ... no single point in common with the perjury of the Jews."*[5][6]

361-363	Roman Emperor Julian the Apostate allowed the Jews to return to *"holy Jerusalem which you have for many years longed to see rebuilt"* and to rebuild the Temple.
337	Christian Emperor Constantius created a law making the marriage of a Jewish man to a Christian punishable by death.[1]
343-381	The Laodician Synod approved Canon XXXVIII, *"It is not lawful [for Christians] to receive unleavened bread from the Jews, nor to be partakers of their impiety."*[2]
386	John Chrysostom of Antioch wrote eight homilies *Adversus Judaeos* (lit: Against the Judaizers).
388	A Christian mob incited by the local bishop plundered and burned down a synagogue in Callinicum. Theodosius I ordered punishment for those responsible, and the rebuilding of the synagogue at the expense of the Christians. Ambrose of Milan insisted in his letter that the whole case be dropped. He interrupted the liturgy in the emperor's presence with an ultimatum that he would not continue until the case was dropped. Theodosius complied.
399	The Western Roman Emperor Honorius called Judaism *superstitio indigna* and confiscated gold and silver collected by the synagogues for Jerusalem.

FIFTH CENTURY

415   Jews were accused of ritual murder during Purim.[7] Christians in Antioch, and Magona confiscated or burned synagogues. Bishop Cyril of Alexandria forced his way into the synagogue, expelled the Jews and gave their property to the mob. Prefect Orestes was stoned almost to death for protesting.

418   The first record of Jews being forced to convert or face expulsion. Severus, the Bishop of Minorca, claimed to have forced 540 Jews to accept Christianity upon conquering the island.

419   The monk Barsauma (subsequently the Bishop of Nisibis) gathered a group of followers and for the next three years destroyed synagogues throughout the province of Palestine.

429   The East Roman Emperor Theodosius II ordered all funds raised by Jews to support schools be turned over to his treasury.

439   The *Codex Theodosianus,* the first imperial compilation of laws. Jews were prohibited from holding important positions involving money, including judicial and executive offices. The ban against building new synagogues was reinstated. The anti-Jewish statutes applied to the Samaritans. The *Code* was also accepted by Western Roman Emperor, Valentinian III.

451	Sassanid, ruler of Yazdegerd II of Persia's decree abolished the Sabbath and ordered executions of Jewish leaders, including the Exilarch Mar Nuna.
465	Council of Vannes, Gaul prohibited the Christian clergy from participating in Jewish feasts.

SIXTH CENTURY

519	Ravenna, Italy. After the local synagogues were burned down by the local mob, the Ostrogothic king Theodoric the Great ordered the town to rebuild them at its own expense.
529-559	Byzantine Emperor Justinian the Great published *Corpus Juris Civilis*. New laws restricted citizenship to Christians. These regulations determined the status of Jews throughout the Empire for hundreds of years: Jewish civil rights restricted: "they shall enjoy no honors". The principle of *Servitus Judaeorum* (Servitude of the Jews) was established: the Jews could not testify against Christians. The emperor became an arbiter in internal Jewish matters. The use of the Hebrew language in worship was forbidden. Shema Yisrael ("Hear, O Israel, the Lord is one"), sometimes considered the most important prayer in Judaism, was banned as a denial of the Trinity. Some Jewish communities were converted by force, their synagogues turned into churches.
535	The First Council of Clermont; Gaul prohibited Jews from holding public office.

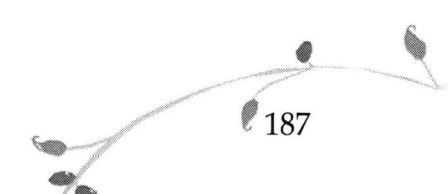

GRAFTED IN THE JEWISH OLIVE TREE

538 The Third Council of Orléans, Gaul forbade Jews to employ Christian servants or possess Christian slaves. Jews were prohibited from appearing in the streets during Easter: "their appearance is an insult to Christianity". A Merovingian king Childebert approved the measure.

576 Clermont, Gaul. Bishop Avitus offered Jews a choice: accept Christianity or leave Clermont. Most emigrated to Marseille.

589 The Council of Narbonne, Septimania, forbade Jews from chanting psalms while burying their dead. Anyone violating this law was fined 6 ounces of gold. The third Council of Toledo, held under Visigothic King Reccared, banned Jews from slave ownership and holding positions of authority, and reiterated the mutual ban on intermarriage.[8] Reccared also ruled children out of such marriages were to be raised as Christians.

590 Pope Gregory I defended the Jews against forced conversion.

SEVENTH CENTURY

610-620 Visigothic Hispania After many of his anti-Jewish edicts were ignored, king Sisebur prohibited Judaism. Those not baptized fled. This was the first incidence where a prohibition of Judaism affected an entire country.

188

614	Fifth Council of Paris decreed that all Jews holding military or civil positions must accept baptism, together with their families.
615	Italy. The earliest referral to the *Juramentum Judaeorum* (the Jewish Oath): the concept that no heretic could be believed in court against a Christian. The oath became standardized throughout Europe in 1555.
629	Mar. 21 - Byzantine Emperor Heraclius with his army marched into Jerusalem. Jewish inhabitants supported him after his promise of amnesty. Upon his entry into Jerusalem the local priests convinced him that killing Jews is a good deed. Hundreds of Jews were massacred, thousands fled to Egypt. Frankish King Dagobert I, encouraged by Byzantine Emperor Heraclius, expelled all Jews from the kingdom.
632	The first case of officially sanctioned forced baptism. Emperor Heraclius violated the *Codex Theodosianus*, which protected them from forced conversions.
681	The Twelfth Council of Toledo, Spain ordered the burning of the Talmud and other "heretic" books.
682	Visigothic king Erwig began his reign by enacting 28 anti-Jewish laws. He pressed for the "utter extirpation of the pest of the Jews" and decreed that all converts must be registered by a parish priest, who must issue travel permits. All holidays, Christian and Jewish, must be spent in the presence of a priest to ensure piety and to prevent the *backsliding*.

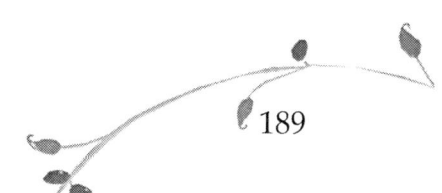

692	Quinisext Council in Constantinople forbade Christians on pain of excommunication to bathe in public baths with Jews, employ a Jewish doctor or socialize with Jews.
694	17th Council of Toledo. King Ergica believed rumors that the Jews had conspired to ally themselves with the Muslim invaders and forced Jews to give all land, slaves and buildings bought from Christians, to his treasury. He declared that all Jewish children over the age of seven should be taken from their homes and raised as Christians.

EIGHTH CENTURY

722	Byzantine emperor Leo III forcibly converted all Jews and Montanists in the empire into mainstream Byzantine Christianity.

NINTH CENTURY

807	Abbassid Caliph Harun al-Rashid ordered all Jews in the Caliphate to wear a yellow belt, with Christians to wear a blue one.
820	Agobard, Archbishop of Lyon, declared in his essays that Jews are accursed and demanded a complete segregation of Christians and Jews. In 826 he issued a series of pamphlets to convince Emperor Louis the Pious to attack "Jewish insolence", but failed to convince the Emperor.

Anti-Semitism Throughout History

898-929   French king Charles the Simple confiscated Jewish-owned property in Narbonne and donated it to the Church.

ELEVENTH CENTURY

1008-1013   Caliph Al-Hakim bi-Amr Allah ("the Mad") issued severe restrictions against Jews in the Fatimid Empire. All Jews were forced to wear a heavy wooden "golden calf" around their necks. Christians had to wear a large wooden cross and members of both groups had to wear black hats.

1012   One of the first known persecutions of Jews in Germany: Henry II, Holy Roman Emperor expelled Jews from Mainz.

1016   The Jewish community of Kairouan, Tunisia was forced to chose between conversion and expulsion.

1026   Probable date of the chronicle of Raoul Glaber. The French chronicler blamed the Jews for the destruction of the Church of the Holy Sepulchre, which was destroyed in 1009 by (Muslim) Caliph Al-Hakim. As a result, Jews were expelled from Limoges and other French towns.

1032   Abul Kamal Tumin conquered Fez, Morocco and decimated the Jewish community, killing 6,000 Jews.

1050   Council of Narbonne, France forbade Christians to live in Jewish homes.

1066	Granada Massacre: Muslim mob stormed the royal palace in Granada, crucified Jewish vizier Joseph ibn Naghrela and massacred most of the Jewish population of the city. "More than 1,500 Jewish families, numbering 4,000 persons, fell in one day."[9]
1078	Council of Gerona decreed that Jews were to pay taxes for support of the Catholic Church to the same extent as Christians.
1090	The Jewish community of Granada, which had recovered after the attacks of 1066, was attacked again at the hands of the Almoravides led by Ibn Iashufin, bringing the golden age of Jewish culture in Spain to end.
1096	The First Crusade. Three hosts of crusaders passed through several Central European cities. The third, unofficial host, led by Count Emicho, decided to attack the Jewish communities, most notably in the Rhineland, under the slogan: "Why fight Christ's enemies abroad when they are living among us?" Eimicho's host attacked the synagogue at Speyer and killed all the defenders. Another 1,200 Jews committed suicide in Mainz to escape his attempt to forcibly convert them. Attempts by the local bishops remained fruitless. All in all, 5,000 Jews were murdered. St. Bernard intervened to minimize the worst of the persecution, preaching vigorously against the killing.[10]

TWELFTH CENTURY

1107	Moroccan Almoravid ruler Yusuf ibn Tashfin ordered all Moroccan Jews to convert or leave.

1143	150 Jews were killed in Ham, France.
1144	March 20 (Passover) The case of William of Norwich, a contrived accusation of murder by Jews in Norwich, England.
1148-1212	The rule of the Almohads in al-Andalus. Only Jews who had converted to Christianity or Islam were allowed to live in Granada. One of the refugees was Maimonides who settled in Fez and later in Fustat near Cairo.
1165	Forced mass conversions in Yemen.
1171	In Blois, France 31 Jews were burned at the stake for blood libel.
1179	The Third Lateran Council, Canon 26: Jews were forbidden to be plaintiffs or witnesses against Christians in the Courts. Jews were forbidden to withhold inheritance from descendants who had accepted Christianity.
1180	Philip Augustus of France after four months in power, imprisoned all the Jews in his lands and demanded a ransom for their release.
1181	Philip Augustus annulled all loans made by Jews to Christians and took a percentage for himself. A year later, he confiscated all Jewish property and expelled the Jews from Paris.

1189	Holy Roman Emperor Frederick I Barbarossa ordered priests not to preach against Jews.
1189	A Jewish deputation attending coronation of Richard the Lionheart was attacked by the crowd. Pogroms in London followed and spread around England.
1190	All the Jews of Norwich, England found in their houses were slaughtered, except a few who found refuge in the castle.
1190	500 Jews of York were massacred after a six day siege by departing Crusaders, backed by a number of people indebted to Jewish money-lenders.[11]
1190	Saladdin took over Jerusalem from Crusaders and lifted the ban for Jews to live there.
1198	Philip Augustus readmitted Jews to Paris, but only after another ransom was paid and a taxation scheme was set up to procure funds for himself. August: Saladdin's nephew al-Malik, caliph of Yemen, summoned all the Jews and forcibly converted them.

THIRTEENTH CENTURY

13th century — Germany. Appearance of *Judensau*: obscene and dehumanizing imagery of Jews, ranging from etchings to Cathedral ceilings. Its popularity lasted for over 600 years.

1205 — Pope Innocent III wrote to the archbishops of Sens and Paris that *"the Jews, by their own guilt, are consigned to perpetual servitude because they crucified the Lord ... As slaves rejected by God, in whose death they wickedly conspire, they shall by the effect of this very action, recognize themselves as the slaves of those whom Christ's death set free ..."*[3]

1209 — Raymond VI, Count of Toulouse, humiliated and forced to swear that he would implement social restrictions against Jews.

1215 — The Fourth Lateran Council headed by Pope Innocent III declared: "Jews and Saracens of both sexes in every Christian province and at all times shall be marked off in the eyes of the public from other peoples through the character of their dress." (Canon 68). The Fourth Lateran Council also noted that the Jews' own law required the wearing of identifying symbols. Pope Innocent III also reiterated papal injunctions against forcible conversions, and added: "No Christian shall do the Jews any personal injury...or deprive them of their possessions...or disturb them during the celebration of their festivals...or extort money from them by threatening to exhume their dead."[12]

1222	Council of <u>Oxford</u>: <u>Archbishop of Canterbury</u> <u>Stephen Langton</u> forbade Jews from building new synagogues, owning slaves or mixing with Christians.
1223	Louis VII of France prohibited his officials from recording debts owed to Jews, reversing his father's policy of seeking such debts.
1229	<u>Raymond VII</u>, <u>Count of Toulouse</u>, heir of Raymond VI, forced to swear that he would implement social restrictions against Jews.
1232	Forced mass conversions in <u>Marrakesh</u>.
1235	The Jews of Fulda, Germany were accused of <u>ritual murder</u>. To investigate the <u>blood libel</u>, Emperor Frederick II held a special conference of Jewish converts to Christianity at which the converts were questioned about Jewish ritual practice. Letters inviting prominent individuals to the conference still survive. At the conference, the converts stated unequivocally that Jews do not harm Christian children or require blood for any rituals. In 1236 the Emperor published these findings and in 1247 <u>Pope Innocent IV</u>, the Emperor's enemy, also denounced accusations of the <u>ritual murder</u> of Christian children by Jews. In 1272, the papal repudiation of the <u>blood libel</u> was repeated by <u>Pope Gregory X</u>, who also ruled that thereafter any such testimony of a Christian against a Jew could not be accepted unless it is confirmed by another Jew. Unfortunately, these proclamations from the highest sources were not effective in altering the beliefs of the Christian majority and the libels continued.[13]

1236	Crusaders attacked Jewish communities of Anjou and Poitou and attempted to baptize all the Jews. Those who resisted (est. 3,000) were slaughtered.
1240	Duke Jean le Roux expelled Jews from Brittany.
1240	Disputation of Paris. Pope Gregory IX put Talmud on trial on the charges that it contained blasphemy against Jesus and Mary as well as attacks on the Church.
1241	In England, first of a series of royal levies against Jewish finances, which forced the Jews to sell their debts to non-Jews at cut prices.[14]
1242	24 cart-loads of hand-written Talmudic manuscripts burned in the streets of Paris.
1242	James I of Aragon ordered Jews to listen to conversion sermons and to attend churches. Friars were given power to enter synagogues uninvited.
1244	Pope Innocent IV ordered Louis IX of France to burn all Talmud copies.
1250	Zaragoza: death of choirboy Saint Dominguito del Val prompted ritual murder accusation. His sainthood was revoked in the 20th century but reportedly a chapel dedicated to him still exists in the Cathedral of Zaragoza.
1253	Henry III of England introduced harsh anti-Jewish laws.[15]

GRAFTED *In* THE JEWISH OLIVE TREE

1254   Louis IX expelled the Jews from France, and their property and synagogues were confiscated. Most move to Germany and further east; however, after a couple of years, some were readmitted back.

1255   Henry III of England sold his rights to the Jews' properties (regarded as royal "chattels") to his brother Richard for 5,000 marks.

c 1260   Thomas Aquinas published *Summa Contra Gentiles*, a summary of Christian faith to be presented to those who reject it. The Jews who refused to convert were regarded as "deliberately defiant" rather than "invincibly ignorant".

1263   Disputation of Barcelona.

1264   Pope Clement IV assigned a Talmud censorship committee.

1264   Simon de Montfort inspired the massacre of Jews in London.[16]

1267   In a special session, the Vienna city council forced Jews to wear *Pileum cornutum* (a cone-shaped headdress, prevalent in many medieval illustrations of Jews). This distinctive dress was an addition to the Yellow badge Jews were already forced to wear. Christians were not permitted to attend Jewish ceremonies.

1267   Synod of Breslau ordered Jews to live in a segregated quarter.

Anti-Semitism Throughout History

1275	King Edward I of England passed the Statute of the Jewry forcing Jews over the age of seven to wear an identifying yellow badge, and making usury illegal, in order to seize their assets. Scores of English Jews were arrested, 300 hanged and their property went to the Crown. In 1280 he ordered Jews to be present as Dominicans preached conversion. In 1287 he arrested heads of Jewish families and demanded their communities pay a ransom of 12,000 pounds.
1278	The Edict of Pope Nicholas III required compulsory attendance of Jews at conversion sermons.
1279	Synod of Ofen: Christians were forbidden to sell or rent real estate to or from Jews.
1282	John Pectin, Archbishop of Canterbury, ordered all London synagogues to close and prohibited Jewish physicians from practicing on Christians.
1283	Philip III of France caused mass migration of Jews by forbidding them to live in the small rural localities.
1285	Blood libel in Munich, Germany resulted in the death of 68 Jews. 180 more Jews were burned alive at the synagogue.
1287	A mob in Oberwesel, Germany killed 40 Jewish men, women and children after a ritual murder accusation.
1289	Jews were expelled from Gascony and Anjou.
1290	July 18 - Edict of Expulsion: Edward I expelled all Jews from England, allowing them to take only what they

could carry; all the other property became the Crown's. Official reason: continued practice of usury.

1291   Philip the Fair published an ordinance prohibiting the Jews to settle in France.

1298   During the civil war between Adolph of Nassau and Albrecht of Austria, German knight Rindfleisch claimed to have received a mission from heaven to exterminate "the accursed race of the Jews". Under his leadership, the mob went from town to town destroying Jewish communities and massacring about 100,000 Jews, often by mass burning at the stake. Among 146 localities in Franconia, Bavaria and Austria are Röttingen (April 20), Würzburg (July 24), Nuremberg (August 1). [17]

FOURTEENTH CENTURY

1305   Philip IV of France seized all Jewish property (except the clothes they wear) and expelled them from France (approx. 100,000). His successor Louis X of France allowed French Jews to return in 1315.

1320   Shepherds' Crusade attacked the Jews of 120 localities in southwest France.

1321   King Henry II of Castile forced Jews to wear the Yellow badge.

1321   Jews in central France were falsely charged of their supposed collusion with lepers to poison wells. After a massacre of an estimated 5,000 Jews, king Philip V of France admitted they were innocent.

1322	King Charles IV expelled Jews from France.
1333	Forced mass conversions in Baghdad
1336	Persecutions against Jews in Franconia and Alsace led by lawless German bands, the Armleder.
1348	European Jews were blamed for the Black Death. The charge laid to the Jews was that they poisoned the wells. Massacres spread throughout Spain, France, Germany and Austria. More than 200 Jewish communities were destroyed by violence. Many communities were expelled and the Jews settled in Poland.
1348	Basel: 600 Jews burned at the stake, 140 children forcibly baptized, and the remaining city's Jews were expelled. The city synagogue was turned into a church and the Jewish cemetery was destroyed.
1359	Charles V of France allowed Jews to return for a period of 20 years in order to pay ransom for his father John II of France, who was imprisoned in England. The period was later extended beyond the 20 years.
1386	Wenceslaus, Holy Roman Emperor, expelled the Jews from the Swabian League and Strasbourg and confiscated their property.
1389	March 18, a Jewish boy was accused of plotting against a priest. The mob slaughtered approx. 3,000 of Prague's Jews, destroyed the city's synagogue and Jewish

	cemetery. Wenceslaus insisted that the responsibility lay with the Jews for going outside during Holy Week.
1391	Violence incited by the Archdeacon of Ecija, Ferrand Martinez, resulted in over 10,000 murdered Jews. The Jewish quarter in Barcelona was destroyed. The campaign quickly spread throughout Spain (except for Granada) and destroyed Jewish communities in Valencia and Palma De Majorca.
1394	November 3, Charles VI of France expelled all Jews from France.
1399	Blood libel in Posen.

FIFTEENTH CENTURY

1411	Oppressive legislation against Jews in Spain as an outcome of the preaching of the Dominican friar Vicente Ferrer.
1413	Disputation of Tortosa, Spain, staged by the Avignon Pope Benedict XIII, was followed by forced mass conversions.
1420	All Jews were expelled from Lyon.
1421	Persecutions of Jews in Vienna, known as *Wiener Gesera* (Vienna Edict), confiscation of their possessions, and forced conversion of Jewish children. 270 Jews burned at the stake. Expulsion of Jews from Austria.
1422	Pope Martin V issued a Bull reminding Christians that Christianity was derived from Judaism and warned the friars not to incite against the Jews. The Bull was

withdrawn the following year on allegations that the Jews of Rome attained it by fraud.

1434 Council of Basel, Sessio XIX: Jews were forbidden to obtain academic degrees and to act as agents in the conclusion of contracts between Christians.

1435 Massacre and forced conversion of Majorcan Jews.

1438 Establishment of *mellahs* (ghettos) in Morocco.

1447 Casimir IV renewed all the rights of Jews of Poland and made his charter one of the most liberal in Europe. He revoked it in 1454 at the insistence of Bishop Zbigniew.

1449 The Statute of Toledo introduced the rule of purity of blood discriminating Conversos (Jews and Muslims who had converted to Christianity, usually by being forced to). Pope Nicholas V condemned it.

1463 Pope Nicholas V authorized the establishment of the Inquisition to investigate heresy among the Marranos.

1473-1474 Spain. Massacres of Marranos of Valladolid, Cordoba, Segovia, Ciudad Real.

1475 A student of the preacher Giovanni da Capistrano, Franciscan Bernardino de Fletre, accused the Jews of murdering an infant, Simon. The entire community was arrested, 15 leaders were burned at the stake, and the rest were expelled. In 1588, Pope Sixtus V confirmed Simon's cultus. Saint Simon was considered a martyr and patron of kidnap and torture victims for almost 500 years. In 1965, Pope Paul VI declared the episode a fraud, and decanonized Simon's sainthood.

1481   The Spanish Inquisition was instituted.

1487-1504   Bishop Gennady exposed the heresy of *Zhidovstvuyushchiye* (Judaizers) in Eastern Orthodoxy of Muscovy.

1490   Tomás de Torquemada burned 6,000 volumes of Jewish mansucripts in Salamanca.

1491   The blood libel in La Guardia, Spain, where the alleged victim Holy Child of La Guardia became revered as a saint.

1492   Mar. 31 - Ferdinand II and Isabella issued *General Edict on the Expulsion of the Jews* from Spain: approx. 200,000. Some returned to the Land of Israel. As many localities and entire countries expelled their Jewish citizens (after robbing them), and others deny them entrance, the legend of the *Wandering Jew*, a condemned harbinger of calamity, gained popularity.

1492   Oct. 24 - Jews of Mecklenburg, Germany were accused of stabbing a consecrated wafer. 27 Jews were burned, including two women. The spot is still called the *Judenberg*. All the Jews were expelled from the Duchy.

1493   Jan. 12 - Expulsion from Sicily: approx. 37,000.

1496	Forced conversion and expulsion of Jews from Portugal. This included many who fled Spain four years earlier.
1498	Prince Alexander of Lithuania forced most of the Jews to forfeit their property or convert. The main motivation was to cancel the debts the nobles owed to the Jews. Within a short time the trade ground to a halt and the Prince invited the Jews back into the country.

SIXTEENTH CENTURY

1505	Ten Ceské Budejovice Jews were tortured and executed after being accused of killing a Christian girl; later, on his deathbed, a shepherd confesses to fabricating the accusation.
1506	April 19 - A marrano expressed his doubts about miracle visions at St. Dominics Church in Lisbon, Portugal. The crowd, led by Dominican monks, killed him, then ransacked Jewish houses and slaughtered any Jew they could find. The countrymen heard about the massacre and joined in. Over 2,000 marranos killed in three days.
1509	August 19 - A converted Jew Johannes Pfefferkorn received authority from Maximilian I, Holy Roman Emperor, to destroy the Talmud and other Jewish religious books, except the Hebrew Bible, in Frankfurt.
1510	July 19 - Forty Jews were executed in Brandenburg, Germany for allegedly desecrating the host; the remainder expelled; November 23 - Less-wealthy Jews

	expelled from Naples; remainder heavily taxed. 38 Jews burned at the stake in Berlin.
1511	June 6 - Eight Roman Catholic converts from Judaism burned at the stake for allegedly reverting to Judaism.
1516	The first ghetto was established, on one of the islands in Venice.
1519	Martin Luther lead the Protestant Reformation and challenged the doctrine of *Servitus Judaeorum* "... to deal kindly with the Jews and to instruct them to come over to us". February 21 - All Jews were expelled from Ratisbon/Regensburg.
1520	Pope Leo X allowed the Jews to print the Talmud in Venice
1527	June 16 - Jews were ordered to leave Florence, but the edict is soon rescinded.
1528	Three *judaizers* were burned at the stake in Mexico City's first auto da fe.
1535	After Spanish troops captured Tunis all the local Jews were sold into slavery.
1543	In his pamphlet *On the Jews and Their Lies* Martin Luther advocated an eight-point plan to get rid of the Jews as a distinct group either by religious conversion or by expulsion:

"...set fire to their synagogues or schools..."

"...their houses also be razed and destroyed..."

"...their prayer books and Talmudic writings... be taken from them..."

"...their rabbis be forbidden to teach henceforth on pain of loss of life and limb..."

"...safe-conduct on the highways be abolished completely for the Jews..."

"...usury be prohibited to them, and that all cash and treasure of silver and gold be taken from them..." and "Such money should now be used in ... the following [way]... Whenever a Jew is sincerely converted, he should be handed [certain amount]..."

"...young, strong Jews and Jewesses [should]... earn their bread in the sweat of their brow..."

"If we wish to wash our hands of the Jews' blasphemy and not share in their guilt, we have to part company with them. They must be driven from our country" and "we must drive them out like mad dogs."

Luther "got the Jews expelled from Saxony in 1537 , and in the 1540s he drove them from many German towns; he tried unsuccessfully to get the elector to expel them from Brandenburg in 1543 . His followers continued to agitate against the Jews there: they sacked the Berlin synagogue in 1572 and the following year finally got their way, the Jews being banned from the entire country."[18]

1540   All Jews were banished from Prague.

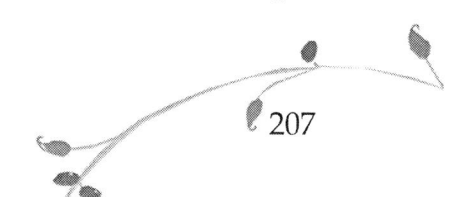

1546   Martin Luther's sermon *Admonition against the Jews* contained accusations of ritual murder, black magic, and poisoning of wells. Luther recognized no obligation to protect the Jews.

1547   Ivan the Terrible became ruler of Russia and refused to allow Jews to live in or even enter his kingdom because they "bring about great evil" (quoting his response to request by Polish king Sigismund II).

1550   Dr. Joseph Hacohen was chased out of Genoa for practicing medicine; soon all Jews were expelled.

1553   Pope Julius III forbade Talmud printing and ordered burning of any copy found. Rome's Inquisitor-General, Cardinal Carafa (later Pope Paul IV) had the Talmud publicly burnt in Rome on Rosh Hashanah, starting a wave of Talmud burning throughout Italy. About 12,000 copies were destroyed.

1554   Cornelio da Montalcino, a Franciscan Friar who converted to Judaism, was burned alive in Rome.

1555   In Papal Bull *Cum nimis absurdum*, Pope Paul IV writes: "It appears utterly absurd and impermissible that the Jews, whom God has condemned to eternal slavery for their guilt, should enjoy our Christian love." He renews anti-Jewish legislation and installs a locked nightly ghetto in Rome. The Bull also forces Jewish males to wear a yellow hat, females - yellow kerchief. Owning real estate or practicing medicine on Christians is forbidden. It also limits Jewish communities to only one synagogue.

1557   Jews were temporarily banished from Prague.

1558	Recanati, Italy: a baptized Jew, Joseph Paul More, entered a synagogue on Yom Kippur under the protection of Pope Paul IV and tried to preach a conversion sermon. The congregation evicted him. Soon after, the Jews were expelled from Recanati.
1559	Pope Pius IV allowed the Talmud on condition that it is printed by a Christian and the text is censored.
1563	February - Russian troops took Polotsk from Lithuania, Jews were given an ultimatum: embrace Russian Orthodox Church or die. Around 300 Jewish men, women and children were thrown into ice holes of Dvina river.
1564	Brest-Litovsk: the son of a wealthy Jewish tax collector was accused of killing the family's Christian servant for ritual purposes. He was tortured and executed in line with the law. King Sigismund II of Poland forbade future charges of ritual murder, calling them groundless.
1565	Jews were temporarily banished from Prague.
1566	Antonio Ghislieri elected and, as Pope Pius V, reinstated the harsh anti-Jewish laws of Pope Paul IV. In 1569 he expelled Jews dwelling outside of the ghettos of Rome, Ancona, and Avignon from the Papal States, thus ensuring that they remain city-dwellers.
1567	Jews were reauthorised to live in France

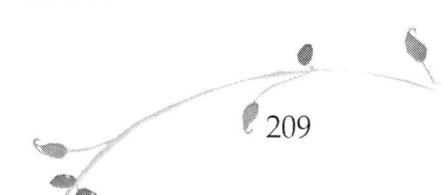

1586   Pope Sixtus V forbade printing of the Talmud.

1590   Jewish quarter of Mikulov (Nikolsburg) burned to the ground and 15 people died while Christians watched or pillaged. King Philip II of Spain ordered expulsion of Jews from Lombardy. His order was ignored by local authorities until 1597 , when 72 Jewish families were forced into exile.

1593   Feb. 25 - Pope Clement VIII confirmed the Papal bull of Paul III that expels Jews from Papal states except ghettos in Rome and Ancona and issues *Caeca et obdurata* ("Blind Obstinacy"): "All the world suffers from the usury of the Jews, their monopolies and deceit. ... Then as now Jews have to be reminded intermittently anew that they were enjoying rights in any country since they left Palestine and the Arabian desert, and subsequently their ethical and moral doctrines as well as their deeds rightly deserve to be exposed to criticism in whatever country they happen to live."

SEVENTEENTH CENTURY

1603   Frei Diogo da Assumpcão, a partly Jewish friar who embraced Judaism, burned alive in Lisbon.

1608   The Jesuit order forbade admission to anyone descended from Jews to the fifth generation, a restriction lifted in the 20th century. Three years later Pope Paul V applied the rule throughout the Church, but his successor revoked it.

Anti-Semitism Throughout History

1612	The Hamburg Senate decided to officially allow Jews to live in the city on the condition there is no public worship.
1614	Vincent Fettmilch, who called himself the "new Haman of the Jews", led a raid on Frankfurt synagogue that turned into an attack which destroyed the whole community.
1615	King Louis XIII of France decreed that all Jews must leave the country within one month on pain of death.
1615	The Guild led by Dr. Chemnitz, "non-violently" forced the Jews from Worms.
1619	Shah Abbasi of the Persian Sufi Dynasty increased persecution against the Jews, forcing many to outwardly practice Islam. Many kept practicing Judaism in secret.
1624	Ghetto established in Ferrara, Italy.
1632	King Ladislaus IV of Poland forbade antisemitic print-outs.
1648-1655	The Ukrainian Cossacks lead by Bohdan Chmielnicki massacred about 100,000 Jews and similar number of Polish nobles, 300 Jewish communities destroyed.
1655	Oliver Cromwell readmitted Jews to England.
1664	Jews of Lvov ghetto organized self-defense against impending assault by students of Jesuit seminary and

Cathedral school. The militia sent by the officials to restore order, instead joined the attackers. About 100 Jews killed.

1670   Jews expelled from Vienna.

1678   Forced mass conversions in Yemen.

EIGHTEENTH CENTURY

1711   Johann Andreas Eisenmenger wrote his *Entdecktes Judenthum* ("Judaism Unmasked"), a work denouncing Judaism and which had a formative influence on modern anti-Semitic polemics.

1712   Blood libel in Sandomierz and expulsion of the town's Jews.

1727   Edict of Catherine I of Russia: "The Jews... who are found in Ukraine and in other Russian provinces are to be expelled at once beyond the frontiers of Russia."

1736   The Haidamaks, paramilitary bands in Polish Ukraine, attacked Jews.

1742   Dec - Elizabeth of Russia issued a decree of expulsion of all the Jews out of Russian Empire. Her resolution to the Senate's appeal regarding harm to the trade: "I don't desire any profits from the enemies of Christ". One of the deportees was Antonio Ribera Sanchez, her own personal physician and the head of army's medical dept.

1744	Frederick II The Great (a "heroic genius", according to Hitler) limited Breslau to ten "protected" Jewish families, on the grounds that otherwise they will "transform it into complete Jerusalem". He encouraged this practice in other Prussian cities. In 1750 he issued *Revidiertes General Privilegium und Reglement vor die Judenschaft*: "protected" Jews had an alternative to "either abstain from marriage or leave Berlin" (Simon Dubnow).
1744	Dec - Archduchess of Austria Maria Theresa ordered: "... no Jew is to be tolerated in our inherited duchy of Bohemia" by the end of Feb. 1745. In Dec. 1748 she reversed her position, on condition that Jews pay for readmission every ten years. This extortion was known as *malke-geld* (queen's money). In 1752 she introduced the law limiting each Jewish family to one son.
1762	Rhode Island refused to grant Jews Aaron Lopez and Isaac Eliezer citizenship stating "no person who is not of the Christian religion can be admitted free to this colony."
1768	Haidamaks massacred the Jews of Uman, Poland.
1771	Voltaire called Jews "deadly to the human race", promoted racial antisemitism.
1775	Pope Pius VI issued a severe *Editto sopra gli ebrei* (Edict concerning the Jews). Previously lifted restrictions were reimposed, Judaism was suppressed.

1782	Holy Roman Emperor Joseph II abolished most persecution practices in *Toleranzpatent* on condition that Yiddish and Hebrew be eliminated from public records and judicial autonomy was annulled. Judaism was branded "quintessence of foolishness and nonsense". Moses Mendelssohn wrote: "Such a tolerance... is even more dangerous play in tolerance than open persecution".
1790	May 20 - Eleazer Solomon was quartered for the alleged murder of a Christian girl in Grodno.
1790	"To Bigotry No Sanction, to Persecution No Assistance" (George Washington's Letter to the Jews of Newport, Rhode Island)
1790-1792	Destruction of most of the Jewish communities of Morocco.
1791	Catherine II of Russia confined Jews to the Pale of Settlement and imposed them with double taxes. Pale of Settlement

NINETEENTH CENTURY

1805	Massacre of Jews in Algeria.
1815	Pope Pius VII reestablished the ghetto in Rome after the defeat of Napoleon.
1819	A series of anti-Jewish riots in Germany that spread to several neighboring countries: Denmark, Poland, Latvia

Anti-Semitism Throughout History

and Bohemia, known as *Hep-Hep riots*, from the derogatory rallying cry against the Jews in Germany.

1827   August 26 - Compulsory military service for the Jews of Russia: Jewish boys under 18 years of age, known as the *Cantonists*, were placed in preparatory military training establishments for 25 years. Cantonists were encouraged and sometimes forced to be baptized.

1835   Oppressive constitution for the Jews issued by Czar Nicholas I of Russia.

1840   The Damascus affair: false accusations caused arrests and atrocities, culminating in the seizure of sixty-three Jewish children and attacks on Jewish communities throughout the Middle East.

1844   Karl Marx praised Bruno Bauer's essays containing demands that the Jews abandon Judaism, and published his work *On the Jewish Question*: "What is the worldly cult of the Jew? What is his worldly god? Money... Money is the jealous God of Israel, besides which no other god may exist... The god of the Jews has been secularized and has become the god of this world". "In the final analysis, the emancipation of the Jews is the emancipation of mankind from Judaism." This probably led to the anti-Semitic feeling within communism.

1853   Blood libels in Saratov and throughout Russia.

1858   Edgardo Mortara, a six-year-old Jewish boy whom a maid had baptised during an illness, was taken from his parents in Bologna, an episode which aroused universal indignation in liberal circles.

1862   During the American Civil War General Grant issued General Order No. 11 (1862), ordering all Jews out of his military district, suspecting them of pro-Confederate sympathy. President Lincoln directed him to rescind the order. Polish Jews were given equal rights. Old privileges forbidding Jews to settle in some Polish cities were abolished.

1871   Speech of Pope Pius IX in regard to Jews: "of these dogs, there are too many of them at present in Rome, and we hear them howling in the streets, and they are disturbing us in all places."

1878   Adolf Stoecker, German anti-Semitic preacher and politician, founded the *Social Workers' Party*, which marks the beginning of the political anti-Semitic movement in Germany.

1879   Heinrich von Treitschke, German historian and politician, justified the anti-Semitic campaigns in Germany, bringing anti-Semitism into learned circles.

1879   Wilhelm Marr coined the term *antisemitism* to distinguish himself from religious Anti-Judaism.

1881-1884   Pogroms swept southern Russia, propelling mass Jewish emigration from the Pale of Settlement: about 2 million Russian Jews emigrated in the period 1880-1924, many of them to the United States (until the National Origins Quota of 1924 and the Immigration Act of 1924 largely halted immigration to the U.S. from Eastern Europe and Russia). The Russian word "pogrom" became international.

1882 The Tiszaeszlár blood libel in Hungary aroused public opinion throughout Europe.

1882 First International Anti-Jewish Congress convened at Dresden, Germany.

1882 May - A series of "temporary laws" by Tsar Alexander III of Russia (the May Laws), which adopted a systematic policy of discrimination, with the object of removing the Jews from their economic and public positions, in order to "cause one-third of the Jews to emigrate, one-third to accept baptism and one-third to starve" (according to a remark attributed to Konstantin Pobedonostsev)

1887 Russia introduced measures to limit Jews access to education, known as the *quota*.

1891 Blood libel in Xanten, Germany.

1891 Expulsion of 20,000 Jews from Moscow, Russia. The Congress of the United States eased immigration restrictions for Jews from the Russian Empire. (Webster-Campster report)

1893 Karl Lueger established anti-Semitic *Christian Social Party* and became the Mayor of Vienna in 1897.

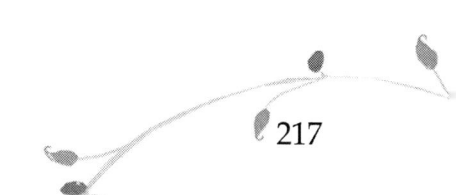

1894   The Dreyfus Affair in France. This was a political scandal which divided France from the 1890s to the early 1900s. It involved the conviction for treason in November 1894 of Captain Alfred Dreyfus, a young Alsatian artillery officer of Jewish descent. Sentenced to life imprisonment for allegedly having been a spy for the German Army, Dreyfus was sent to the penal colony at Devil's Island in French Guiana and placed in solitary confinement.

Two years later, in 1896, evidence came to light identifying a French Army major named Ferdinand Walsin Esterhazy as the real culprit. However, high-ranking military officials suppressed this new evidence, and Esterhazy was unanimously acquitted on just the second day of his trial. Instead of being exonerated, Dreyfus was further implicated in false documents designed by French counter-intelligence officers to re-confirm Dreyfus's conviction.

Word of the military court's framing of Dreyfus and the attendant cover-up began to spread in January of 1898, largely due to a vehement, public protestation by the writer Emile Zola. The case had to be re-opened, and Dreyfus was brought back from Guiana in 1899 to be tried again. The intense political and judicial scandal that ensued divided French society between those who supported Dreyfus (the Dreyfusards[11]) and those who condemned him (the anti-Dreyfusards, such as Edouard Drumont and Hubert-Joseph Henry, respectively, the director and publisher of the anti-semitic newspaper *La Libre Parole*.

Eventually, all the accusations against Alfred Dreyfus were demonstrated to be baseless. Dreyfus was exonerated and reinstated as a major in the French Army in 1906. He later served during the whole of World War I, ending his service with the rank of Lieutenant-Colonel.

1895 A. C. Cuza organized the *Alliance Anti-semitique Universelle* in Bucharest, Romania.

1899 Houston Stewart Chamberlain, racist and anti-Semitic author, published his *Die Grundlagen des 19 Jahrhunderts* which later became a basis of National-Socialist ideology.

1899 Blood libel in Bohemia (the Hilsner case).

TWENTIETH CENTURY

IN THE LATE NINETEENTH and early twentieth centuries, the Roman Catholic Church adhered to a distinction between "good antisemitism" and "bad antisemitism". The "bad" kind promoted hatred of Jews because of their descent. This was considered un-Christian because the Christian message was intended for all of humanity regardless of ethnicity; anyone could become a Christian. The "good" kind criticized alleged Jewish conspiracies to control newspapers, banks, and other institutions, to care only about accumulation of wealth, etc. Many Catholic bishops wrote articles criticizing Jews on such grounds, and, when accused of promoting hatred of Jews, would remind people that they condemned the "bad" kind of antisemitism.[19]

1903 The Kishinev pogrom: 49 Jews murdered.

1903	The first publication of *The Protocols of the Elders of Zion hoax* in St. Petersburg, Russia (by Pavel Krushevan). (Added note: this work has become popular again in resent years).
1909	Salomon Reinach and Florence Simmonds referred to "this *new anti-Semitism*, masquerading as patriotism, which was first propagated at Berlin by the court chaplain Stöcker, with the connivance of Bismarck." [20] Similarly, Peter N. Stearns' commented that "the ideology behind the new anti-Semitism [in Germany] was more racist than religious." [21]
1911	The Blood libel trial of Menahem Mendel Beilis in Kiev.
1915	World War I prompted expulsion of 250,000 Jews from Western Russia. The Leo Frank trial and lynching in Atlanta, Georgia turned the spotlight on anti-Semitism in the United States and led to the founding of the Anti-Defamation League.
1917-1921	Attacked for being revolutionaries or counter-revolutionaries, unpatriotic pacifists or warmongers, religious zealots or godless atheists, capitalist exploiters or bourgeois profiteers, masses of Jewish civilians (by various estimates 70,000 to 250,000, the number of orphans exceeded 300,000) were murdered in pogroms in the course of Russian Civil War.
1919-1922	Soviet Yevsektsiya (the Jewish section of the Communist Party) attacked Bund and Zionist parties for "Jewish cultural particularism". In April 1920, the

All-Russian Zionist Congress was broken up by Cheka led by Bolsheviks, whose leadership and ranks included many anti-Jewish Jews. Thousands were arrested and sent to Gulag for "counter-revolutionary... collusion in the interests of Anglo-French bourgeoisie... to restore the Palestine state." Hebrew language was banned, Judaism was suppressed, along with other religions.

1920   The Jerusalem pogrom of April, 1920 of old Yishuv.
The idea that the Bolshevik revolution was a Jewish conspiracy for world domination sparked worldwide interest in *The Protocols of the Elders of Zion*. In a single year, five editions were sold out in England alone. In the US Henry Ford printed 500,000 copies and began a series of anti-Semitic articles in *The Dearborn Independent* newspaper.

1921   May 1-4 Jaffa riots in Palestine.

1921-1925 Outbreak of anti-Semitism in USA, led by Ku Klux Klan.

1924   The National Origins Quota of 1924 and Immigration Act of 1924 largely halted immigration to the U.S. from Eastern Europe and Russia; many later saw these governmental policies as having anti-Semitic undertones, as a great many of these immigrants coming from Russia and Eastern Europe were Jews (the "outbreak of anti-Semitism" mentioned in the above entry may have also played a part in the passage of these acts).

1925   Adolf Hitler published *Mein Kampf*.

1929 August 23 - The ancient Jewish community of Hebron was destroyed in the Hebron massacre. [22]

1933-1941 Persecution of Jews in Germany rose until they were stripped of their rights not only as citizens, but also as human beings. During this time anti-Semitism reached its all-time high.[2]

- Law against Overcrowding of German Schools and Universities
- Law for the Reestablishment of the Professional Civil Service (ban on professions)

1934 2,000 Afghani Jews expelled from their towns and forced to live in the wilderness.

1934 The first appearance of The Franklin Prophecy on the pages of William Dudley Pelley's pro-Nazi weekly magazine *Liberation*. According to the US Congress report:

"The Franklin "Prophecy" is a classic anti-Semitic canard that falsely claims that American statesman Benjamin Franklin made anti-Jewish statements during the Constitutional Convention of 1787. It has found widening acceptance in Muslim and Arab media, where it has been used to criticize Israel and Jews..."[23]

1935 Nuremberg Laws introduced. Jewish rights rescinded. The Reich Citizenship Law stripped them of

Anti-Semitism Throughout History

citizenship. The Law for the Protection of German Blood and German Honor:

- Marriages between Jews and citizens of German or kindred blood are forbidden.
- Sexual relations outside marriage between Jews and nationals of German or kindred blood are forbidden.
- Jews will not be permitted to employ female citizens of German or kindred blood as domestic servants.
- Jews are forbidden to display the Reich and national flag or the national colors. On the other hand they are permitted to display the Jewish colors.

1938   Anschluss, pogroms in Vienna, anti-Jewish legislation, deportations to concentration camps.

- Decree authorizing local authorities to bar Jews from the streets on certain days
- Decree empowering the justice Ministry to void wills offending the "sound judgment of the people"
- Decree providing for compulsory sale of Jewish real estate
- Decree providing for liquidation of Jewish real estate agencies, brokerage agencies, and marriage agencies catering to non-Jews
- Directive providing for concentration of Jews in houses

1938   Father Charles E. Coughlin, Roman Catholic priest, started anti-Semitic weekly radio broadcasts in the United States.

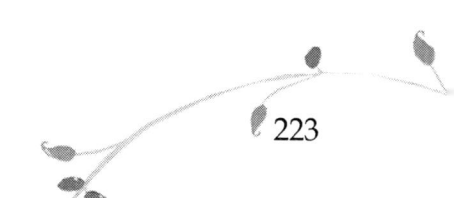

GRAFTED IN THE JEWISH OLIVE TREE

1938   July 6-15 - Evian Conference: 31 countries refused to accept Jews trying to escape Nazi Germany (with exception of Dominican Republic). Most find temporary refuge in Poland.

1938   November 9-10 - Kristallnacht (Night of The Broken Glass). In one night most German synagogues and hundreds of Jewish-owned German businesses were destroyed. Almost 100 Jews were killed, and 10,000 were sent to concentration camps.[24]

1938   November 17 - Racial legislation introduced in Italy. Anti-Jewish economic legislation in Hungary.

1939   The "Voyage of the Damned": S.S. St. Louis, carrying 907 Jewish refugees from Germany, was turned back by Cuba and the US.[25] Also turned away by Canada.

1939   February - The Congress of the United States rejected the Wagner-Rogers Bill, an effort to admit 20,000 Jewish refugee children under the age of 14 from Nazi Germany.[26]

1939-1945   **The Holocaust**. About 6 million Jews, including 1.5 million children, systematically killed by Nazi Germany.

1941   The Farhud pogrom in Baghdad resulted in 200 Jews dead, 2,000 wounded.

1946   The Kielce pogrom. 39 Jews were massacred and 80 wounded out of about 200 who returned home after

World War II. There were also killed 2 non-Jewish Poles.

1946   Nikita Khrushchev, then the first secretary of Communist party of Ukraine, closed many synagogues (the number declined from 450 to 60) and prevented Jewish refugees from returning to their homes: "It is not in our interests that the Ukrainians should associate the return of the Soviet power with the return of the Jews."[27]

1948   January 13 - Solomon Mikhoels, actor-director of the Moscow State Jewish Theater and chairman of Jewish Anti-Fascist Committee was killed in suspicious car accident. Mass arrests of prominent Jewish intellectuals and suppression of Jewish culture followed under the banners of campaign on *rootless cosmopolitanism* and *anti-Zionism*.

1948-2001   Anti-Semitism played a major role in the Jewish exodus from Arab lands. The Jewish population in the Arab Middle East and North Africa has decreased from 900,000 in 1948 to less than 8,000 today.

1948   The day after Israel declared herself an independent State, she was attacked by a coalition of her Arab neighbors, including Egypt, Jordan, Lebanon, Syria and Iraq. Although outnumbered by 20 to 1, the Israelis prevailed.[4]

During the Siege of Jerusalem of the Arab-Israeli War, Arab armies were able to conquer part of the West Bank and Jerusalem; they expelled all Jews (about 2,000) from

	the Old City (the Jewish Quarter) and destroyed the ancient synagogues that were in Old City as well.
1952	August 12-13 - The Night of the Murdered Poets. Thirteen most prominent Soviet Yiddish writers, poets, actors and other intellectuals were executed, among them Peretz Markish, Leib Kwitko, David Hofstein, Itzik Feffer, David Bergelson.[28] [29] In 1955 UN General Assembly's session a high Soviet official still denied the "rumors" about their disappearance.
1952	The Prague Trials in Czechoslovakia.
1953	The Doctors' plot - false accusation in the USSR. Scores of Soviet Jews dismissed from their jobs, arrested, some executed. The USSR was accused of pursuing a "new antisemitism." [30] Stalinist opposition to "rootless cosmopolitans" – a euphemism for Jews – was rooted in the belief, as expressed by Klement Gottwald, that "treason and espionage infiltrate the ranks of the Communist Party. This channel is Zionism." [31] This newer anti-Semitism was, in effect, a species of anti-Zionism.
1956	The Suez War broke out when Egypt closed the Suez canal to Israeli ships. Egypt, under her President Nasser, refused to follow a UN order to keep the canal open, and instead sent terrorists into Israel. Nasser's foreign minister said, "We shall not be satisfied except by the final obliteration of Israel from the map of the Middle east."⁵
1964	The Roman Catholic Church under Pope Paul VI issued the document *Nostra Aetate* as part of Vatican II,

Anti-Semitism Throughout History

repudiating the doctrine of Jewish guilt for the Crucifixion.

1967 — The Six Day War. President Nasser of Egypt announced, "The armies of Egypt, Jordan. Syria and Lebanon are poised on the borders of Israel ... while standing behind us are the armies of Iraq, Algeria, Kuwait, Sudan and the whole Arab nation. This act will astound the world. Today they will know that the Arabs are arranged for battle, the critical hour has arrived. We have reached the stage of serious action and not declarations."[6]

1960-1991 — The rise of Zionology in the Soviet Union. In 1983, the Department of Propaganda and the KGB's Anti-Zionist committee of the Soviet public orchestrated formally an "anti-Zionist" campaign.

1968 — Polish 1968 political crisis. The state-organized anti-Semitic campaign in the People's Republic of Poland under the guise of "anti-Zionism" drove out most of the remaining Jewish population.

1968 — The ancient Jewish community of Hebron, which had been destroyed in the 1929 Hebron massacre, was revived at Kiryat Arba. The community, in 1979 and afterwards, moved into Hebron proper and rebuilt the demolished Abraham Avinu Synagogue, the site which had been used by Jordan as a cattle-pen.

1983 — The Lutheran Church – Missouri Synod officially disassociated itself from "intemperate remarks about Jews" in Luther's works. Since then, many Lutheran

GRAFTED *IN* THE JEWISH OLIVE TREE

church bodies and organizations have issued similar statements.

1994   Second Hebron massacre. Baruch Goldstein, a Jew, killed several Muslim worshippers; this led to riots that killed both Muslims and Jews.

1999   August 10 - Buford O. Furrow, Jr. killed mail carrier Joseph Santos Ileto and shot five people in the August 1999 Los Angeles Jewish Community Center shooting.

TWENTY-FIRST CENTURY

2002   Massive European wave of attacks on Jews and Jewish institutions between March and May, with largest number of attacks occurring in France.

2002   Third Hebron massacre. Palestinians killed Israeli soldiers and rescue workers, as well as others, on the road from the Tomb of the Patriarchs to Kiryat Arba. [3]

2003   October 16 - The Malaysian Prime Minister Dr. Mahathir Mohammed drew standing ovation at the 57-member Organization of the Islamic Conference for his speech. An excerpt: "[Muslims] are actually very strong. 1.3 billion people cannot be simply wiped out. The Nazis killed 6 million Jews out of 12 million. But today the Jews rule this world by proxy. They get others to fight and die for them. They invented socialism, communism, human rights and democracy so that persecuting them would appear to be wrong so they may enjoy equal rights with others. With these they have now gained control of the most powerful countries. And they, this tiny community, have become a world power."

2004   April - United Talmud Torah school library was firebombed in Montreal, Canada.

2004   June - A series of attacks on Jewish cemeteries in Wellington, New Zealand.

2004   September - The European Commission against Racism and Intolerance, a part of the Council of Europe, called on its member nations to "ensure that criminal law in the field of combating racism covers anti-Semitism" and to penalize intentional acts of public incitement to violence, hatred or discrimination, public insults and defamation, threats against a person or group, and the expression of anti-Semitic ideologies. It urged member nations to "prosecute people who deny, trivialize or justify the Holocaust". The report was drawn up in wake of a rise in attacks on Jews in Europe. The report said it was Europe's "duty to remember the past by remaining vigilant and actively opposing any manifestations of racism, xenophobia, anti-Semitism and intolerance... Anti-Semitism is not a phenomenon of the past and... the slogan 'never again' is as relevant today as it was 60 years ago." ([4])

2005   September - Throughout the Polish election Radio Maryja continued to promote anti-Semitic views, including denial of the facts of the Jedwabne pogrom in 1941. Their support of right-wing conservative Law and Justice party is considered a major factor in their electoral victory.[32]

GRAFTED IN THE JEWISH OLIVE TREE

2005   October - A nazi swastika was spray-painted to the side of Temple Beth El synagogue in Portland, Maine.

2005   A group of 15 members of the State Duma of Russia demanded that Judaism and Jewish organizations be banned from the country. In June, 500 prominent Russians demanded that the state prosecutor investigate ancient Jewish texts as "anti-Russian" and ban Judaism. The investigation was launched, but halted amidst international outcry.

2005   December - Iranian president Mahmoud Ahmadinejad widened the hostility between Iran and Israel by denying the Holocaust during a speech in the Iranian city of Zahedan. He made the following comments on live television: "They have invented a myth that Jews were massacred and place this above God, religions and the prophets." Continuing, he suggested that if the Holocaust had occurred, that it was the responsibility of Europeans to offer up territory to Jews: "This is our proposal: give a part of your own land in Europe, the United States, Canada or Alaska to them [the Jews] so that the Jews can establish their country."

2006   February - A French Jew, Ilan Halimi was kidnapped and tortured to death for 23 days in what Paris police have officially declared an anti-Semitic act.[33] The event caused international outcry.[34] On May 9, the Helsinki Commission held a briefing titled "Tools for Combating Anti-Semitism: Police Training and Holocaust Education". [35]

Anti-Semitism Throughout History

2006	March - Two synagogues in Montreal, Canada were vandalized with spray-painted swastikas and Nazi SS symbols.[36]
2006	Naveed Afzal Haq killed Pamela Waechter and injured five others in the July 2006 Seattle Jewish Federation shooting.
2006	September - A school in Ontario had one wall spray painted in anti-Jewish phrases and Nazi symbols.
2006	December - The International Conference to Review the Global Vision of the Holocaust was a two-day conference that opened on December 11, 2006 in Tehran, Iran; many saw it as a conference rife with antisemitism, anti-Zionism, and Holocaust denial.
2007	August/September - The Jewish state, Israel, was shocked to find a neo-Nazi group of immigrants (from Russia) committing vandalism and voicing anti-Semitic rhetoric within its borders; also, this group had members that came in under the Law of Return. One of that group's members was a grandchild of a Holocaust survivor, and all were of Jewish descent. The group was violent against gays, Ethiopian Jews, haredi Jews, and drug addicts. [5]
2007/2008	Pope Benedict XVI, via the document *Summorum Pontificum*, officially revived the Tridentine mass, which contains a Good Friday prayer asking for the conversion of the Jews. This led to criticism from Jewish leaders, charging that the prayer is anti-Semitic. The Vatican subsequently issued a statement condemning

anti-Semitism, but was reluctant to remove the prayer. Benedict visited the Park East Synagogue in an April 2008 visit to New York, which was apparently well-received, with the congregants and the Pope exchanging gifts with each other. [6][7]

2009 Anti-Semitism is said to be higher today than at any time since the second World War. As we have seen, Iran is constantly threatening to wipe Israel off the map. The very real fact that Iran is on the brink of producing enough nuclear energy for weapons should bring us all to our knees. And it is not only in Iran that we see antisemitism. It is happening across Europe as well as in our universities in the United States and here at home in Canada.

Israel has been fighting for her very survival for many years, essentially since becoming an independent state in 1948. US presidents have been trying for years to broker a peace accord, encouraging the Israelis to give away 'land for peace', which, incidently, never happens.

REFERENCES FROM WIKIPEDIA

1. "Against Apion" Bk 2.7)
2. (*Symposiacs* Bk 4.5).
3. e-text at Project Gutenberg
4. Lehmann, Clayton Miles (May-September 1998). "Palestine: History: 135–337: Syria Palaestina and the Tetrarchy". *The On-line Encyclopedia of the Roman Provinces*. University of South Dakota. http://www.usd.edu/erp/Palestine/history.htm#135-337. Retrieved on 2006-07-19.
5. The Epistle of the Emperor Constantine, concerning the matters transacted at the Council, addressed to those Bishops who were not present
6. *Life of Constantine* Vol. III Ch. XVIII by Eusebius
7. Socrates Scholasticus, *Ecclesiastical History* VI,16
8. "Toledo", *Catholic Encyclopedia* [1]
9. Granada by Richard Gottheil, Meyer Kayserling, *Jewish Encyclopedia*. 1906 ed.
10. Benbassa, Esther (2001). *The Jews of France: A History from Antiquity to the Present*. Princeton University Press. ISBN 0-691-09014-9.
11. German chronicler's account in Medieval Sourcebook
12. Halsall, Paul (1996). "Innocent III: Letter on the Jews 1199". *Internet Medieval Source Book*. Fordham University. http://www.fordham.edu/halsall/source/inn3-jews.html. Retrieved on 2006-11-27.
13. [Ben-Sasson, H.H., Editor; (1969). *A History of The Jewish People*. Harvard University Press, Cambridge, Massachusetts. ISBN 0-674-39731-2 (paper).]
14. Stephen Inwood, *A History of London*, London: Macmillan, 1998 p.70.

15. Inwood, *loc. cit.*
16. Inwood, *loc. cit*
17. Rindfleisch article in the Jewish Encyclopedia (1906) by Gotthard Deutsch, S. Mannheimer
18. Paul Johnson, A History of the Jews (New York: HarperCollins Publishers, 1987), 242.
19. David Kertzer, *The Popes Against the Jews.*
20. Reinach, Salomon & Simmonds, Florence. *Orpheus: A General History of Religions*, G. P. Putnam & Sons, 1909, p. 210.
21. Stearns, Peter N. *Impact of the Industrial Revolution: Protest and Alienation.* Prentice Hall, 1972, p. 56.
22. Hebron Massacre
23. *Anti-Semitism in Europe: Hearing Before the Subcommittee on European Affairs of the Committee on Foreign Relations* by United States Congress. Senate. Committee on Foreign Relations. Subcommittee on European Affairs. 2004. p.69
24. Kristallnacht and The World's Response
25. The Tragedy of the S.S. St. Louis
26. A Decision Not to Save 20,000 Jewish Children
27. Joseph Schechtmann, *Star in Eclipse: Russian Jewry Revisited*
28. Stalin's Secret Pogrom: The Postwar Inquisition of the Jewish Anti-Fascist Committee (introduction) by Joshua Rubenstein
29. Seven-fold Betrayal: The Murder of Soviet Yiddish by Joseph Sherman
30. Schwarz, Solomon M. "The New Anti-Semitism of the Soviet Union," *Commentary*, June 1949.
31. *Pravda 1952, November 21*
32. Stephen Roth Institute, Annual Report, Poland

33. Rally honors legacy of slain French Jew by Norm Oshrin (NJ Jewish News)
34. Rutgers University Students Pay Tribute to Hate-Crime Victim May 01, 2006
35. OSCE at 'Critical Point' in Fight Against Anti-Semitism May 12, 2006
36. "Global Anti-Semitism:Selected Incidents Around the World in 2006" Retrieved from "http://en.wikipedia.org/wiki/Timeline_of_antisemitism" except where otherwise noted.

Categories: Antisemitism | Jewish history timelines | Anti-Semitic attacks and incidents Hidden category: Articles needing additional references from May 2007

All above text is available under the terms of the GNU Free Documentation License.

Chapter 17
Hindrances To Understanding

IN THE PREVIOUS CHAPTER WE LOOKED at the anti-Semitism which has taken place throughout history. We noticed, hopefully, that a great deal of this anti-Semitism was carried out by people who professed to be Christians. Indeed, even our revered Martin Luther, whose Reformation removed believers from the clutches of the Roman Catholic Church, was, himself, terribly anti-Semitic.

I believe in order to be freed from this anti-Semitic spirit which still exists in the Church today, we must repent of the sins of our fathers, as well as the anti-Semitism which remains among us. Just as Daniel repented on behalf of his people in the 9th chapter of the book called by his name, saying, **"O Lord, great and awesome God, who keeps His covenant and mercy with those who love Him, and with those who keep His commandments, we have sinned and committed iniquity, we have done wickedly and rebelled, even by departing from Your precepts and Your judgments. Neither have we heeded Your servants the prophets, who spoke in Your name to our kings and our princes, to our fathers and all the people of the land. O Lord, righteousness belongs to You, but to us shame of face ....because of the unfaithfulness which they have committed against You. O Lord, to us belongs shame of** face, to our kings, our princes, and our fathers, because we have sinned against You. To the Lord our God belong mercy and forgiveness, though we have rebelled against Him. We have not obeyed the voice of the LORD our God, to walk in His laws, which He has set before us by His servants the prophets." (Dan. 9:4-10) The Church needs to repent of the sin of anti-Semitism which has existed and still exists in the hearts of some in the Church today.

Daniel's prayer goes on for several more verses, and then he says, **"O my God, incline Your ear and hear; open Your eyes and see our desolations, and the city which is called by Your name; for we do not present our supplications before You because of our righteousness, but because of Your great mercies. O Lord, hear! O Lord, forgive! O Lord, listen and act! Do not delay for Your own sake, my God, for Your city and Your people are called by Your name"** (Dan. 9:18-19).

Many, if not most Christians, seem to not fully understand the importance the Jewish people and Israel have to the church. Although they know that Jesus came through the line of David and was, indeed, brought up in the Jewish customs and was a Jewish rabbi, yet there seems to be a block in their understanding of what that means to us today.

Until the time that Paul was struck blind on the road to Damascus, believers in Jesus (the "church") largely consisted of Jewish men and women, with the exception of Cornelius and his household. Paul was also a Jew, who was given the responsibility to preach the Good News of the Gospel to the Gentiles. However, he first went to the Jews. After Paul and Barnabus were set apart by the Holy Spirit they went to Salamis, where **they preached the word of God in the synagogues of the Jews** (Acts 13:5). Again in verse 14 the Scriptures tell us, **"But when they departed from Perga, they came to Antioch in Pisidia, and went into the synagogue on the Sabbath day,"** and after the reading of the Law and the Prophets, Paul spoke to the rulers about Messiah. Verse 43 tells us, **"Now when the congregation had broken up, many of the Jews and devout proselytes followed Paul and Barnabus, who, speaking to them, persuaded them to continue in the grace of God."** Again at Iconium (Acts 14:1) they went to the Jews first. Later in Acts 17:1-2 we see the same pattern, **"... they came to Thessalonica, where there was a synagogue of the Jews. Then Paul, as his custom was, went in to them, and for three Sabbaths reasoned with them from the Scriptures."** This was his custom, and continued to take place in Berea (Acts 17:10), in Athens (Acts 17:17), in Corinth (Acts 18:4), and in Ephesus (Acts 19:8). In Acts 26:20, before King Agrippa he testified that he **"declared first to those in Damascus and in Jerusalem, and throughout all the region of Judea, and *then* to the Gentiles."** He wrote in Romans 1:16, **"For I am not ashamed of the gospel of Christ, for it is the power of God to salvation for everyone who believes, *for the Jew first* and also for the Greek"** (emphasis mine).

Although Paul stated in the above verse that the gospel was to be preached to the Jew first, even though he was called to preach the gospel to the Gentiles, the Church, unfortunately, has not continued this practice through the centuries. We have sent missionaries off to practically ever other people group in the world, but not "to the Jew first," wherever they have been scattered. Is not every word of God as important as another?

Paul did not become "Christian." Rather, he often referred to his "Jewishness" and was proud of his Jewish heritage. In Romans 11:1 Paul says, **"For I also am an Israelite, of the seed of Abraham, of the tribe of Benjamin."** In Romans 9:2-3 he says, **"I have great sorrow and continual grief in my heart. For I could wish that I myself were accursed from Christ for my brethren, my countrymen according to the flesh."** Those are very strong words! Would we be willing to give up our salvation if it would mean another could take our place? Of course, it doesn't work that way, as each person must make his or her own decision to accept the wonderful gift that Jesus offers us through His shed blood. However, it is very obvious that Paul's heart breaks for his Jewish brethren who don't know their Messiah.

Why is it that 2000 years after Jesus came to shed His blood, His church is so powerless and fragmented? In the 17th chapter of the Gospel of John, Jesus prayed that we would be one. I am convinced that He meant all believers, both Jew and Gentile, to be one. Paul writes about this in his letter to the Ephesians when he tells them the middle wall of separation has been broken down by Jesus, so He could create in Himself "one new man." That has not yet happened. In fact, even within the Gentile church there is so much division and fragmentation. Why?

I believe this is because of historical error in teaching. Two such errors are predominant in the church's history: Replacement Theology and Dual Covenant Theology. We will examine each of these separately.

REPLACEMENT THEOLOGY

ESSENTIALLY, REPLACEMENT THEOLOGY teaches the church has replaced Israel in God's scheme of things, and that all the promises God gave to Israel and the Jews now belong to the church and not to them. Following are a few examples of what early Church Fathers believed:

- Justin Martyr (about 100 – 165 AD) – "For the true spiritual Israel ... are we who have been led to God through this crucified Christ."[1]
- Hippolytus of Rome (martyred 235 AD) – [The Jews] "have been darkened in the eyes of your soul with a darkness utter and everlasting."[2]
- Origen (about 185 – 254 AD) – [The Jews] "will never be restored to their former condition."[3]

- Augustine (354 – 430 AD) – followed the above views, but introduced a new angle on the importance to Christianity of the continued existence of the Jewish people, "The Jews ... are thus by their own Scriptures a testimony to us that we have not forged the prophecies about Christ."[4]

Of course, all the promises God gave to the Jews *do* belong to the church, but it is because we have been *grafted in* to the Jewish olive tree, and *not* because we have replaced Israel and the Jewish people. God has *not* given up on His own Jewish people!

When Jesus began His ministry He chose Jews to be His disciples, because His Father had made a covenant with Abraham and called out a people for Himself. Jesus preached to Jewish multitudes, and healed many. When He sent out the twelve He told them not to go to the Gentiles, or to the Samaritans (Matt. 10:5), but said, **"... go rather to the lost sheep of the house of Israel"** (Matt. 10:6). Later, in chapter 15 of Matthew, a Canaanite woman approached Him to heal her daughter of demon possession, but He ignored her and said in verse 24, **"I was not sent except to the lost sheep of the house of Israel."** However, because of the faith this Gentile woman displayed, He relented and healed her daughter.

It has been argued that Jesus Himself was against the scribes and Pharisees, calling them hypocrites. He was against their hypocrisy and their pride and their wrong teaching, but He wasn't against them as people or as Jews. He was trying to teach them, but they didn't want to learn.

He loved His people. Recall how He wept over Jerusalem because the people did not recognize the time of their visitation. And God still loves His chosen people and His holy city Jerusalem.

Replacement Theology has been handed down to us since the 4th century, when the Church, in order to prevent being persecuted, made a pact with their enemies, the Romans, and it has been a plague upon the church ever since. It didn't stop with the Roman

Catholic Church. Luther, who finally broke away, was very anti-Semitic, as we saw in the last chapter. Today we have countless denominations, but all are tinted to some degree with Replacement Theology.

Another contributor to Replacement Theology is incorrect translations of the Scriptures. Unfortunately, the Greek of the New Testament often did not have exact words which corresponded to the Hebrew thought behind it, so at times they used the word closest to the meaning, and sometimes they made up a new word. However, Greek thought and idiom is far removed from Hebrew thought and idiom. This obviously presented problems with both understanding and translation.

Dual Covenant Theology

DUAL COVENANT THEOLOGY essentially teaches that Jews need only keep the Laws of Moses in order to have eternal life, because of the eternal covenant God made with Abraham; whereas Gentiles need to believe that Jesus shed His blood for the forgiveness of our sins and receive Him as our Savior and Lord.

Paul makes it clear that this is false in Romans 1:16 when he said, **"For I am not ashamed of the gospel of Christ, for it is the power of God to salvation** *for everyone who believes, for the Jew first and also for the Greek."* (emphasis mine). There is not one way for Christians and another way for Jews. It is only through Jesus for all of us. Later in the 8th verse of the 9th chapter of Romans Paul states, **"... that if you confess with your mouth the Lord Jesus and believe in your heart that God has raised Him from the dead, you will be saved,"** and he adds in verse 10, **"For with the heart one believes unto righteousness, and with the mouth confession is made unto salvation."**

Hindrances to Understanding

Some have argued the Jerusalem Council in Acts 15:24-29 suggests a dual covenant theology. After Paul began preaching to the Gentiles, some Judaizers said that Gentiles should be circumcised into the custom of Moses first in order to be saved, before joining Jewish believers in Yeshua (Jesus). Paul experienced great dissension over this, so he and Barnabas as well as others went to Jerusalem to speak to the leadership there. The Jerusalem Council was in response to this, and formulated a decree saying Gentile believers did not have to be circumcised, but that they should **"abstain from things offered to idols, from blood, from things strangled, and from sexual immorality."** Simply put, the Gentiles did not have to become Jewish through circumcision before believing in Yeshua's sacrifice. This does not suggest, however, that Jewish people do not need the blood of Jesus to be saved.

Anyone from any background can be saved, as long as they believe that Jesus paid the penalty for their sins, and receive Him as the Savior and Lord of their life. Jews remain Jews, Gentiles remain Gentiles. The term "Gentile" refers to all people of every tribe, tongue and kindred who are not Jewish. Of course we need to give up pagan practices; this applies to all.

THE BOTTOM LINE

> All Scripture is given by inspiration of God, and is profitable for doctrine, for reproof, for correction, for instruction in righteousness. *2 Timothy 3:16*

WE WOULD DO WELL to heed this. If something doesn't line up with God's Word, we need to do away with it. Replacement Theology and Dual Covenant Theology are two of these things. They are hindrances to our understanding of God's Word. In a word, they are heresies.

Daniel Gruber, in his book entitled "The Separation of Church and Faith, Vol. 1, Copernicus and the Jews" has this to say:

> Historical Christianity has theologically defined itself in opposition to, or at least in separation from, the Jewish people. As a theological system, Christianity is based upon the Divine rejection, momentary or eternal, of the Jewish people. It is a system crafted in replacement of Israel. It has produced a history that has grown from that definition.[5]

Daniel Gruber further suggests in his book that misunderstanding grew out of the difficulty of the original writers writing in Greek and thinking in Hebrew. Sometimes there was not an accurate word in Greek to completely convey the intended meaning. As well, translators of the Bible from Greek to English or any other language would have encountered difficulties which would extend from that. Gruber states:

> "But the translator may have a different mindset than the author, or a different mindset than the audience. He, or she, may not understand what is being said, or what is being heard. He may assign incorrect meanings to the original words, because

he does not understand the context in which they were used. Additionally, the language into which he is translating may not have any equivalent way of reproducing the original."[6]

In addition to possible misunderstandings as a result of translations of God's Word, we would be wise to heed the Bible's warnings of a last-days apostasy. Paul wrote to Timothy in 1 Tim. 4:1, **"Now the Spirit expressly says that in latter times some will depart from the faith, giving heed to deceiving spirits and doctrines of demons."** We would be wise to read and study the word of God carefully, so that we will not be led astray.

Chapter 18
The Olive Tree

AFTER THE DIVERGENCE OF THE LAST chapter describing theologies not found in the Bible, let us now look at God's word, in particular regarding the Christian's relationship with the Jews.

In Jeremiah 11, God laments over the stubbornness of His people, the Jews, and their waywardness with the Baals. He tells Jeremiah not to pray for the people, for He will not hear. In verse 16 the Lord says, "**The Lord called your name, Green Olive Tree, Lovely and of Good Fruit. With the noise of a great tumult He has kindled fire on it, And its branches are broken.**"

It is obvious, then, the olive tree refers to the Jewish people, and through the mouth of His prophet, He is warning them what will happen to them - that this olive tree, cultivated lovingly by God to be lovely and bearing good fruit, would be set afire and its branches would be broken. The roots are the Patriarchs, Abraham, Isaac and Jacob. God cultivated this olive tree, but finally, in His anger, pronounced doom against His people for offering incense to Baal. (Jeremiah 11:17)

Does this mean that God has rejected His Jewish people and replaced them with believing Gentiles? Paul states unequivocally in the first verse of the eleventh chapter in his letter to the Romans that this is not the case. "**I say then, has God cast away His** people? Certainly not!" (Romans 11:1). He continues in verse 2, "**God has not cast away His people whom He foreknew.**" Further along in verse 11, he asks a question and answers it himself. "**I say then, have they stumbled that they should fall? Certainly not! But through their fall, to provoke them to jealousy, salvation has come to the Gentiles.**"

As believers, we are to provoke the Jews to jealousy so they would want to get to know this Jewish Messiah of theirs. Instead, over the centuries, we have stripped Jesus of His Jewishness and made Him a "gentile god" in the eyes of the Jewish people. We have taken part in anti-Semitic acts or thought, or we have been silent in the face of it. God forgive us! As believers, we are called to pray for Israel, and the peace of Jerusalem (Psalm 122:6). But I often wonder how many Christians do pray for Israel. How many Christians are even aware that we should?

I've been going over my sermon notes which I have taken of many different pastors' sermons since I became a Christian and began going to church over twenty years ago. I have not one set of sermon notes on Romans Chapter 11. I don't think I have *ever* heard a sermon on Romans Chapter 11 preached in a church service. I can't help but wonder why that is. I've heard many sermons on spiritual warfare, many on prayer and faith, many on the fruit of the Spirit. I've heard sermons on the Book of Job, the Book of James, the Gospels, Romans Chapters 2 through 9. However, not too much is spoken of Romans Chapter 10, where Paul describes Israel's need of the Gospel, and states that his heart's desire is that they may be saved (v.1). Or Chapter 11, where he makes it clear that God is not finished with His Jewish people, and that the Gentiles have been grafted in to the Jewish Olive Tree.

Paul speaks at great length about the olive tree in chapter 11 of Romans. Due to the unbelief of the majority of the Jews in regard to the Messiah, Paul says these unbelievers were cut off from the olive tree, and wild branches, the Gentiles, were grafted in. Does this mean that God has cast away His people? We have already seen that it does not.

God has always kept for Himself a remnant of Jewish people chosen by His grace.

In verse 14 of Romans Chapter 10, Paul asks a few questions, **"How then shall they call on Him whom they have not believed? And how shall they believe in Him of whom they have not heard? And how shall they hear without a preacher?"** He goes on to say in verse 15, **"And how shall they preach unless they are sent?"**

Paul is talking about his fellow Jews here, although it *can* include world evangelism as well. In fact, the latter is the only way I have heard verse 15 used. In verse 19 he refers to Moses' words from Deuteronomy 32:21b regarding the Jewish people, **"I will provoke you to jealousy by those who are not a nation, I will move you to anger by a foolish nation."** Those "who are not a nation" refer to all those who are not Jews – in other words, the Gentiles. Have we Gentiles, especially Christian Gentiles, provoked the Jews to jealousy? I think not. There has been far too much anti-Semitism in the historical church for them to become jealous of us. Rather, sad to say, they fear us, and for good reason as we have seen in a previous chapter.

THE UNPREACHED SERMON

THEN COMES ROMANS 11, the unpreached sermon, and a message that desperately needs to be heard. The Church needs to know this chapter, because Paul gives us a few warnings within it. We need to pay attention to them.

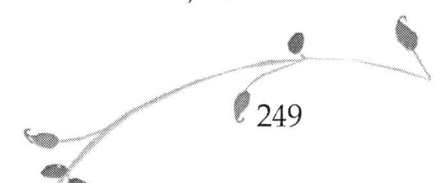

He begins by asking a question, **"Has God totally rejected and disowned His people?"** He answers his own question for us, **"Certainly not!"** He goes on to speak of his own Jewish heritage from the tribe of Benjamin. He reminds us about Elijah, who complained to God about the Israelites, and God told him that He has kept for Himself "seven thousand men who have not bowed the knee to Baal (v.4). Paul then goes on to say, **"So too at the present time there is a remnant (a small believing minority), selected (chosen) by grace (by God's unmerited favor and graciousness.)"** (v.5 AMP)

Paul reminds us about what grace is – God's unmerited favor, and not dependent upon man's works. Consequently, although Israel did not obtain God's favor by obedience to the Law, and most were blinded, those chosen by God from the beginning of time received the necessary grace, and believed. For the rest, according to God's mysterious plan, blindness was brought upon them, so they could not see or understand the truth. Verse 8 states, **"As it is written, God gave them a spirit (an attitude) of stupor, eyes that should not see and ears that should not hear, [that has continued] down to this very day."** (AMP).

Why did God do this to His chosen people, allowing only a few to believe in Jesus, and not the many? Paul answers that question for us, **"... through their false step and transgression salvation [has come] to the Gentiles, so as to arouse Israel [to see and feel what they forfeited] and so to make them jealous"** (v. 11 AMP). God, in His graciousness and love and mercy, did not want to limit His wonderful gift of salvation only to His chosen people, the Jews, but to open it up to all mankind, to whomever would believe, in order to make His chosen ones who had rejected Him jealous. We, as the Gentile church, have not, however, done a very good job of provoking them to jealousy. Rather, through the anti-Semitism that has for centuries been evident in the church, we have made the Jewish people hate us and fear us, as well as the Name of Jesus. Instead of lifting up His Name as the Jewish Messiah, we have made Him into a "Gentile" God in the eyes of the Jewish people. God forgive us!

As stated above, the Gentile Church is called to provoke the Jews to jealousy. It is our mandate to come together with the Jewish people and become "one new man" according to Ephesians 2:14-15, 22 (AMP, emphasis added), **"For He is [Himself] our peace (our bond of unity and harmony). He has made us both [Jew and Gentile] one [body], and has broken down (destroyed, abolished) the hostile dividing wall between us, by abolishing in His [own crucified] flesh the enmity [caused by] the Law with its decrees and ordinances [which He annulled]; that He from the two might create in Himself one new man [one new quality of humanity out of the two], so making peace. .... In Him [and in fellowship with one another] you yourselves also are being built up [into this structure] with the rest, to form a fixed abode (dwelling place) of God in (by, through) the Spirit."**

In The Complete Jewish Bible, translated by David H. Stern, verses 13 through 15 are translated thus: **"But now, you who were once far off have been brought near through the shedding of the Messiah's blood. For he himself is our** *shalom* **(peace) – he has made us both one and has broken down the** *m'chitzah* (divider which separates people into two groups) **which divided us by destroying in his own body the enmity occasioned by the** *Torah*, **with its commands set forth in the form of ordinances. He did this in order to create in union with himself from the two groups a single new humanity and thus make** *shalom*.**"**

Paul goes on to say in Romans 11:12, **"Now if their stumbling (their lapse, their transgression) has so enriched the world [at large], and if [Israel's] failure means such riches for the Gentiles, think what an enrichment and greater advantage will follow their full reinstatement!"** (AMP) What does he mean by this? He answers this question for us in verse 15. **"For if their rejection and exclusion from the benefits of salvation were [overruled] for the reconciliation of a world to God, what will their acceptance and**

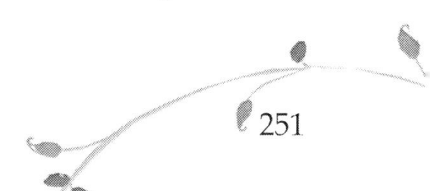

admission mean? [It will be nothing short of] life from the dead!" (AMP)

I have often wondered what Paul meant by the phrase "life from the dead." I now believe it means that when believing Jews and Gentiles join hands and hearts and become "one new man" it will usher in a great worldwide revival. Personally, I have heard about a great revival coming for a long time, and although there have been revivals here and there around the world, I have never had the opportunity or the blessing to be a part of it. This end-time revival, however, when Jew and Gentile come together as "one new man" will be much greater than anything the world has experienced! It will be similar to what took place on the day of Pentecost in Acts 2!

It is up to believers, the Church, to show the Jewish people that Jesus (Yeshua) is indeed their long-awaited Messiah! In order for us to do this, we need to show them that we repent of the anti-Semitism that has abounded. We need to show them our love for them by publicly and privately praying for and supporting Israel and Messianic ministries. When talking with Jewish friends and acquaintances, we need to use language that they can understand. We cannot refer to "Christ," but rather the Messiah. We need to use the name Yeshua, His Hebrew name, rather than Jesus. We need to have more interaction with the Messianic community. We are brothers!

The very first ones to believe that Jesus was the long-awaited Messiah were Jews, and largely, until Paul was sent to the Gentiles, this was the case. However, the Gentile numbers increased over the years and unfortunately, most of them eventually distanced themselves from the Jewish people, especially after making a pact with the Roman authorities, as we saw in a previous chapter.

When the world sees Jew and Gentile believers coming together, it will usher in the greatest end time harvest the Church has ever known! There has been much talk and expectancy in recent years regarding the great end time harvest. I believe that in order for this to take place, the Church must first join with the Jews and become the "One New Man" that Paul spoke about. Then the harvest can be complete. Sid Roth, in his book "The Incomplete Church" says:

> "When the Jew and Gentile converge together as One New Man, it will spark an end-time revival such as the world has never seen."[1]

I look to that day!

THE OLIVE TREE

LET US TAKE A CLOSER LOOK at the Olive Tree which Paul describes. Abraham and the patriarchs are the roots of the olive tree. Paul says if the roots are holy, so are the branches. The first branches on the tree were Jewish. But some of the (Jewish) branches were cut off because they did not believe that Yeshua was who He said He was, so that a "wild olive shoot" (the Gentiles) could be grafted in, **"to share the richness [of the root and sap] of the olive tree."** (verse 17 AMP). He then issues a warning to us which we would be wise to heed, **"Do not boast over the branches and pride yourself at their expense. If you do boast and feel superior, remember it is not you that support the root, but the root [that supports you]"** (verse 18 AMP). Paul cautions us further, **"So do not become proud and conceited, but rather stand in awe and be reverently afraid. For if God did not spare the natural branches [because of unbelief], neither will He spare you [if you are guilty of the same offense"].** (Rom. 11:20b – 21 AMP).

So often I have heard preachers take verses from the Old Testament and apply them to the Church today. This in itself is fine, because as believers they do apply to us. However, without the understanding that **we** are the grafted in ones, many branches of the Church have usurped their rightful place and think the

Church has replaced Israel, which is "Replacement Theology," a modern-day heresy. The Church has not replaced Israel, as we have already seen.

Today there are many Messianic Jews throughout the world who believe that Jesus (Yeshua in Hebrew) is their Messiah, proving the truth of verse 23 AMP, that **"if they do not persist in [clinging to] their unbelief, will be grafted in, for God has the power to graft them in again."** We have a great deal to learn from them, because they have a much deeper knowledge of the riches to glean from the Old Testament regarding the holiness of God and the Feasts of the Lord. These Messianic Jews have not given up their Jewishness to become "Gentiles," although prior to the "Jesus Movement" of the late 60s and early 70s, believing Jews were expected to do just that. Today they enjoy the richness of both Old and New Covenants, both in their lifestyle and in congregations very often made up of not only believing Jews, but also Gentiles, who desire the rich heritage these Messianic Jews offer.

The "Mystery"

PAUL REMINDS US NOT to be conceited, and miss this mystery: that **"a hardening (insensibility) has [temporarily] befallen a part of Israel [to last] until the full number of the ingathering of the Gentiles has come in"** (Rom. 11:25 AMP). However, God has not forgotten His Jewish people, for **"from the point of view of God's choice (of election, of divine selection), they are still the beloved (dear to Him) for the sake of their forefathers. For God's gifts and His call are irrevocable."** (verses 28b-29a AMP).

He wants us to know the meaning of this, and its importance. He explains his allegory of the olive tree:

> "In that case, I say, isn't it that they have stumbled with the result that they have permanently fallen away? Heaven forbid! Quite the contrary, it is by means of their stumbling that the

The Olive Tree

deliverance has come to the Gentiles, in order to provoke them to jealousy. Moreover, if their stumbling is bringing riches to the world - that is, if Israel's being placed temporarily in a condition less favored than that of the Gentiles is bringing riches to the latter - how much greater riches will Israel in its fullness bring them!" (Rom. 11: 11-12; *Complete Jewish Bible*, an English Version by David H. Stern, Jewish New Testament Publications, Inc.)

In nature, the roots of an olive tree are deep and strong, and can thrive in rocky soil in an arid climate for centuries. It is renowned for its longevity. While in Israel recently I saw these olive trees for the first time. They are amazing! One particular gnarled-looking tree was pointed out as being about 400 years old!

Spiritually, this olive tree's roots go back to the Patriarchs, all the way back to Abraham, who believed God, and it was accounted to him as righteousness. It goes back to Abraham, Isaac and Jacob. And God called His chosen people, the Jews, His olive tree.

When the majority of the Jews didn't accept Jesus as their Messiah, they were cut off from the olive tree, and Gentiles were grafted in. In addition to giving Gentiles the opportunity to know the One God and to partake of the benefits of knowing Him through faith in the Messiah, the purpose of being grafted in was to provoke the Jews to jealousy.

Throughout history the Christian Church has failed to do this. God's desire was for His believers, Jew and Gentile to be "one new man" together, but this has not continued (see Eph. 2:14-18). Instead, we have seen the separation of the Church and the Jewish people, much to the detriment of both. Instead of provoking the Jewish people to jealousy (because we believe in and have received their One God and their Messiah), and instead of helping them to see that Jesus (Yeshua) is their long-awaited Messiah, we have pushed them away from Him. Through much persecution and

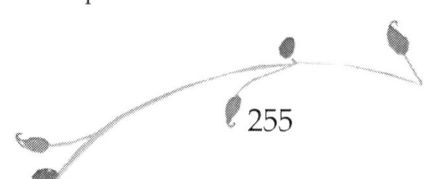

GRAFTED *IN* THE JEWISH OLIVE TREE

death at the hand of those who called themselves "Christians," the Church has caused them to hate Him and fear us.

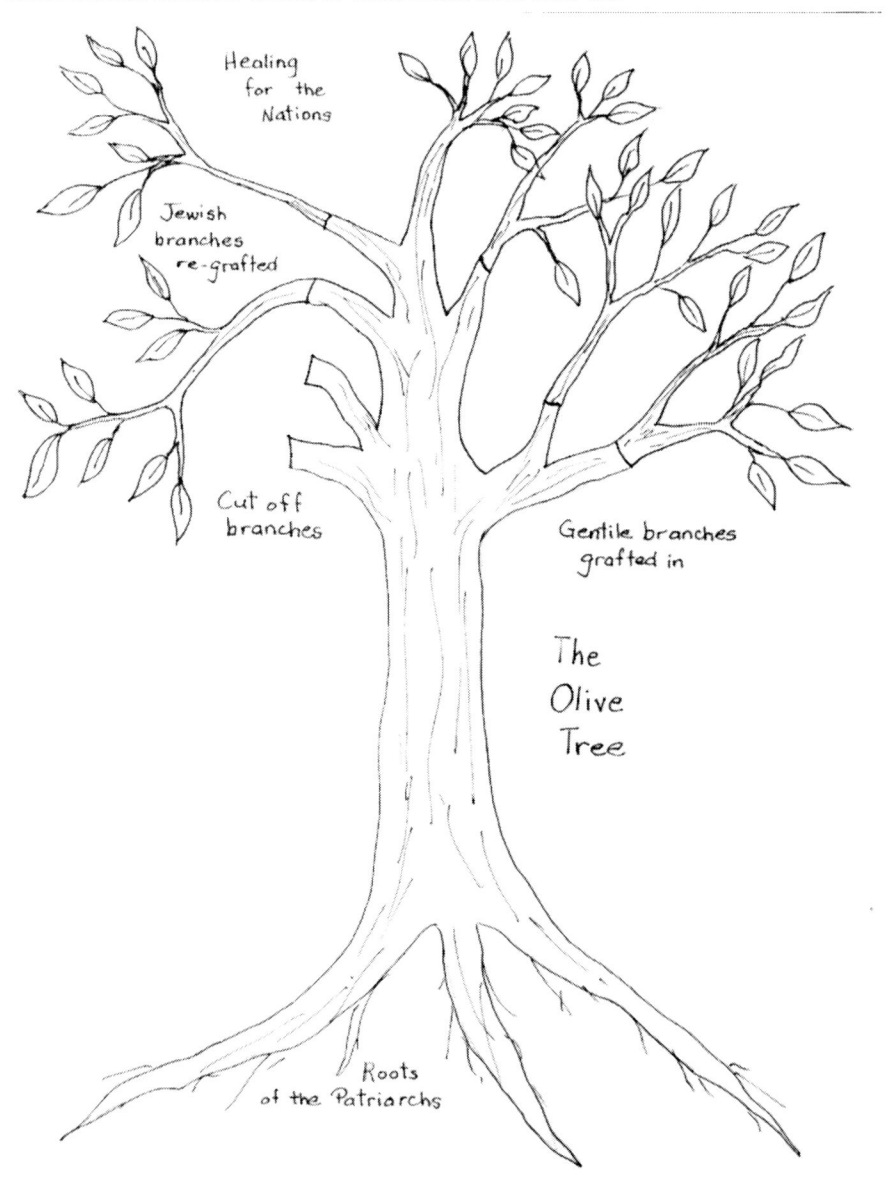

Healing for the Nations

Jewish branches re-grafted

Cut off branches

Gentile branches grafted in

The Olive Tree

Roots of the Patriarchs

This separation of Jew and believing Gentile is not in God's will. David Stern says in his book *Restoring the Jewishness of the Gospel* that it is the "worst schism in the history of this planet" and is "completely out of God's will."[2]

> "For if God did not spare the natural branches, he certainly won't spare you! So take a good look at God's kindness and his severity: on the one hand, severity toward those who fell off; but, on the other hand, God's kindness toward you - provided you maintain yourself in that kindness! Otherwise, you too will be cut off! Moveover, the others, if they do not persist in their lack of trust, will be grafted in; because God is able to graft them back in. For if you were cut out of what is by nature a wild olive tree and grafted, contrary to nature, into a cultivated olive tree, how much more will these natural branches be grafted back into their own olive tree!
>
> "For, brothers, I want you to understand this truth which God formerly concealed but has now revealed, so that you won't imagine you know more than you actually do. It is that stoniness, to a degree, has come upon Israel, until the Gentile world enters in its fullness; and that it is in this way that all Israel will be saved." (vv. 21-26, Complete Jewish Bible)

Chapter 19
Messianic Judaism

THE BOOK OF ACTS REFERENCES "multitudes" and "myriads" of Jews joining the number of those who believed in Yeshua as their Messiah. Today that number has grown exponentially as many of God's chosen people come to believe in Yeshua and are regrafted into the Olive Tree. The growth of Messianic Judaism has allowed many Christians and Messianic Jews to share in the blessing of revivals and evangelical movements throughout the course of history.

Messianic Judaism is essentially the doctrine of Jewish people who believe that Yeshua, the Hebrew name for Jesus, is the Messiah. It differs from Christianity in that they retain many of their Jewish customs and traditions, particularly the keeping of the Feasts (Appointed times of God).

In the following pages we will examine the history and growth of Messianic Judiasm in the world today.

Beginnings

THE FIRST MESSIANIC JEWS WERE, of course, the apostles and disciples of Jesus, as recorded in the Bible. They were those Jews who recognized that Yeshua was the long-awaited Messiah. They learned from Him. They did not become 'Christians'. The Bible records that believers weren't referred to as Christians until Paul's outreach to the Gentiles at Antioch (see Acts 11:26), and then it was really more of a derogatory term, much like the term "Jesus Freaks' in the 1970s.

Did these early Jewish believers cease to be Jews when they believed that Yeshua was the Messiah? Of course not!

> So continuing daily with one accord in the temple, and breaking bread from house to house, they ate their food with gladness and simplicity of heart, praising God and having favor with all the people. And the Lord added to the church (Assembly) daily those who were being saved. Acts 2:46-47

We have seen in previous chapters how the early believers, both Jew and Gentile, were scattered with the destruction of Jerusalem, as well as how the church was eventually taken over by Rome.

HISTORICALLY

THE FACT THE CHURCH became primarily Gentile does not mean there were no longer Jews who believed. Jewish congregations continued to exist in the Middle east until around 600 AD. It is assumed that they were wiped out by Islam. Eventually, however, those Jews who did believe became part of the Church, essentially forced to give up their 'Jewishness'. These people were sometimes referred to as 'Hebrew Christians'. There were times throughout history, as we have seen, that Jews were forced to be baptized, or be put to death. Those who did convert were forced to eat pig; if they refused they were executed. The practice of having Jews eat pork continues today in Protestant churches, especially in Israel. As time went on, these Jewish believers simply became part of the many denominations of the Church.

THE 60S REVOLUTION

YOU WILL RECALL THE 'HIPPIE' movement of the 60s when the young people turned from the values of their parents, calling out the slogan "Make love, not war", with the rise of anti-government rhetoric, rebellion, drug use, and a new rock and roll.

Beginning in 1967 when Jerusalem went back into the hands of the Jews many Jewish people became believers in Yeshua and are now the Rabbi leadership of congregations around the world. Many of the congregational leaders in Israel became believers that year and the years that followed.

THE 70S AND THE 'JESUS MOVEMENT'

THE DECADE OF THE 70S SAW the rise of the 'Jesus Movement' when terms such as "Jesus people' and 'Jesus freaks' became common. These young people were an antidote to the drug culture of the hippie movement, and sought to return to a simpler, more meaningful life similar to that of the early Christians. They believed in signs and wonders and miracles of the Holy Spirit. According to Wikipedia, "... a miracle-filled revival at Asbury College in 1970 grabbed the attention of the secular news media and became known nation-wide."[1]

The movement was strong on evangelism. According to Wikipedia, "Some of the most read books by those within the movement included Ron Sider's *Rich Christians in an Age of Hunger* and Hal Lindsay's *The Late Great Planet Earth*.[2]

The Jesus Movement left a lasting legacy on several fronts. Christian music benefited greatly, with the likes of Keith Green, Second Chapter of Acts, Petra, Phil Keaggy, and Larry Norman. As well, according to Wikipedia, "Some of the fastest growing US denominations of the late 20th century, such as Calvary Chapel,

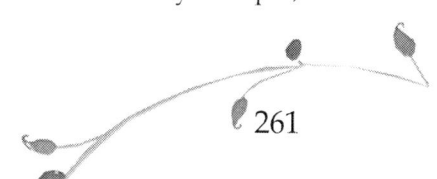

Hope Chapel Churches, and the Vineyard Churches, trace their roots directly back to the Jesus movement, as do parachurch organizations like Jews for Jesus and the multi-million-dollar contemporary Christian music industry."[3]

Jews for Jesus, mentioned in the above paragraph, is an organization, not a Messianic congregation. However, its birth in the midst of the Jesus Movement indicates that during this time Jewish people were coming to faith in Jesus as their Messiah, and, I believe, was a forerunner of the present-day Messianic Movement.

One Messianic music group, Joel Chernoff and Paul Wilbur of Lamb, had their beginnings during this time. I have several cassette tapes of Lamb, two of which were recorded in 1973 and 1974. Some of the songs on these albums are hauntingly beautiful - 'The Sacrifice Lamb', 'The Night is Far Spent' and 'Yeshua Hope of Israel' are cries from the heart.

MESSIANIC JUDAISM TODAY

I HAVE BEEN TRYING TO FIND an online listing of the number of Messianic congregations around the world today, and thus far have been unsuccessful. However, I do know there are congregations in many countries of the world.

According to an article on Messianic Judaism on Wikipedia, "By 2003, there were at least 150 Messianic houses of worship in the United States and over 400 worldwide, often members of larger Messianic organizations or alliances.[4] "In 2008, the movement was reported to have between 6,000 and 15,000 members in Israel."[5]

Messianic Judaism believes that Yeshua (Jesus) was not only a man who lived on earth, but that He was God's promised Son. Adherents believe, as do Christians, that salvation is necessary through believing in His sacrifice of the shedding of His blood for the remission of our sins. They affirm the Trinity, as do Christians.

Essentially, Messianic Judaism has the same beliefs as evangelical Christians, except that along with those beliefs, they maintain their 'Jewishness' in the keeping of the Feasts of the Lord, including the Sabbath (Shabbat). Most Messianic Jews, as well, keep the dietary laws as laid out in the Torah (the five books of Moses).

Messianic congregations are generally made up of both believing Jews and Gentiles who desire to learn more about the Jewish roots of their faith. Both see themselves as having been grafted into the Jewish Olive Tree spoken of in Romans 11. In this way, Messianic congregations are a picture of the 'one new man' that Paul speaks of in Ephesians 2:14-15, which says:

> For He Himself is our peace, who has made both one, and has broken down the middle wall of separation, having abolished in His flesh the enmity, *that is*, the law of commandments *contained* in ordinances, so as to create in Himself one new man *from* the two, *thus* making peace.

Essentially, the purpose of Messianic congregations is, first of all, to glorify God. The *Shema* is recited, and often sung, at every Shabbat (Sabbath) gathering:

Shema, Yisrael, Adonai Elohenu, Adonai Echad.
Hear, O Israel, the Lord our God, the Lord is One.

Messianic congregations meet on Saturday morning, or Friday evening, which is the beginning of the Sabbath, at sundown, for God sanctified the seventh day, making it holy. As we have seen in a previous chapter, when God gave the children of Israel His feasts, he began with the Sabbath,:

> Six days shall work be done, but the seventh day is a Sabbath of solemn rest, a holy convocation. You shall do no

work on it; it is the Sabbath of the Lord in all your dwellings. (Lev. 23:3)

Another purpose of Messianic congregations is to equip God's people for the work of the ministry, according to Ephesians 4:16. Consequently congregants are encouraged to use their God-given gifts.

From whom the whole body, joined and knit together by what every joint supplies, according to the effective working by which every part does its share, causes growth of the body for the edifying of itself in love.

Messianic congregations believe that Israel, as a nation, is chosen by God to be a blessing to the nations of the earth, and the return of Jewish people to the land is fulfillment of Biblical prophecy. They also believe that Yeshua (Jesus) will return again to the earth to establish His worldwide reign from Jerusalem.

Messianic Jews generally believe that they are to maintain their Biblical Jewish heritage. This they are able to do in a Messianic congregation. This differentiates them from 'Hebrew Christians' who, although they are ethnically Jewish, have chosen to identify with believers in a Christian setting rather than become part of a Messianic congregation.

Non-Jewish believers are welcomed into Messianic congregations, and indeed, sometimes outnumber those of Jewish descent. These believers generally want to learn more about the Jewish roots of Christianity and/or have a heart for Israel. They are every bit as much a member of the congregation as their Jewish counterparts. They become part of the 'mishpocha' or family.

An important function of the Messianic congregation is that of a bridge to the Christian community, to promote love and unity. They can foster friendships with one another, to help Christians understand the Jewish roots of their faith, correct misconceptions due to replacement theology, and share with them the richness of the Lord's Feasts. Many congregations welcome non-members, either Jewish or Gentile, to their celebrations of Purim, Passover, Shavuot, (or Pentecost), Feast of Trumpets, Succot (Tabernacles) and Hannukah, and even Yom Kippur, the Day of Atonement, although it is not a 'celebration', strictly speaking. It can be very exciting and rewarding for a Gentile who has never taken part, especially in a Passover dinner, to do so, as eyes are often opened, and they come away, excitedly saying, "I didn't know that!"

In Israel

IN ISRAEL, IT IS NOT SO EASY to be a Messianic Jew, for in the land they are persecuted by the Orthodox and Ultra-Orthodox. In fact, a Messianic Jew from another country desiring Israeli citizenship is denied it, as he is seen as having given up his 'Jewishness' by believing that Yeshua is the Messiah!

A few years ago a young man was very badly injured at the Feast of Purim. It is common during this celebration to give gifts, and on this particular day a young teen-aged boy answered a knock at the door. Seeing a brightly-wrapped gift on the doorstep, he picked it up, and it exploded, injuring him severely. He has had many surgeries, and still requires more. This young teen and his family are Messianic believers.

The Orthodox and Ultra-Orthodox wield a great deal of power in Israel, and persecute Messianic Jews. In spite of this, Messianic Judaism is growing in the land, and there are many ministries, as well as congregations.

Chapter 20
The Land And The Promises

GOD PROMISED ABRAM "A land that I will show you" (Gen. 12:1). In verse 7 the LORD appeared to him and said, **"To your descendants I will give this land."**

The area on which Israel sits today is much smaller than the original land given to the Jewish people by God. Even so, this land that Jewish people have been fighting for since the day after David Ben-Gurion proclaimed the Declaration of Independence on May 14, 1948 is the most disputed piece of property in the whole earth. They are literally surrounded by their enemies, some of whom want to push them into the sea, and wipe them off the map.

We saw in Genesis 17:5-8 that the Lord said to Abram, **"No longer shall your name be called Abram, but your name shall be Abraham; for I have made you a father of many nations. I will make you exceedingly fruitful; and I will make nations of you, and kings shall come from you. And I will establish My covenant between Me and you and your descendants after you in their generations, for an** *everlasting covenant* **to be God to you and your descendants after you. Also I give to you and your descendants after you the land in which you are a stranger,** *all the land of Canaan, as an everlasting possession;* **and I will be their God"** (emphasis mine). Notice the land mentioned here is an *everlasting* possession. Everlasting means forever.

God's heart is for Israel to have that land. The world thinks the "Palestinians" should have it. Several US presidents have tried to broker a "peace accord" between Israel and the Arab people living in the land, essentially the idea of Israel giving away parts of their land, which they won in the 1967 war, in exchange for peace. However, in exchange for giving up a portion of their land, instead of peace they have received violence, suicide bombers, and rockets.

On and on it goes. Just as in Moses' day, it is "once more around that mountain."

However, when we look at God's word, in spite of what the world says, that land belongs to the Jewish people, covenanted to them by God. He is not going to stand by forever while the world cuts up His land and wars against His people.

We need to read to the end of the Book!

WARS AND RUMORS OF WARS

IN SPITE OF WARS AND RUMORS of wars, God ultimately wins, no matter how much human beings fight Him or disregard Him. Things are shaping up in the world on many fronts, bringing to mind things that Jesus spoke about in His "end of days" explanation to His disciples in Matt. 24 and Luke 21.

Alliances are being made. Armaments are becoming more and more deadly.

It is not my intent in this book to describe end time scenarios. However, we know from Scripture there are two major battles that will take place, the War of Gog and Magog as described in Ezekiel 38, and the Battle of Armageddon described in the Book of Revelation.

WE NEED TO PRAY

EVEN THOUGH GOD'S WORD TELLS us that He will bring judgment upon Gog, He also tells us there will be a terrible earthquake in the land of Israel at that time. An earthquake isn't particular with regard to whom its victims are. Not only will Gog and his armies suffer many casualties in this earthquake, but so will the people of Israel.

Most Jewish people do not know their Messiah. Most are secular. Most of the rest adhere to several branches of Judaism, such as the Ultra-Orthodox, the Orthodox, the Reformed, or the Conservative. Percentage-wise, few are Messianic, believing that Yeshua (Jesus) is their Messiah.

Who is going to pray them into the Kingdom if we, as Christian believers, don't? These are the descendants of those whom God chose and made His people, the ones whom He cut covenant with. Psalm 122:6 commands us to **"Pray for the peace of Jerusalem,"** and follows this with a promise, saying, **"May they prosper who love you."** It is vital at this time in the history of the world for Christians to realize our heritage in the faith, and pray for Israel and the Jewish people all over the world. Pray them "home" to Israel.

In the eleventh chapter of Isaiah, verses 11 and 12, God says:
"It shall come to pass in that day
That the LORD shall set His hand again the second time
To recover the remnant of His people who are left,
From Assyria and Egypt,
From Pathros and Cush,
From Elam and Shinar,
From Hamath and the islands of the sea.
He will set up a banner for the nations,
And will assemble the outcasts of Israel,

And gather together the dispersed of Judah
From the four corners of the earth."

Conclusion
God's Heart For His People

[The Lord was speaking to Jacob,] "Also your descendants shall be as the dust of the earth; you shall spread abroad to the west and the east, to the north and the south; and in you and in your seed all the families of the earth shall be blessed. Behold, I am with you and will keep you wherever you go, and will bring you back to this land; for I will not leave you until I have done what I have spoken to you." Gen. 28:14-15

GENTILES HAVE BEEN GRAFTED IN to the Jewish Olive Tree, and it is from its roots and sap that we receive our nourishment.

God did not turn His back or His face from His Jewish people, but rather opened His arms to include us along with them!

Even though the majority of Jewish people today do not believe the Messiah has come, and did not recognize Him when He came, there are a growing number of Jewish men and women who recognize Yeshua as their Messiah. That number is growing daily, thanks be to God! There are Messianic Jewish congregations in many countries of the world, including Israel!

ISRAEL'S REJECTION IS NOT FINAL! Luke's gospel tells us that **"Jerusalem will be trampled by Gentiles until the times of the Gentiles are fulfilled"** (Luke 21:24), and Paul tells us in Romans

11:25 that **"blindness in part has happened to Israel until the fullness of the Gentiles has come in."** I used to think that this "fullness of the Gentiles" perhaps referred to a specific number of Gentiles that God had in mind. However, when we include Luke's "times of the Gentiles" that conclusion doesn't make any sense. We know the Temple in Jerusalem was burned and sacked in AD 70 by the Romans. Josephus claims that 1,100,000 people were killed during the siege and that 97,000 were captured and enslaved. Still others escaped and fled the area. Then in AD 135 Bar Kochba led a rebellion against the still reigning Romans which resulted in the Jews being expelled from Jerusalem. Over the centuries Israel became desolation. However, there have always been Jews who have maintained their presence in the land of Israel. Never has the territory God promised to Abraham been without Jews living there, though they may have lived in less than ideal circumstances.

In 1948, after the Second World War and the Holocaust, Israel became a sovereign State once more. She has had to fight for her existence ever since, but once again the Jews are in their promised land. I think this could indicate that Luke's reference to the "times of the Gentiles" may be at or nearing an end, especially since the war of 1967, when Jerusalem was captured, and is once again the capital of Israel. The fact remains the Temple Mount is presently in Arab hands, and this is significant and problematic.

We know from the Scriptures that Jesus will be returning to Jerusalem to the Mount of Olives after He comes to fight the nations (Zech.14). We also know that He won't return until the Jewish people say, **"Blessed is He who comes in the name of the Lord"** (Matt. 23:39). God has not rejected His people. Paul says in Romans 11:28-29, **"Concerning the gospel they are enemies for your sake, but concerning the election they are beloved for the sake of the fathers. For the gifts and the calling of God are irrevocable."**

Conclusion

GOD LOVES, WITH AN EVERLASTING LOVE. He has not stopped loving His chosen people. He chose them carefully, through the line of Abraham, to Isaac, and through to all the descendents of Jacob. He is looking to the day when **"they in turn may one day, through the mercy you are enjoying, also receive mercy [that they may share the mercy which has been shown to you – through you as messengers of the Gospel to them]"** (Romans 11:31b AMP). We, the Church, need to gain a better understanding of Romans 11, as well as a deeper sense of the Father's heart for His people Israel. We have a job to do!

Hear the Father's heart for His chosen people:

> O Israel, return to the LORD your God, For you have stumbled because of your iniquity; Take words with you, and return to the LORD. Say to Him, "Take away all iniquity; Receive us graciously, for we will offer the sacrifices of our lips." (Hos. 14:1-2)

> "I will heal their backsliding, I will love them freely, For My anger has turned away from him." (Hos. 14:4)

> "Comfort, yes, comfort My people!" says your God. (Is. 40:1)

> "But you, Israel, are My servant, Jacob whom I have chosen, The descendants of Abraham My friend. You whom I have taken from the ends of the earth, And called from its farthest regions, and said to you, "You are My servant, I have chosen you and have not cast you away; Fear not, for I am with you; Be not dismayed, for I am your God. I will strengthen you, yes, I will help you, I will uphold you with My righteous right hand." (Is. 41:8-10)

But Zion said, "The LORD has forsaken me, and my LORD has forgotten me." "Can a woman forget her nursing child, and not have compassion on the son of her womb? Surely they may forget, yet I will not forget you. See, I have inscribed you on the palms of My hands; Your walls are continually before Me." (Is. 49:14-16)

I have set watchmen on your walls, O Jerusalem; They shall never hold their peace day or night. You who make mention of the LORD, do not keep silent, And give Him no rest till He establishes And till He makes Jerusalem a praise in all the earth. (Is. 62:6-7)

"But this is the covenant that I will make with the house of Israel after those days," says the LORD: "I will put My law in their minds, and write it on their hearts; and I will be their God, and they shall be My people." (Jer. 31:33)

Thus says the LORD, Who gives the sun for a light by day, The ordinances of the moon and the stars for a light by night, Who disturbs the sea, And its waves roar (The LORD of hosts is His name); If those ordinances depart from before Me, says the LORD, *Then* the seed of Israel shall also cease from being a nation before Me forever. (Jer. 31:35-36)

GOD HAS ALWAYS KEPT a faithful remnant of His people. Until the rise of Messianic Judaism, any Jewish people who believed in Yeshua as their Messiah had to become "Christian" and attend a Christian church because there was no alternative. They were essentially required to give up their Jewishness.

With the rise of Messianic Judaism, some Jewish people are beginning to take note, and are becoming curious about these followers of Jesus who keep the Jewish feasts and traditions. They have become a bridge, not only to their own people, but also to the Church, to help her discover her Jewish roots. David Stern, translator of the "Complete Jewish Bible" and the "Jewish New Testament" says, "...it is possible for us, today, to dare expect that Messianic Judaism will succeed in reaching its goal of healing the split between the Church and the Jewish people."[1]

This is an important era in which we live. As the Church gets back to her roots, and begins to pray for the salvation of the Jewish people and the peace of Jerusalem, it will hasten the return of the Lord. The Church has a vital role to play in intercessory prayer, for Jesus said He would not return until His people, the Jews, say, **"Baruch haba baShem Adonai" - Blessed is He who comes in the Name of the Lord** (Matt. 23:39). The Christian Church and the Jewish believers in Messiah have much in common, and we need to work together toward these two goals: To heal the rift between Jews and Christians, and to pray that the natural branches of the olive tree will be grafted in again.

A final quote from Stern's book, *Restoring the Jewishness of the Gospel* says:

> "The Jewish people must be brought to understand - freely, willingly, not by coercion or deception - that the age-old goals of Jewish endeavor will be achieved only when the Jewish people come to understand and trust in Yeshua, the Jewish Messiah. The Church must be brought to understand - freely, willingly, not by coercion or deception - that its goal will be achieved only when any form of overt or covert anti-Semitism or stand-offishness has disappeared, and intimate unity with the Jewish people has been acknowledged. ...it is essential that we be armed with a right understanding of the relationship between Israel and the Church."[2]

God wants us, Jew and Gentile together, to be one in our Messiah. Today there are more believing Jews than ever before; so much so that Messianic congregations and fellowships are being planted in many countries of the world, including up to one hundred in Israel. As followers of Yeshua (Jesus), they are all our brothers and sisters. There is no room on our part for boasting. Indeed, Paul warned us against boasting, reminding us that we don't support the root, but the root supports us, and that if God did not spare the natural branches, He won't spare the grafted branches either!

It is true that the majority of Jews today do not believe that Jesus is their Messiah. This is part of the "mystery" Paul speaks about, referring to God putting a veil over the eyes of their understanding, so they could not receive the truth. Why? So the Gentiles could be grafted in. God in His wonderful mercy and grace extended to us the invitation to partake of all the spiritual blessings that He has in store, **"that the Gentiles should be fellow heirs, of the same body, and partakers of His promise in Christ through the gospel"** (Eph. 3: 6). Notice how Paul says that we Gentiles should be "fellow heirs" along with His chosen people, the Jewish people, a people God called out for Himself. Remember that the original believers in Jesus the Messiah were Jewish.

When the time is right, when the fullness of the Gentiles has come, (it is at our very doorstep) all Israel will be saved (Romans 11:26)! God will remove their blindness as He extends His love and reveals His goodness to them through the witness of loving believers. Then they will say, "Blessed is He who comes in the name of the Lord!"

In the meantime, it is important for us, as followers of the Messiah, to "pray for the peace of Jerusalem" (Psalm 122:6)', and for the Jewish people to recognize that Yeshua is their Messiah. The number of Messianic Jews is increasing throughout the world. May we truly bless the Jewish people, as God's promise to Abraham indicates we should. May we truly provoke them to jealousy by showing them the love of God as we are called to do.

Conclusion

How should we pray for God's chosen people? The following is a guideline which will be helpful. Sid Roth, of Messianic Vision, suggests that "Bible-believers should be changing their tactics in this new era of spiritual warfare on behalf of the people of Israel and of the nations." Scriptures from the Psalms follow, to be used in our prayers for the Jewish people:

Biblical Accounts of Terrorism - the intentions of the adversary:
Ps. 10:7-10; Ps. 17:11-12; Ps. 35:20; Ps. 37:12-14; Ps. 37:32; Ps. 94:5-6; Ps. 140:1-5

Active Intercession - a pre-emptive strike:
Ps. 18:37-42; Ps. 37:15; Ps. 69: 22; Ps. 75:10; Ps. 91:13; Ps. 140:9-11; Ps. 141:10; Ps.144:1

Entreating God for His protection against the enemy:
Ps. 7:6; Ps. 10:12-15; Ps. 17:8-9; Ps. 22:19-21; Ps. 27:11-13; Ps. 31:1-5; Ps. 35:1-8; Ps. 35:17; Ps. 64:1-10; Ps. 94:16-19

The Lord is the ultimate defense against terror:
Ps. 20:1; Ps. 18:47-48; Ps. 21:8-12; Ps. 31:2; Ps. 31:15; Ps. 60:12; Ps. 94:22-23; Ps. 97:3; Ps. 129:4"[3]

BIBLIOGRAPHY

A Rabbi Looks at the Last Days © 2008 Rabbi Jonathan Bernis, JVMI Publishing, a division of Jewish Voice Ministries International

Complete Jewish Bible © 1998 by David H. Stern, Jewish New Testament Publications, Inc. PO Box 615, Clarksville, MD 21029

God's Appointed Times © 1993 Barney Kasdan, Messianic Jewish Publishers, a Division of Lederer/Messianic Jewish Communications, 6204 Park Heights Avenue, Baltimore MD 21215

Halley's Bible Handbook © Henry H. Halley 1927, 1928, 1929, 1931, 1932, 1933, 1934, 1936, 1938, 1939, 1941, 1943, 1944, 1946, 1948, 1951, 1955, 1957, 1959, publisheed by arrangement with Halley's Bible Handbook, Inc.

How Saved Are We © 1990 Michael Brown, Destiny Image ® Publishers, Inc., PO Box 310, Shippensburg, PA 17257-0310

Israel, the Church and the Last Days, © 1990 Dan Juster and Keith Intrater, Destiny Image Publishers, PO Box 351, Shippensburg, PA 17257

Jewish Roots, A Foundation of Biblical Theology, Daniel C. Juster © 1995 Daniel C. Juster, Destiny Image® Publishers, Inc., PO Box 310, Shippensburg, PA 17257

One New Man, © 1993-1999, Reuven Doron, Embrace Israel Ministries, One New Man Call, PO Box 164, Hayfield MN 55940 www.onenewman.injesus.com

Our Hands are Stained with Blood, the Tragic Story of the "Church" and the Jewish People © 1992 Michael L. Brown, Destiny Image ® Publishers, Inc., PO Box 310, Shippensburg, PA 17257-0310

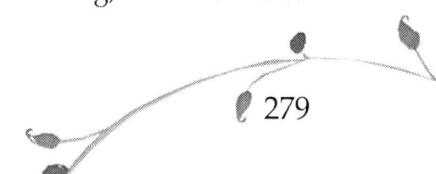

Restoring the Jewishness of the Gospel, A Message for Christians, David H. Stern, Second Edition © David H. Stern 1935, 1988, 1990, Jewish New Testament Publications Inc., PO Box 615, Clarksville, MD 21029

The Cry of Mordecai, Awakening an Esther Generation in a Haman Age © 2009 Robert Stearns, Destiny Image ® Publishers, Inc., PO Box 310, Shippensburg, PA 17257-0310

The Everlasting Tradition, Galen Peterson © 1995 by Kregel Publications, a division of Kregel Inc., PO Box 2607, Grand Rapids, MI 49501

The Hebraic Roots Version Scriptures, James Scott Trimm, ©2004, 2005 James Scott trimm, Published by Institute for Scripture Research, PO Box 1830, 2162 Northriding, Republic of South Africa

The Incomplete Church, Bridging the Gap Between God's Children, ©2007, Sid Roth, Destiny Image® Publishers, Inc., PO Box 310, Shippensburg, PA 17257-0310

The Messianic Church Arising! Restoring the Church to Our Covenant Roots © 2006 Robert D. Heidler, Glory of Zion International Ministries

The New Strongs Exhaustive Concordance of the Bible, James Strong, LL.D., S.T.D., © 1990 by Thomas Nelson Publishers, Nashville, Tennessee; Publishers and distributed in Canada by Lawson Falle, Ltd., Cambridge, Ontario

The Separation of Church and Faith, Vol. 1, Copernicus and the Jews, © Daniel Gruber, Elijah Publishing, PO Box 776, Hanover, NH 03755, www.Elijahnet.org

The Two Babylons or The Papal Worship, © 1916 Rev. Alexander Hislop, First American Edition 1943, 2nd American Edition 1959; Published in America by Loizeaux Brothers Inc.

Bibliography

Wanderings: Chaim Potok's History of the Jews © 1978 by Chaim Potok, Ballantine Books

Watchmen on the Wall – A Practical Guide to Prayer for Jerusalem and Her People © 2005 by Robert Stearns, Published by Kairos Publishing, PO Box 450, Clarence NY 14031 www.kairos.us

Yeshua, A Guide to the Real Jesus and the Original Church © Ronald Wayne Moseley, Messianic Jewish Publishers, a Division of Lederer/Messianic Jewish Communications, 6204 Park Heights Avenue, Baltimore MD 21215

Your People Shall Be My People, How Israel, the Jews and the Christian Church Will Come Together in the Last Days, © 2001 Don Finto, Regal Books, a Division of Gospel Light, Ventura, CA

NOTES

Introduction

[1] The Separation of Church and Faith, Vol. 1, Copernicus and the Jews, p. 18, ©Daniel Gruber, 2005, Elijah Publishing, PO Box 776, Hanover, NH 03755, www.Elijahnet.org

[2] ibid., p. 19

[3] The Hebraic Roots Version Scriptures, Introduction pp ix – xi, James Scott Trimm, ©2004, 2005 James Scott Trimm, Published by Institute for Scripture Reasearch, PO Box 1830, 2162 Northriding, Republic of South Africa

[4] ibid p.ix

[5] The New Strongs Exhaustive Concordance of the Bible, James Strong, LL.D., S.T.D., © 1990 by Thomas Nelson Publishers, Nashville, Tennessee; Publishers and distributed in Canada by Lawson Falle, Ltd., Cambridge, Ontario

[6] The Hebraic Roots Version Scriptures, Introduction pp ix – xi, James Scott Trimm, ©2004, 2005 James Scott Trimm, Published by Institute for Scripture Reasearch, PO Box 1830, 2162 Northriding, Republic of South Africa

Chapter Two

[1] Spirit-Filled Life Bible ©1991 by Thomas Nelson, Inc. Note at Genesis 15:17

[2] www.sacred-texts.com/chr/apo/jasher/index.htm

[3] ibid

[4] A Rabbi Looks at the Last Days by Rabbi Jonathan Bernis, JVMI Publishing, a division of Jewish Voice Ministres International

[5] Spirit-Filled Life Bible, © 1991 by Thomas Nelson, Inc.

[6] The New Compact Bible Dictionary © 1967 by Zondervan Publishing House, Grand Rapids, Michigan

Notes

Chapter Five

[1] The Messianic Church Arising © 2006, Robert D. Heidler, Glory of Zion Internationsl Ministries, pp. 19-20. Used with persmission.

[2] ibid. p.21. Used with permission.

[3] Spirit Filled Life Bible © 1991, Jack W. Hayford, General Editor, Thomas Nelson Publishers, Nashville, p.1647

Chapter Six

[1] Wanderings, Chaim Potok's History of the Jews ©1978, Chaim Potok, p.370

[2] ibid, p.383

[3] The following are taken from Wikipedia: Constantine: Sickness and death (#217-224):

   217 – Eusebius, Vita Constantini 4.58-60; Barnes, CE, 259

   218 – Eusebius, Vita Constantini 4.61; Barnes, CE, 259

   219 – Eusebius, Vita Constantini 4.62

   220 - Eusebius, Vita Constantini 4.62.4

   221 – Pohlsander, *Emperor Constantine*, 75-76; Lenski, "Reign of Constantine" (CC), 82

   222 – Because he was so old, he could not be submerged in water to be baptized, and therefore the rules of baptism were changed to what they are today, having water placed on the forehead alone. In this period, infant baptism, though practiced (usually in circumstances of emergency) had not yet become a matter of routine in the west. Thomas M. Finn, *Early Christian Baptism and the Catechumenate: East and West* (Collegeville: The Liturgical Press/Michael Glazier, 1992); Phillip Rousseau, "Baptism," in *Late Antiquity: A Guide to the Post Classical World*, ed. G.W. Bowersock, Peter brown, and Oleg grabar (Cambridge, MA, Belknap Press, 1999).

   223 – Marilena Amerise, "Il battesimo di Costantino il Grande."

   224 – Eusebius, *Vita Constantini* 4.64; Fowden, "Last Days of Constantine,: 147; Lenski, "Reign of Constantine" (CC), 82

[4] Stefano Assemani, *Acta Sanctorum Martyrum Orientalium*, Vol. 1.1

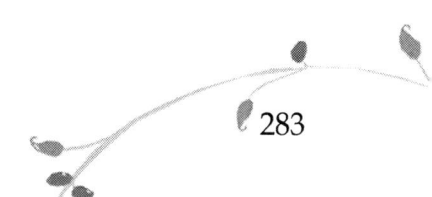

(Rome, 1748), p.105, quoted in The Everlasting Tradition, Galen Peterson, p.17

[5] Watchman on the Wall, © 2005 Robert Stearns, General Editor, Kairos Publishing, PO Box 450, Clarence, NY 14031, www.kairos.us

Chapter Seven

[1] Christmas, or Pagan-Mass? by Reb Yeshayahu Helliczer, www.messianicart.com/paganism/xmas.htm

[2] ibid, p.3

[3] The Two Babylons or The Papal Worship, © 1916 Rev. Alexander Hislop, First American Edition 1943, 2nd American Edition 1959; Published in America by Loizeaux Brothers Inc., p. 93

[4] ibid p. 97

[5] The Mystery of Iniquity (The Feast of Trumpets and the Rapture or What are Christian Holidays?) © Michael J. Rood 2001, Messiah's Branch Yahoo Group, www.6001.com/satanic.htm

[6] What About Hallowe'en? © 1995 Bob and Gretchen Passantino, Answers in Action, P.O. Box 2067, Costa Mesa, CA 92628

[7] ibid

[8] © 1997-99 Akasha, Herne and The Celtic Connection, wicca.com

[9] ibid

[10] ibid

Chapter Eight

[1] www.encountersnetwork.com

[2] ibid

[3] www.fmoran.com/moray.html © Elizabeth H. Harris, 1997

[4] www.moravian.org © 2001-2009 The Moravian Church in North America

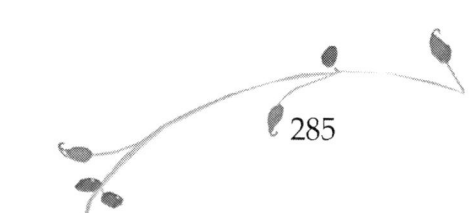

Notes

[5] Catechism of the Catholic Church, Latin text copyright ©1994 Libreria Editrice Vaticanam Città del Vaticano, English Translation of the *Catechism of the Catholic Church* for the United States of America copyright © 1994, United States Catholic Conference, Inc. – Libreria Editrice Vaticana; An Image Book, published by Doubleday, a division of Bantam Doubleday Dell Publishing Group, Inc., 1540 Broadway, New York, New York 10036, p.291

[6] ibid., p.291

[7] ibid., p.411

[8] A History of Christianity, Chapter 5, The Reformation ©2005 Charles Kimball, www.xenohistorian.faithweb.com

[9] ibid

[10] ibid

[11] ibid

[12] Ulrich Zwingli, ©Richard Hooker, www.wsu.edu/~dee/REFORM/ZWINGLI.HTM

[13] ibid

[14] ibid

[15] ibid

[16] ibid

[17] John Calvin, © Richard Hooker, www.wsu.edu/~dee/REFORM/CALVIN.HTM

[18] A History of Christianity, Chapter 5, The Reformation ©2005 Charles Kimball, www.xenohistorian.faithweb.com

[19] ibid

[20] ibid

[21] ibid

[22] A History of Christianity, Chapter 5, The Reformation ©2005 Charles Kimball, www.xenohistorian.faithweb.com

[23] ibid

[24] ibid

Chapter 10

[1] Complete Jewish Bible, © 1998 by David H. Stern, Jewish New Testament Publications, Inc., Clarkesville, Maryland, USA

[2] ibid., p. 1497

[3] Christians and the Sabbath: The Seventh Day by Chuck Missler, Koinonia House, www.store.khouse.org

Chapter 11

[1] www.judaismvschristianity.com/Passover_dates

[2] The New Strong's Concordance of the Bible, Jems Strong, LL/D., S.T.D. © 1990 by Thomas Nelson Publishers

[3] www.bethshechinah.com/shavuot2001.htm

[8] God's Appointed Times © 1993 by Barney Kasdan, Messianic Jewish Publishers, a division of Lederer/Messianic Jewish Communications, 6204 Park Heights Avenue, Baltimore, Maryland 21215

[9] Babylonian Talmud, p.60, HYPERLINK "http://www.sacred-texts.com/jud/t03.yom09.htm" www.sacred-texts.com/jud/t03.yom09.htm (emphasis added)

[10] ibid, p.89

[11] The Everlasting Tradition by Galen Peterson ©1995 by Kregel Publications, a division of Kregel, Inc.
  P.O. Box 2607, Grand Rapids, MI 49501

[12] Good News Bible with Deutercanonicals/Apocrypha © American Bible Society 1979

[13] Josephus, The Complete Works, translated by William Whiston, A.M.,© 1998 by Thomas Nelson Publishers

[14] ibid, page 388

[15] The Everlasting Tradition by Galen Peterson, © 1995 by Kregel Publications, a division of Kregel, Inc., PO Box 2607, Grand Rapids, MI 49501

[16] ibid, page 393

Chapter 14

[1] www.ReturnToGod.com/hebrew/wedding

Chapter 16

[1] Watchmen on the Wall, ©2005 by Robert Stearns, Published by Kairos Publishing, PO Box 450, Clarence, NY 14031

[2] ibid

[3] ibid

[4] A Rabbi Looks at the Last Days by Rabbi Jonathan Bernis, JVMI Publishing, a division of Jewish Voice Ministres International

[5] ibid, from www.sixdaywar.org

[6] ibid, from www.sixdaywar.org

Chapter 17

[1] Justin Martyr, Dialogue With Trypho 11, in *Ante-Nicene Fathers* 1:200.

[2] Hippolytus, Treatise Against the Jews 6, in Ante-Nicene Fathers 5.220.

[3] Origen, Against Celsus 4.22, in Ante-Nicene Fathers' 4.506.

[4] Augustine, The City of God 18.46, in Nicene and Post-Nicene Fathers 2:389.

[5] The Separation of Church and Faith, Vol. 1, Copernicus and the Jews © Daniel Gruber, 2005, Elijah Publishing, PO Box 776, Hanover, NH 03755, www.Elijahnet.org, p.11

[6] ibid., p.18

Chapter 18

[1] The Incomplete Church © 2007, Sid Roth, Destiny Image ® Publishers, Inc., P.O. Box 310, Shippensburg, PA   17257-0310

[2] Restoring the Jewishness of the Gospel © 1988, David H. Stern, 1st.

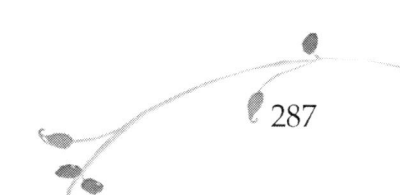

ed. – Jerusalem, Israel: Jewish New Testament Publications, Inc. 2nd ed. 1990 Jewish New Testament Publications, Inc., PO Box 615, Clarksville, MD 21029, p.17

Chapter 19

[1] Revival Breaks Out at Asbury College in 2006 (http://forerunner.com/asbury2006,html)

and *One Divine Moment* (http://francisasburysociety.com/booksprayer.htm)

[2] Larry Eskridge, "Jesus People" in Erwin Fahlbusch, Geoffrey William Bromily, David B. Barrett, *Encyclopedia of Christianity* " ... the popularity of books like Hal Lindsay's *Late great Planet Earth* (1970) mirrored hippie perceptions of the apocalyptic direction of modern America"

[3] Wikipedia, Jesus Movement (citation needed for this entry.)

[4] Wikipedia, Messianic Judaism, Schoeman, Roy H. (2003) *Salvation is from the Jews: the role of Judaism in salvation history from Abraham to the Second Coming.* San Francisco, California: Ignatius Press. P. 351.LCCN 2003-105176 (http://lccn.loc.gov/2003105176). ISBN 089870975X. "By the mid 1970s, *Time* magazine placed the number of Messianic Jews in the U.S. at over 50,000; by1993 this number had grown to 160,000 in the U.S. and about 350,000 worldwide (1989 estimate).... There are currently over 400 Messianic synagogues worldwide, with at least 150 in the U.S."

[5] Wikipedia, McGirk, Tim (June 6, 2008). "Israel's Messianic Jews Under Attack" (http://www.time.com/time/world/article/0,8599,1812430,00.htm . *Time* http://www.time.com/time/world/article/0,8599,1812430,00.html . Retrieved August 4, 2010

Conclusion

[1] Restoring the Jewishness of the Gospel © 1988, David H. Stern, 1st.

ed. – Jerusalem, Israel: Jewish New Testament Publications, Inc. 2nd ed. 1990 Jewish New Testament Publications, Inc., PO Box 615, Clarksville, MD 21029, p.27

[2] ibid, p.28

[3] 2007 Messianic Vision. All rights reserved. This article is not reproducible except with permission from Messianic Vision. Used with permission.

About the Author

Maureen Moss was brought up in the Catholic Church, but even from a young age felt dissatisfied. Feeling that the truth was not in the Church, she looked for it in the world only to be led on a search fraught with eventual alcoholism and despair. Calling out to God, Jesus answered her, which began a new life. As she learned His truth she discovered why she felt drawn to Israel and the Jewish people from her childhood age. Maureen initially became involved in a Pentecostal church then later took the opportunity to become part of a congregation of Messianic believers. Her heartfelt for desire has been for the Church to learn about and embrace its Jewish roots.